I0901087

IMAGES
of America

LEESBURG

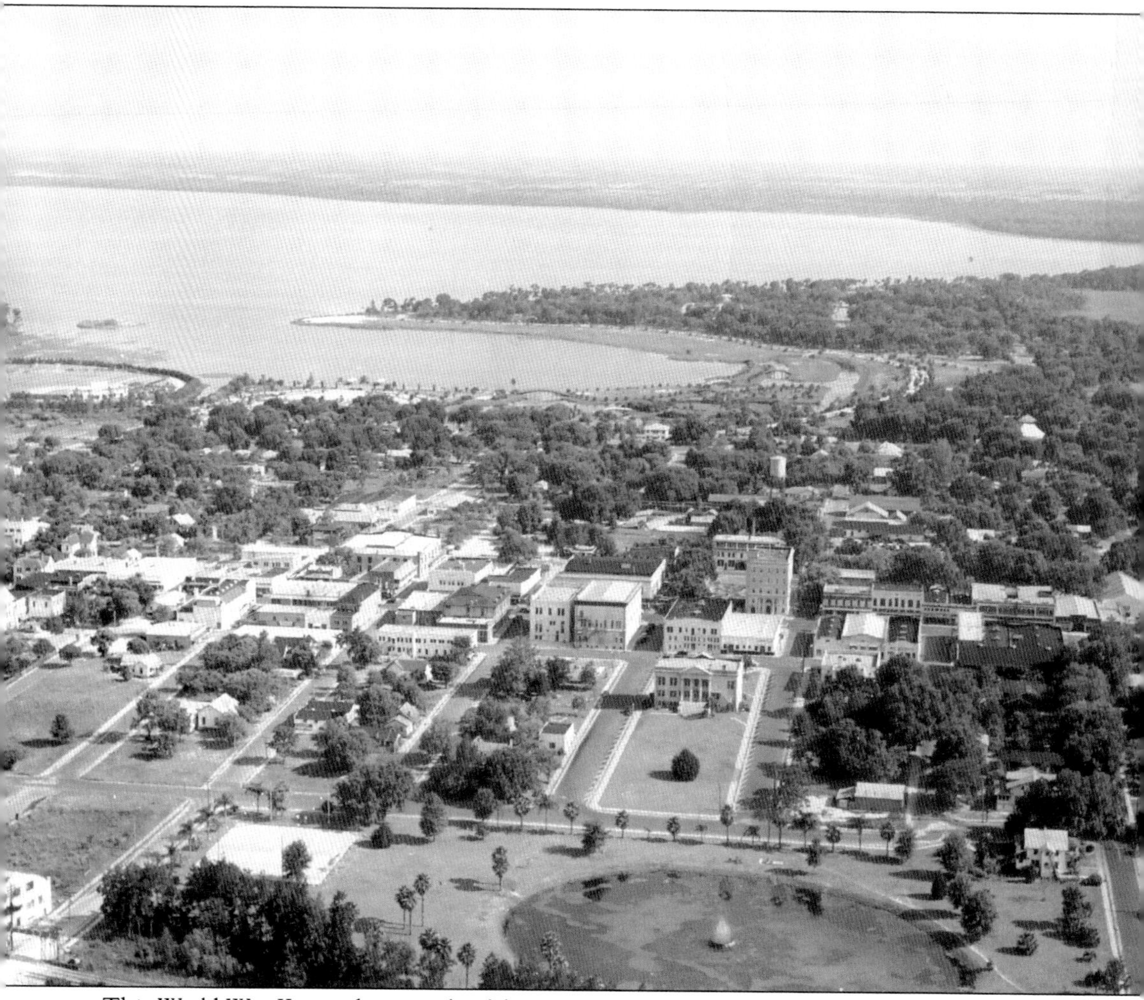

This World War II–era photograph of downtown Leesburg looks south at Lake Harris. Featured in the aerial of "the Lakefront City" are Albert S. Herlong's packinghouse (built in 1929), Edward Mote's Lake View Hotel, Fountain Lake Park, city hall, and Thomas Field at Venetian Gardens. (Courtesy of the Leesburg Heritage Society.)

On the Cover: The Whippoorwills, a popular Leesburg bachelor club, gather for a relaxing group photograph at the boardinghouse of Isabella May Haynes Keeling in 1913. Prominent club members include W.H. Wade, Frank Gillespie, Clarence Hawkins, and G.G. Ware. The Keeling boardinghouse was on Main Street. (Courtesy of James A. Bragdon.)

IMAGES
of America

LEESBURG

Glorianne Seymour Fahs
and Bob Grenier

ARCADIA
PUBLISHING

ISBN 978-0-7385-9079-0

Published by Arcadia Publishing
Charleston, South Carolina

Printed in the United States of America

Library of Congress Control Number: 2012943010

For all general information, please contact Arcadia Publishing:
Telephone 843-853-2070
Fax 843-853-0044
E-mail sales@arcadiapublishing.com
For customer service and orders:
Toll-Free 1-888-313-2665

Visit us on the Internet at www.arcadiapublishing.com

Dedicated to our families, the Leesburg Heritage Society, and the citizens of Leesburg.

Contents

Acknowledgments

Leesburg's storied history and the treasure trove of vintage photographs that have been collected and preserved could easily inspire and produce several more editions of this book.

Glorianne and I are grateful to everyone who made this photographic journey through Leesburg history possible, including Kay Adair, Vi Pfahler, John "Jack" Fahs, Kathy Stevens, Sanna Henderson, Bob Moody, Gerald Lacey, Phil Cross, Dan Smith, Judy Hux Rainey, R.G. Teese, James A. Bragdon, Pam Hester, Gerald McClelland, Joe Shipes, Jan Wideman, Carol Anderson and Tom Wilcox of the Leesburg Public Library, Bonnie Wicher Photography, and Kathy Carter, who proofread and edited the entire manuscript.

There are many outstanding organizations to thank, including the Leesburg Heritage Society, the Leesburg Partnership, the Leesburg Masonic Lodge, the Lake County Historical Society, Lone Oak Cemetery, United Daughters of the Confederacy, the Leesburg Chamber of Commerce, and the City of Leesburg. Our appreciation to Maggie Bullwinkel, Liz Gurley, and Arcadia Publishing as well.

These publications were great resources: *Lake County, Florida: A Pictorial History* by Emmett Peter Jr.; *History of Lake County, Florida* by professor William Kennedy; *My First 100 Years* by George Rast with Lee King; and *Woodlea: Life on the Lake of the Dancing Sunbeams* by yours truly, Bob Grenier. Rick Reed's book *City of Leesburg: Sesquicentennial Celebration* and his popular weekly *Daily Commercial* historical column, *Reminisce*, were also invaluable resources.

I wish to express my gratitude and respect for my coauthor Glorianne Seymour Fahs. She has leadership roles in many organizations, including the National Society United States Daughters of 1812, Land of Lakes Chapter; the National Society Colonial Dames XVII Century, Mercy Hurd Chapter; the Kinseekers Genealogical Society; the Leesburg Heritage Society and Museum; the Daughters of the American Revolution; the Lake County Historical Society; and Lone Oak Cemetery. In 2012, Glorianne was awarded the Florida State Genealogical Society's Outstanding Achievement Award.

We appreciate everyone who worked diligently to help us identify faces and spell names correctly. Unless otherwise noted, all images appear courtesy of the Leesburg Heritage Society.

And finally, for me, Bob, this book was made possible by the support and encouragement of my mom and dad, Dave Clevinger, Patrick Adams, Wahine, Flash, Capt. Melton Haynes, and, of course, God!

INTRODUCTION

Some of Lake County's richest and most colorful history took place in Leesburg. The family names of its early settlers are still among the most well known and remembered in the Lake Region.

Settlers arrived to what is now Leesburg prior to the city's official birth year of 1857. War of 1812 veteran Thomas Robertson, on the strength of the Armed Occupation Act of 1842, arrived in Moss Bluff from South Carolina. On July 27, 1843, after scouting the area for a place to farm, he received his permit to homestead on the south shore of Lake Griffin. Robertson's 21-year-old son John arrived eight days later.

In the spring of 1845, brothers Melton and Bunberry Haynes arrived from Whiteville, North Carolina, and settled on Lake Harris in an area known as Sunnyside, east of what would become downtown Leesburg. Melton Haynes started the orange-growing industry in the Lake Region when he planted a quarter acre of sweet orange seeds on his property.

Leesburg's namesake family, the Lees of Barbour County, Alabama, came to Florida in 1849. Arthur and Mary Lee and their 10 children settled near Adamsville in Sumter County. In 1857, a year after Arthur died, his son Evander moved to what would become Leesburg with his wife, Susannah, and their eight sons and daughters. The city's official birth year was determined by Evander Lee's arrival in Leesburg in 1857. Evander's brothers Josiah and Calvin soon followed, with Josiah homesteading along Lake Griffin. The Lee brothers began major operations in Leesburg, with Evander and Calvin opening the first general merchandise store on Main Street and Josiah operating a cotton gin and gristmill.

The 1840s and 1850s saw the arrival of many more settlers to the area, including the Fussell, Dozier, Love, Stivender, and Dabney families. Leesburg began to take shape shortly before the start of the War Between the States in 1861. When the men returned home following the war, Leesburg began to grow at a rapid pace.

Leesburg received its name in 1866 when Evander and Calvin Lee were on a trip to New York to purchase goods for their store. The wholesale supplier asked the brothers where he should ship their goods. After pausing for a moment to think, Calvin replied, "Ship 'em to Leesburg, Florida, by way of Silver Springs." Calvin commented to his brother later, "If people don't like the name, they can change it." No one ever did.

Over the following century, Leesburg became home to legends, icons, and commercial, agricultural, and industrial movers and shakers. Legends include famous western sharpshooter Annie Oakley, who was a resident of the Lake View Hotel along with her husband, Frank Butler, and their hunting dog Dave.

The world-famous Lake View Hotel was built by entrepreneur and civic icon Edward Mote and his partner Gen. Davis Tilson. Mote, an eight-term Leesburg mayor, and his wife, Lucretia, built a beautiful Victorian-style home on Main Street in 1892, highlighted by a distinctive four-story turret. The home was listed in the National Register of Historic Places in 1974 and moved to a new location on Magnolia Street on September 1, 1990. It remains a popular tourist attraction today.

Another legend who called Leesburg home was author and sportsman David Newell, who hosted a popular radio show for ABC and coproduced one of the first television shows about hunting and fishing. He was a well-known author of children's books and historic novels about Florida, and was the editor of *Field and Stream* magazine.

Leesburg's African American history began with the arrival of John Butler Dabney and his wife, Mackey. Other families included Dennis Mike, who came to Leesburg in 1860, Joseph Silas in 1862, Thornton Sanders in 1864, and Lewis Thompson in 1875.

The 20th century brought Leesburg a World War II German prisoner of war camp, the Coca-Cola, Minute Maid, and Gulf Oil companies, professional major league baseball teams, the Leesburg International Airport, Leesburg Regional Medical Center, the beautiful Venetian Gardens, and watermelon festivals.

Images of America: *Leesburg* will take you on a tour of some of the communities that grew up around Leesburg. Fruitland Park, about four miles north, was founded in 1876 by Maj. O.P. Rooks of Cincinnati. Major Rooks named the town after the Fruitland Nurseries of Augusta, Georgia, and named the town's main thoroughfare, Berckmann Street, after his friend J.P. Berckmann, who owned the nurseries.

Okahumpka was settled to the south of Leesburg in 1880 by Edmund Snyder of Germantown, Pennsylvania. It is located between Lake Dunham on the north, Lake Harris on the east, and Helena Run on the northeast. Okahumpka is the English translation of the Indian word Okeehumpkee, which means "deep waters," because of a spring that lies near the town called Bugg Spring.

Whitney, located on the western edge of the county, was given its name by Florida treasurer John Christian Luning, who owned a large citrus grove there. He named it for a Seaboard Air Line Railroad official. Most of the land was homesteaded by original Leesburg pioneer John Robertson after the War Between the States.

Silver Lake Estates was a 2,500-acre parcel of land on Silver Lake, about five miles west of downtown Leesburg, which was purchased by R.J. Tuller of Illinois in 1913. Other Leesburg area communities this book highlights are Slighville, Orange Bend, Moss Bluff, Montclair, and Lady Lake.

Today, Leesburg's history and heritage serve as an economic engine for the city's future. Many of the city's social and community festivals and events possess a nostalgic theme. Leesburg's history is a drawing card for its residents, visitors, guests, and business investors. Organizations such as the Leesburg Heritage Society and the Leesburg Partnership protect, preserve, and promote their city's history. This book will serve as a souvenir and keepsake for a city that truly embraces its history. Enjoy your stroll down memory lane!

One

"SHIP 'EM TO LEESBURG, FLORIDA"

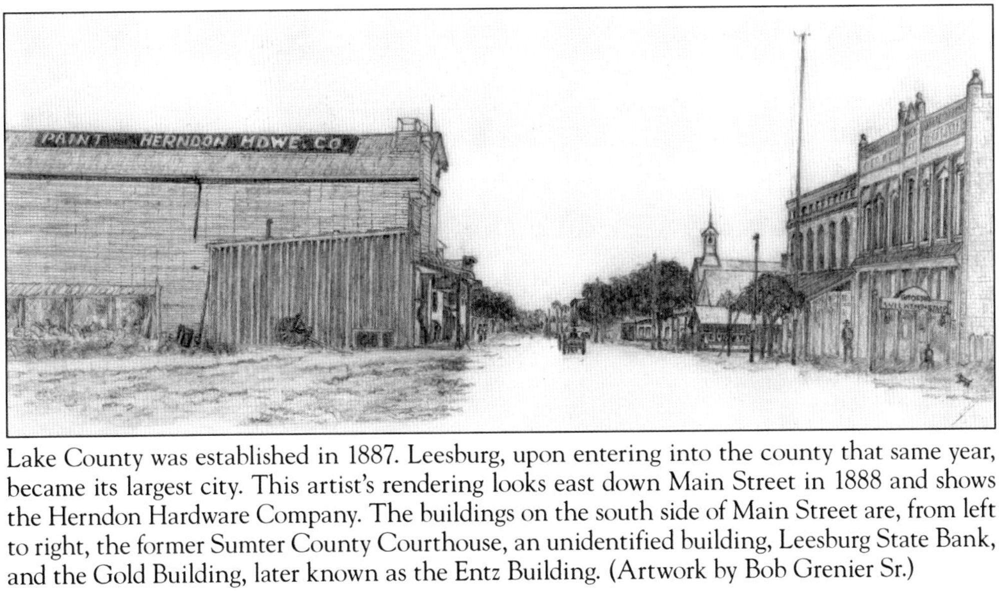

Lake County was established in 1887. Leesburg, upon entering into the county that same year, became its largest city. This artist's rendering looks east down Main Street in 1888 and shows the Herndon Hardware Company. The buildings on the south side of Main Street are, from left to right, the former Sumter County Courthouse, an unidentified building, Leesburg State Bank, and the Gold Building, later known as the Entz Building. (Artwork by Bob Grenier Sr.)

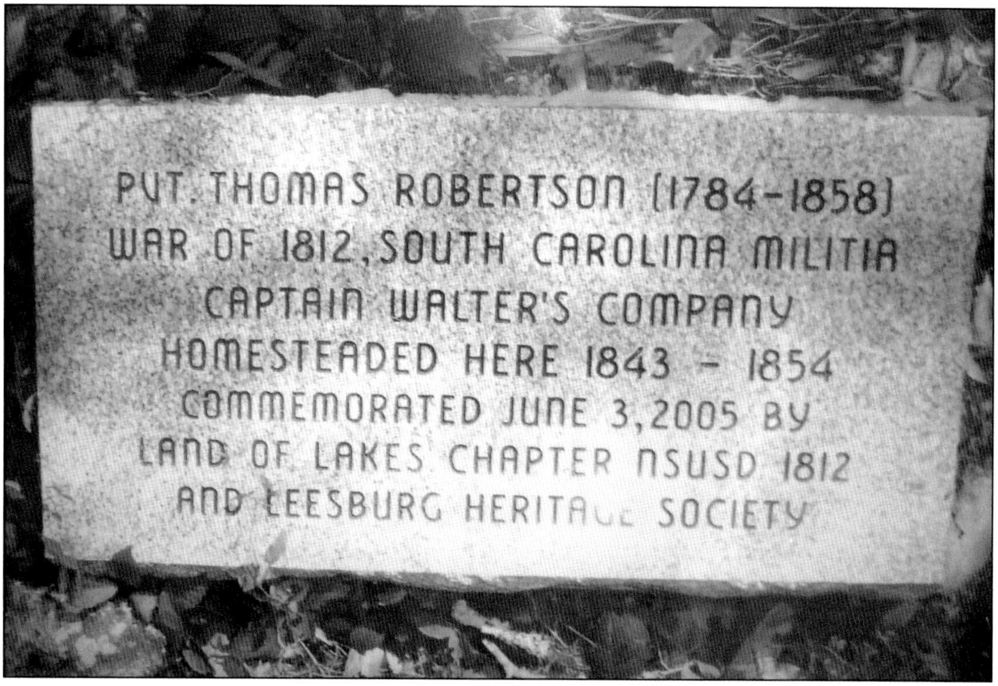

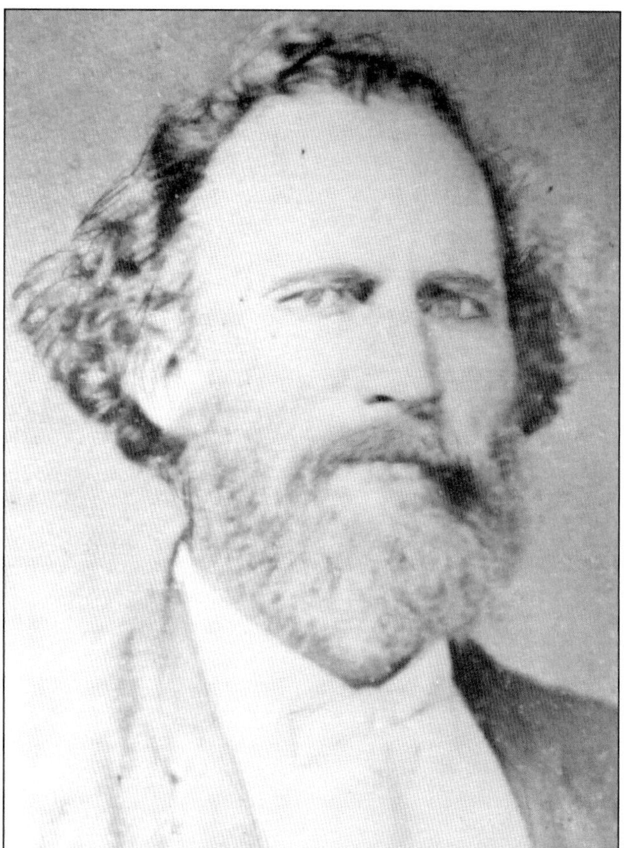

The marker above is located at the Bourlay Historic Nature Park. The park, on the south shore of Lake Griffin, was part of the original 160-acre patent of Thomas Robertson, the area's first settler. Robertson was born around 1784 in South Carolina, where he married Janet Capers and raised eight children. In 1842, at the end of the Second Seminole War, the Robertsons moved to Florida.

Thomas Robertson's son John Marmaduke Robertson arrived at Lake Griffin in August 1843. He received a patent for 160 acres in an area that would become Palmora Park. John served in the Confederate army as a private in the 2nd Florida Cavalry during the War Between the States. In 1868, he was a charter member of Leesburg Masonic Lodge No. 58. John left the area in 1854 and settled the community of Whitney. (Courtesy of Leesburg Masonic Lodge No. 58.)

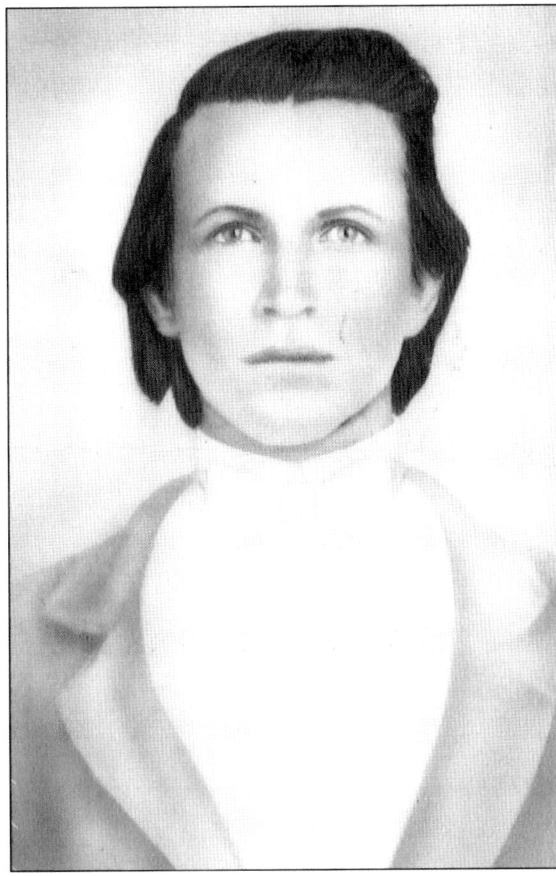

Melton Haynes (right) arrived in the Leesburg area in 1845 at age 18, along with his younger brother Bunberry. They settled along the north shore of Lake Harris on the Sunnyside peninsula (below), where the brothers planted a quarter acre of sweet orange seeds. This planting became the birth of the citrus industry in the region. Melton Haynes married Sarah Isabella Vaught in 1849. Sarah was the daughter of Col. Joseph Vaught, who moved his family to the area from South Carolina in 1846. The Vaughts' homestead, Bachelor's Hall, was located along the creek that connected Lake Eustis and Lake Griffin. That creek was later named Haynes Creek after Melton Haynes, who served as a Confederate cavalry captain during the War Between the States, and, in 1868, was the first Worshipful Master of Leesburg Masonic Lodge No. 58. (Right, courtesy of the Haynes family collection.)

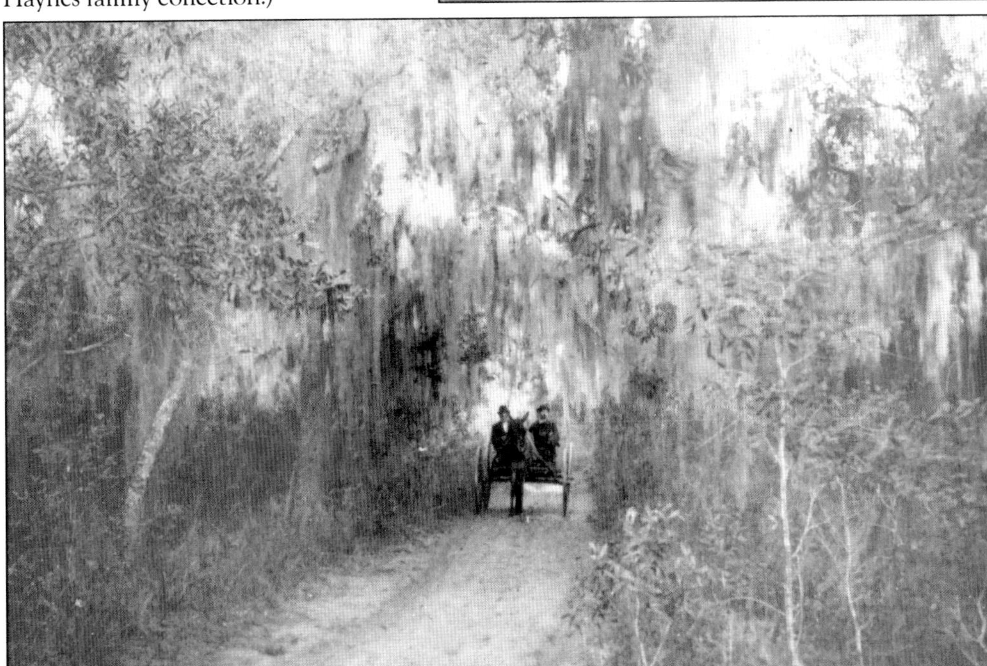

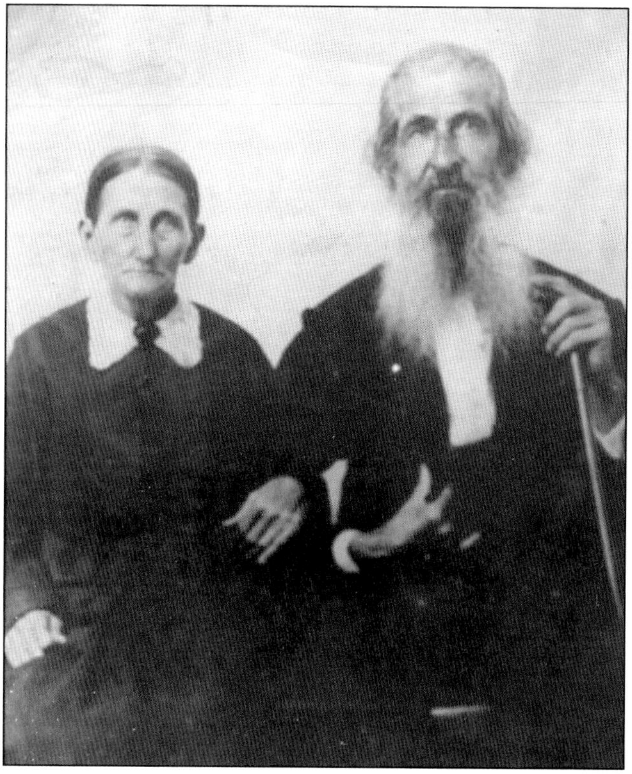

In 1857, Evander and Susannah Lee (left) became the first permanent settlers of Leesburg. Evander had been living in Florida, near Adamsville, since 1849, when his parents, Arthur and Mary Lee, moved their family to Florida from Alabama. Shortly after Evander purchased his first property in the area, his brother Josiah joined him, purchasing land near Montclair Road. In 1863, Evander's youngest brother, John Calvin Lee, settled on Lake Griffin. Evander partnered with him to open their first general store in 1866, at the southeast corner of West Main and Third Streets. Evander died in 1881 and Susannah in 1888. They are buried in Lone Oak Cemetery. Seen below are Evander and Susannah's son Needham with his first wife, Commans Fontaine Bouknight.

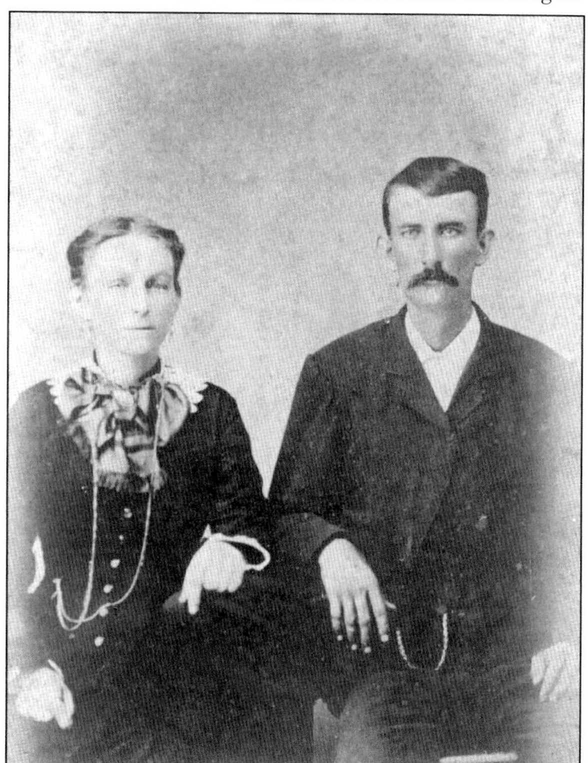

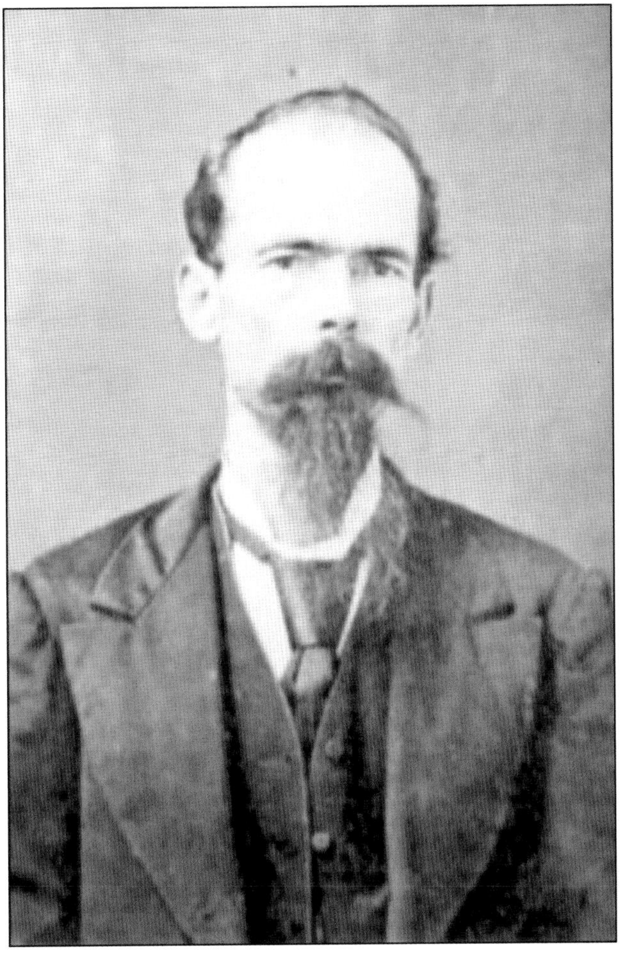

Akin A. Stivender, a nephew of the Lees, was born in 1844 in Alabama. He was a dredger, building and operating a barge he called the *Dry Doe*. He cleared a channel in the Ocklawaha so boats could have a safer and more direct path to Leesburg. When Leesburg was incorporated in 1875, Stivender was elected an alderman as well as the town marshal. He was also a past master of Leesburg Masonic Lodge No. 58.

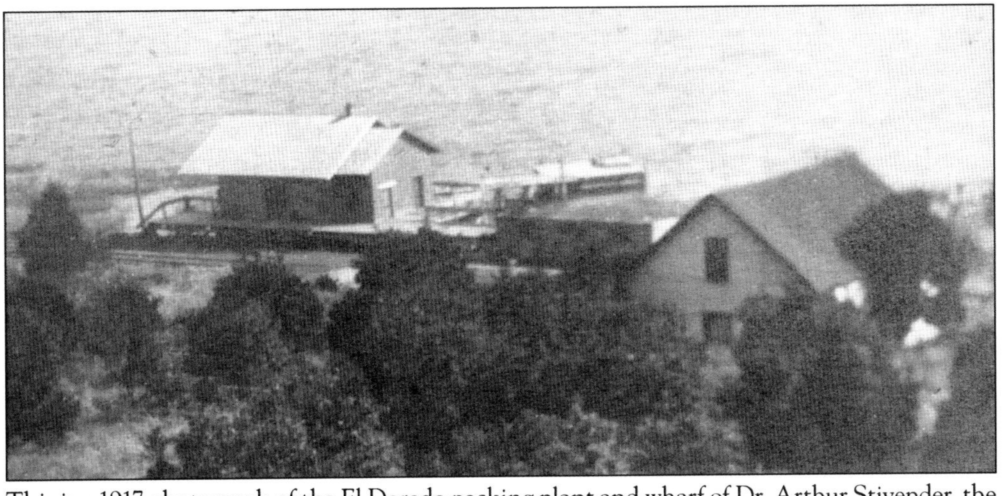

This is a 1917 photograph of the El Dorado packing plant and wharf of Dr. Arthur Stivender, the brother of Akin. Arthur came to Leesburg in 1861 with his mother and siblings after his father died. He settled on the El Dorado–Sunnyside peninsula, where he built a home in 1885. The orange groves he planted surrounding the home are still owned and managed by the family.

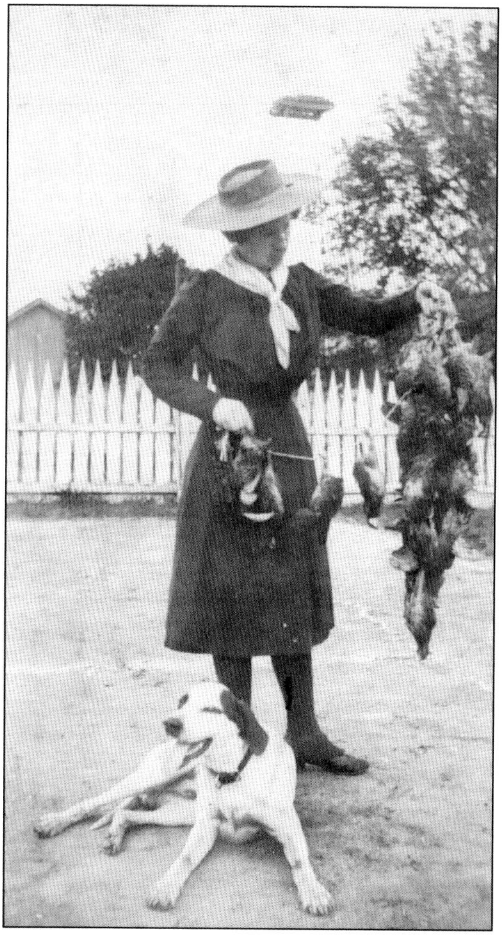

Legendary Wild West sharpshooter Annie Oakley is seen here with her beloved dog Dave, a black-and-white setter. Oakley, along with her husband, Frank Butler, made regular trips to Leesburg between 1912 and 1921 to hunt and visit friends, staying at the Lake View Hotel. Annie began handling guns at age nine and married Butler at 15, in 1876.

The George Edward Winter home (below) is where Annie Oakley's dog Dave is supposedly buried. Winter's granddaughter Eloise Pemble attended the famous dog's funeral and confirmed that Dave was buried near her family's home. Dave was killed in an automobile accident in 1923 near the Lake View Hotel. George Winter and his wife, Annie D. Lee, became close hunting friends with Annie and Frank Butler.

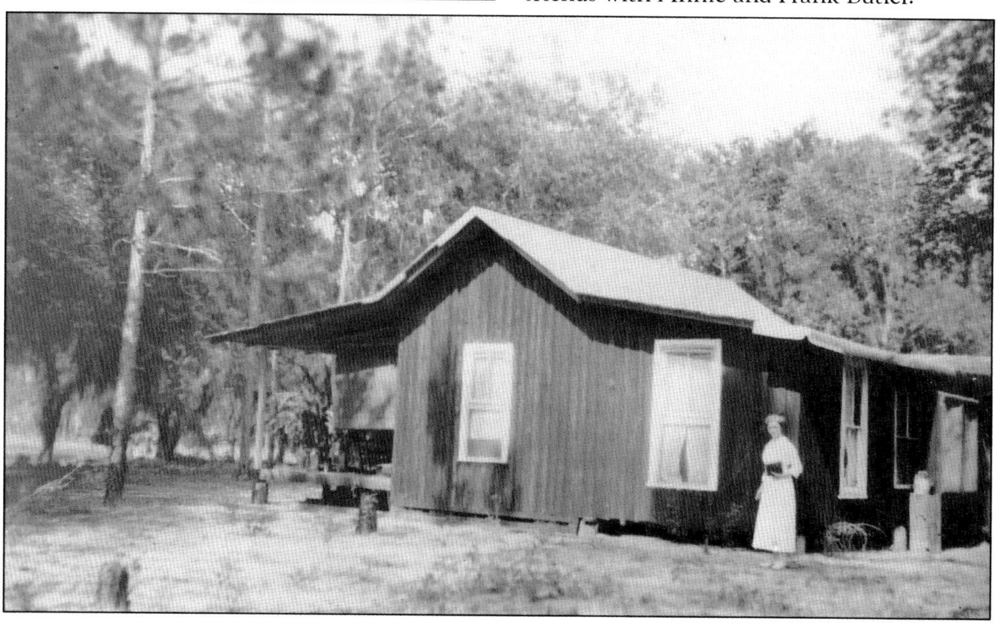

This is a 1923 photograph of Lucretia Hansbrough Mote, the wife of Edward H. Mote. The *Tampa Sunday Tribune* wrote the following about Lucretia in 1923: "A type of woman in Lake County who are taking an active part in the forwarding of the new and better order of things for man and woman alike. Mrs. Mote is one of the most charming matrons of the state."

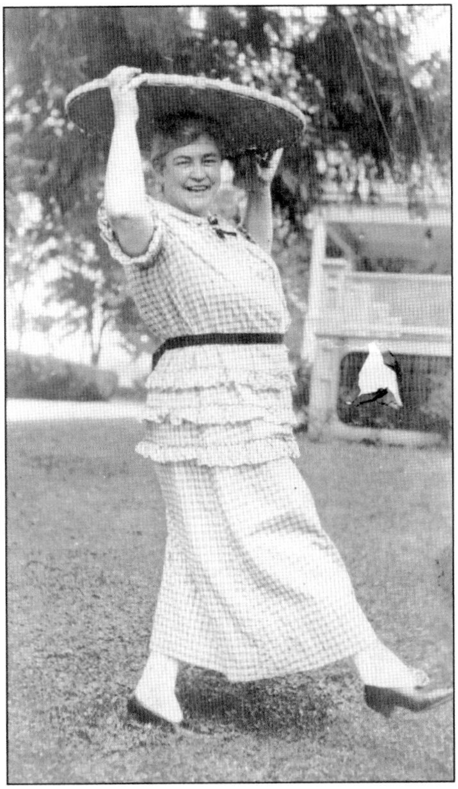

Seen below from left to right are (seated) Edward H. Mote and Nellie Elizabeth Johnson Watts; (standing) Benjamin Franklin Watts Jr., unidentified, and Benjamin Franklin Watts Sr. Edward H. Mote operated a livery business, a stagecoach line, a mercantile, and citrus groves. He also owned and developed Treasure Island and the Lake View Hotel. He established the first waterworks and served as fire chief and mayor, and in the state legislature.

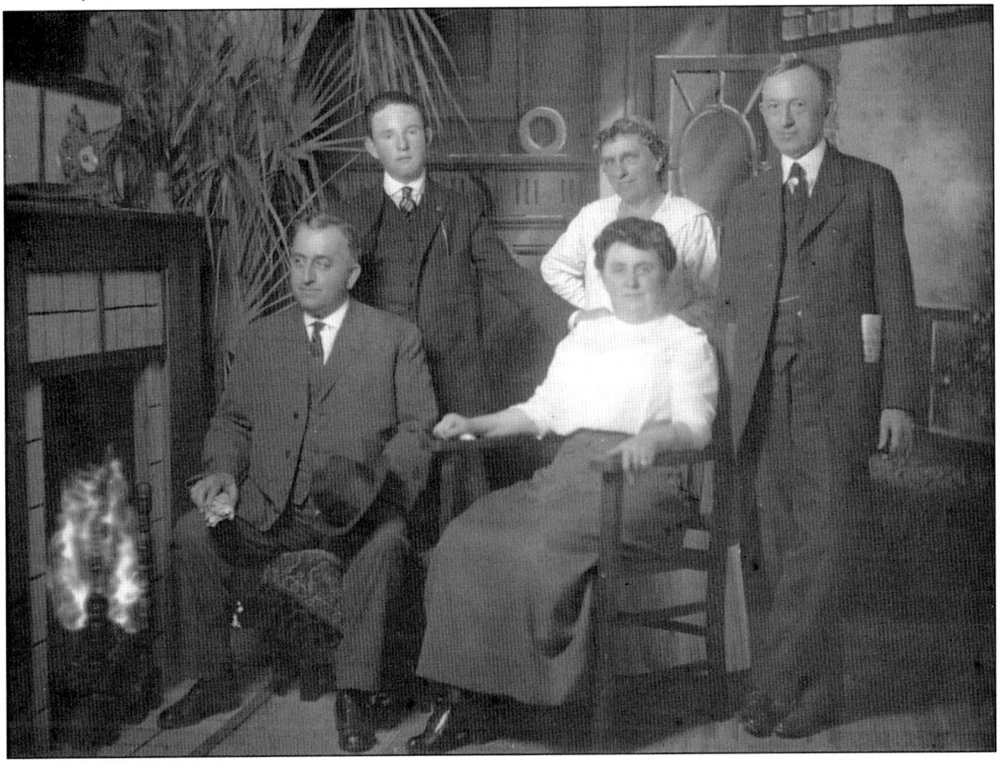

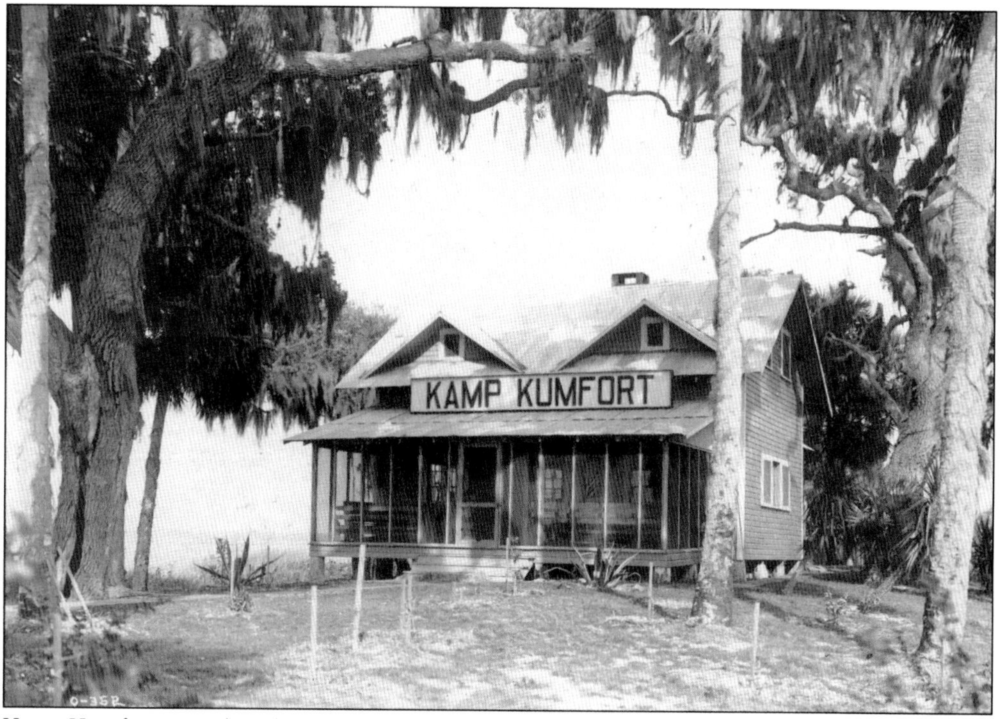

Kamp Kumfort was Edward and Lucretia Mote's country home on Treasure Island, near Leesburg. Edward, a self-made man and one of Leesburg's greatest success stories, was born on January 24, 1860, in Newark, Delaware. He was the son of Jacob Henry and Mary McDowell Mote. When he was 11, he traveled alone to Philadelphia and took a job for $3 a week shoveling snow off roofs. In 1876, he moved to Washington, DC, and then, in 1881, due to lung problems, he traveled to Florida and settled in Leesburg. On October 5, 1885, Edward married Lucretia Hansbrough. The fabulous *Lucretia* cruiser (below) was named for Mrs. Mote. It was docked at Lake Griffin and was used to take the Motes to Kamp Kumfort.

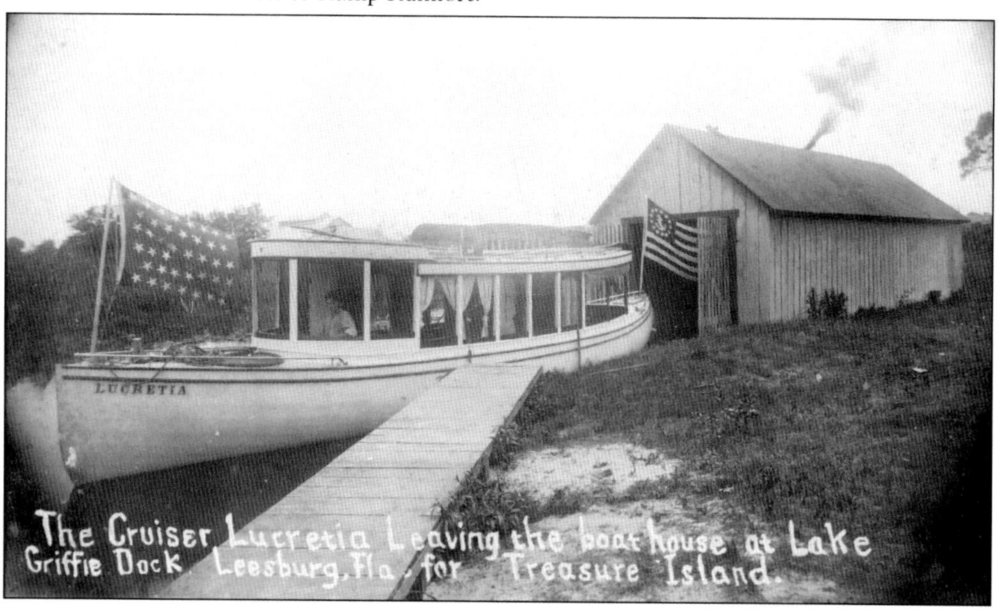

Dennis "Pop" Mike arrived in Leesburg from South Carolina in 1860. His original name was Dennis Dickey, but when he was freed, he changed his last name to Mike after his former owner's son. His death certificate states that he lived to be 110 years and 11 months old. His wife, Priscilla, a midwife, delivered many of Leesburg's early residents. The Mikes had six children. In 1928, Mike Street was named for the family.

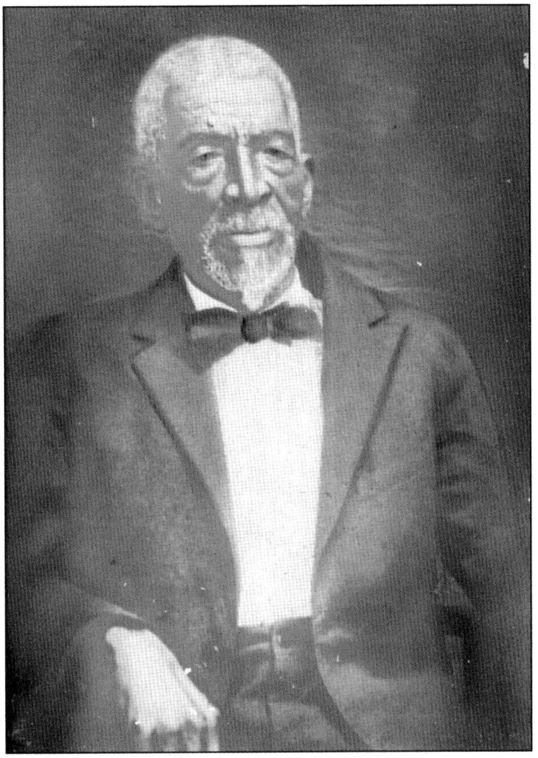

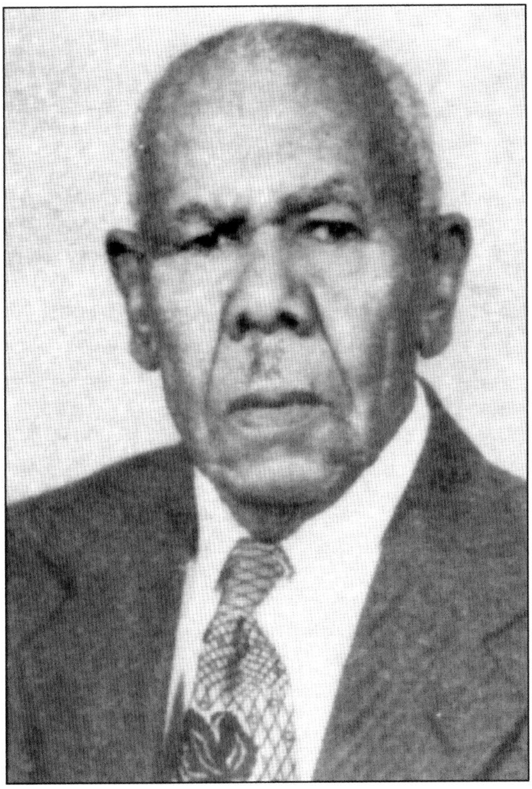

John Morgan Dabney was the son of John Butler and Mackey Dabney, the first black family to settle in Leesburg. They arrived in 1857 from Marion County, Florida, where they first lived when they moved from Virginia. The Dabneys had 10 children, all of whom moved away except for John Morgan, who became the first black teacher in Leesburg and then a school principal. Dabney Elementary School was named in honor of him.

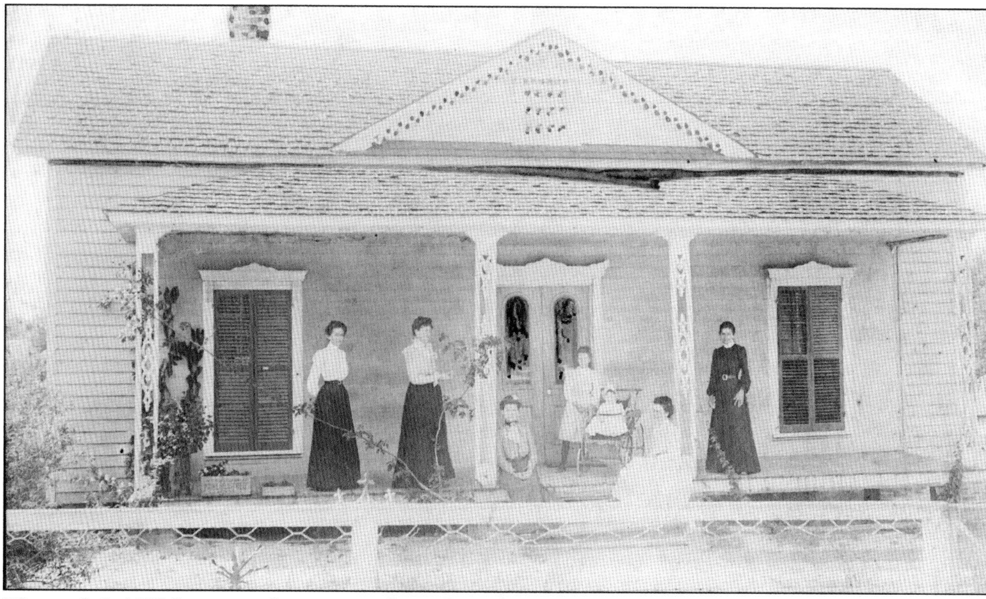

This stylish 1879 house at the corner of Ninth and Main Streets is believed to be the first clapboard house constructed of planks instead of logs in Leesburg's downtown district. It was built by grocer A.L. Miller's father, John Henry Miller. However, the first clapboard house may have been built on Magnolia Street in 1877 by Mary P. Thomas. The ladies and children on the porch are unidentified.

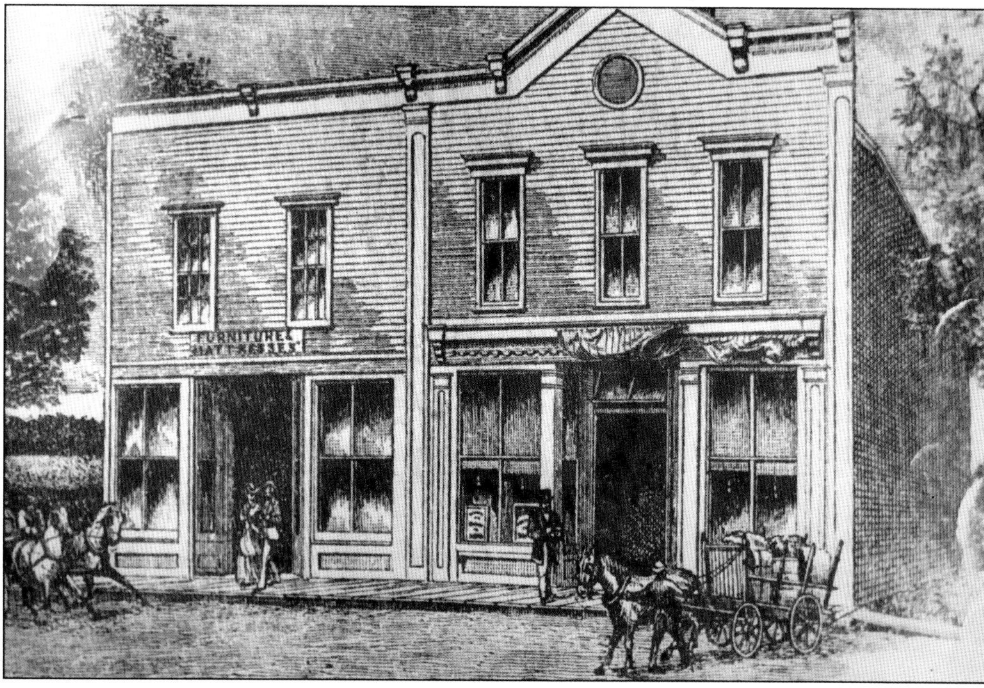

John G. Herndon, with his brothers Pomfrett and Thomas, opened Herndon & Company, depicted in this sketch, at the northwest corner of Main and Sixth Streets. The brothers sold hardware, furniture, and groceries. They were the sons of Cotesworth Pinckney Herndon. A.L. Miller, whose family settled in Leesburg in 1879, purchased a half-interest in the Herndon store and eventually became the sole owner.

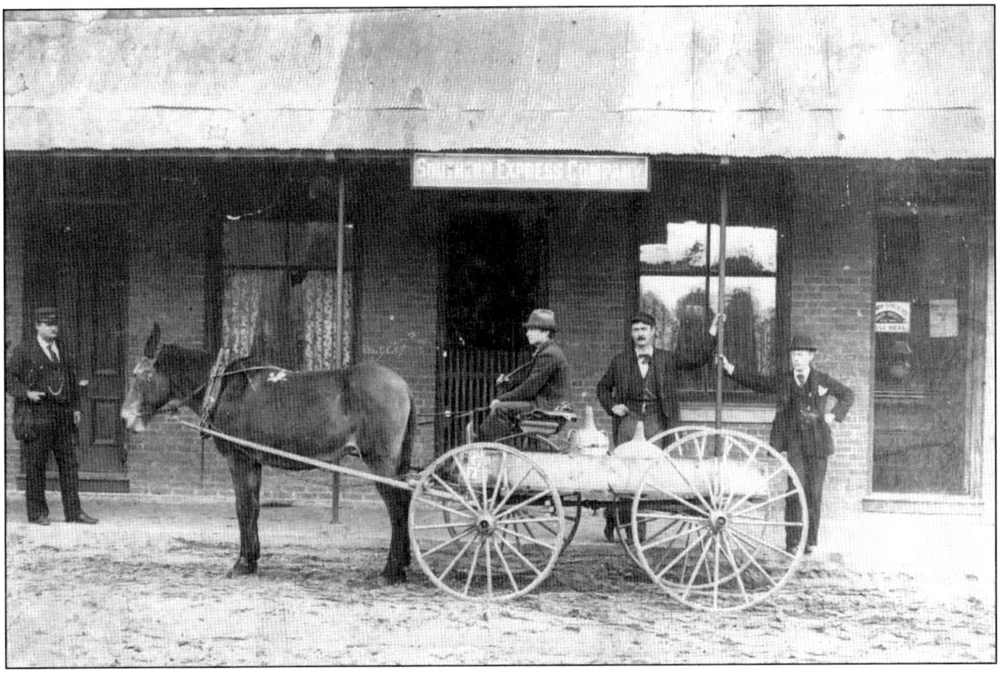

New Jersey–born Arthur B. Lees (far right) came to Florida in 1880 with his parents when he was 10 years old. In November 1907, he married Henrietta Abney in Leesburg. Arthur was the express agent for the Southern Express Company, which had offices in Leesburg and neighboring Tavares. He also owned a furniture store in the early 1900s.

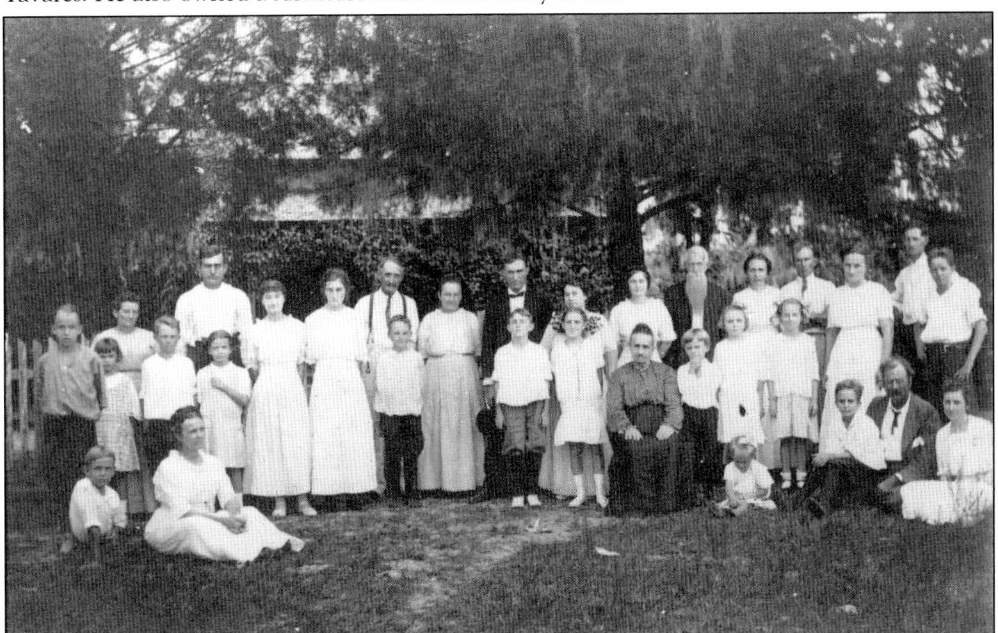

This Hester family photograph was taken in Whitney in the early 1900s. Seated in the first row in the black dress is Mary Ann Permelia Ward Robertson, the wife of John Marmaduke Robertson. Frederick Cummins Hester is standing second from the right with his wife, Annie DeLoss Robertson, on his right. Their son Earle Hester is standing to his left.

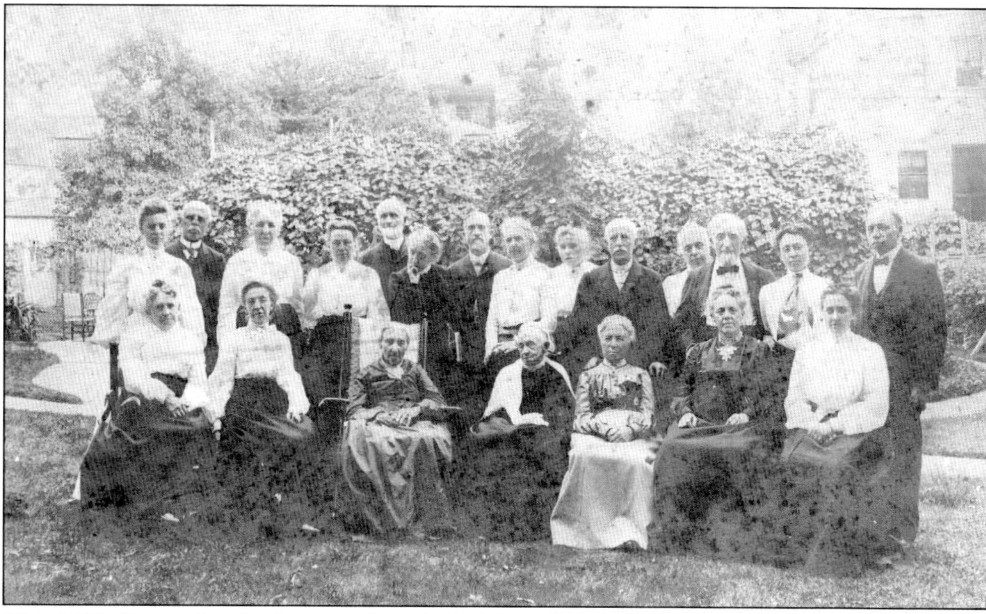

This 1920s Barcus family photograph includes Harry E. Barcus (standing, center), who was born in Marion County, Florida, in 1877. In 1914, he came to Leesburg and operated a shingle mill in Tavares as well as a lumber brokerage business. In later years, Barcus ventured into the citrus and watermelon business, becoming one of Lake County's largest watermelon growers. He was also one of Florida's most successful watermelon shippers. He was married to Olga "Ollie" McAlpin and had five children.

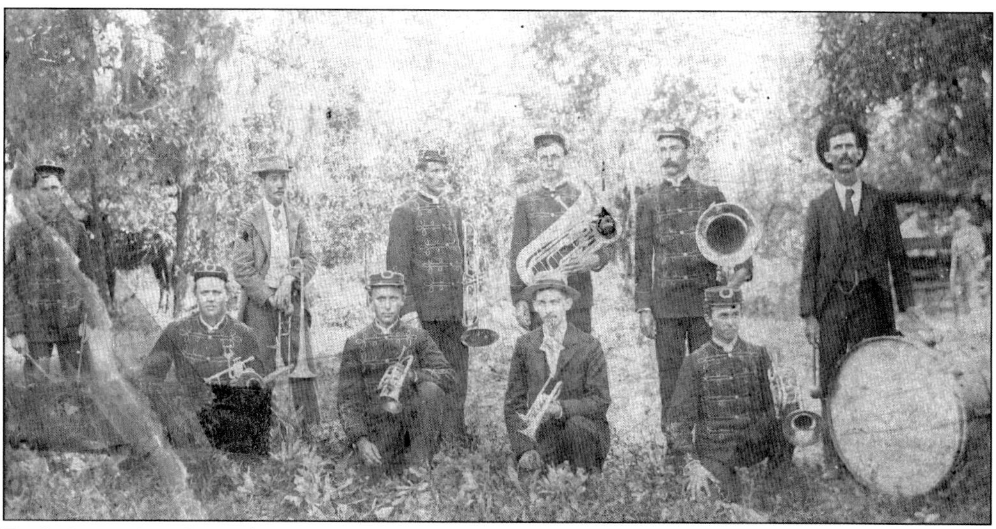

Eggl's Cornet Band, seen here in 1894, performed during the 1895 reelection campaign of incumbent state senator Maj. Alexander St. Clair Abrams of Tavares, although the members of the band supported the challenger, Benjamin Earnest McLin of Umatilla, who won the election and served in the state senate for three terms. Later, McLin became Florida's commissioner of agriculture.

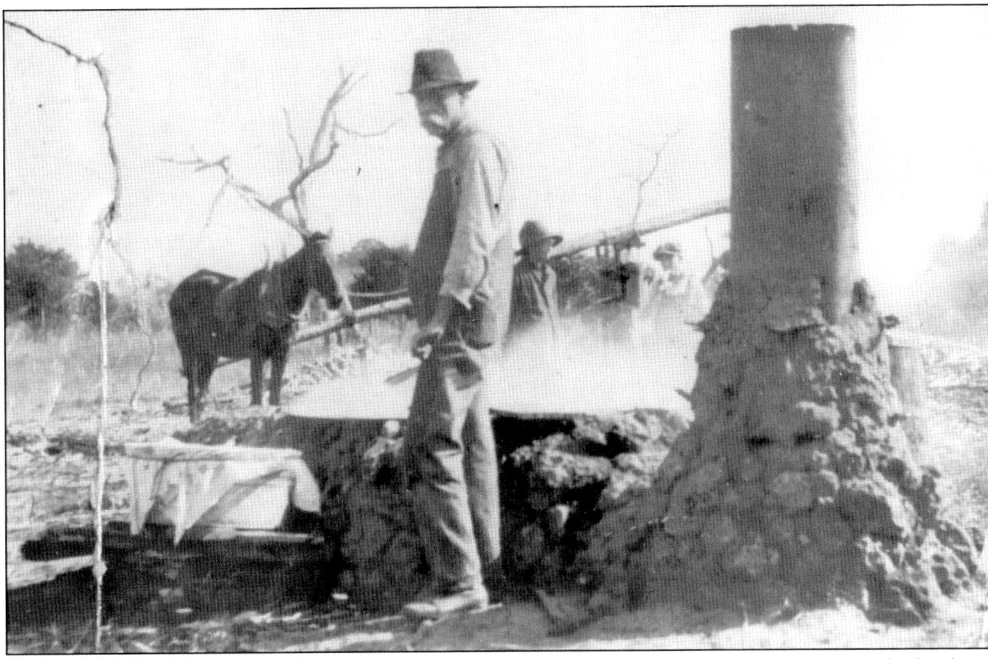

Robert Thomas Padgett was born in Clay County in 1873 to Thomas Eller Padgett and Charlotte Prescott Padgett. Robert owned and operated a sugar cane mill, where he processed cane into syrup and sugar. Other Leesburg growers brought their sugar cane to Padgett's mill for grinding. He married Laura Jane Brantley in 1894.

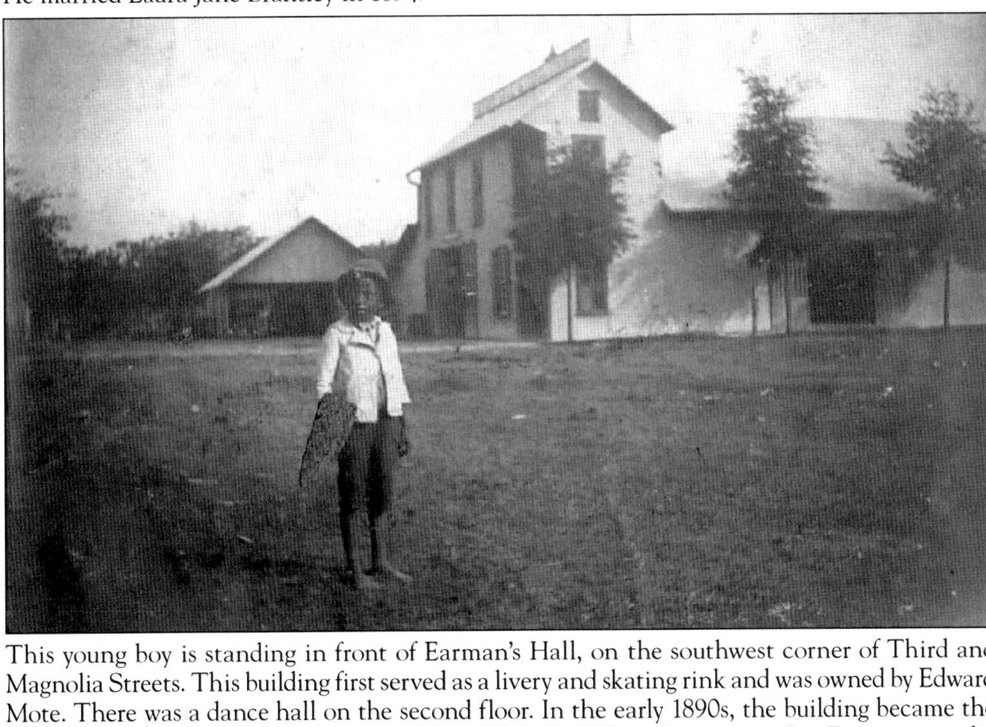

This young boy is standing in front of Earman's Hall, on the southwest corner of Third and Magnolia Streets. This building first served as a livery and skating rink and was owned by Edward Mote. There was a dance hall on the second floor. In the early 1890s, the building became the Maude & Neve Livery and Hall. Former Grand Central Hotel proprietor Joe Earman was the livery's new owner.

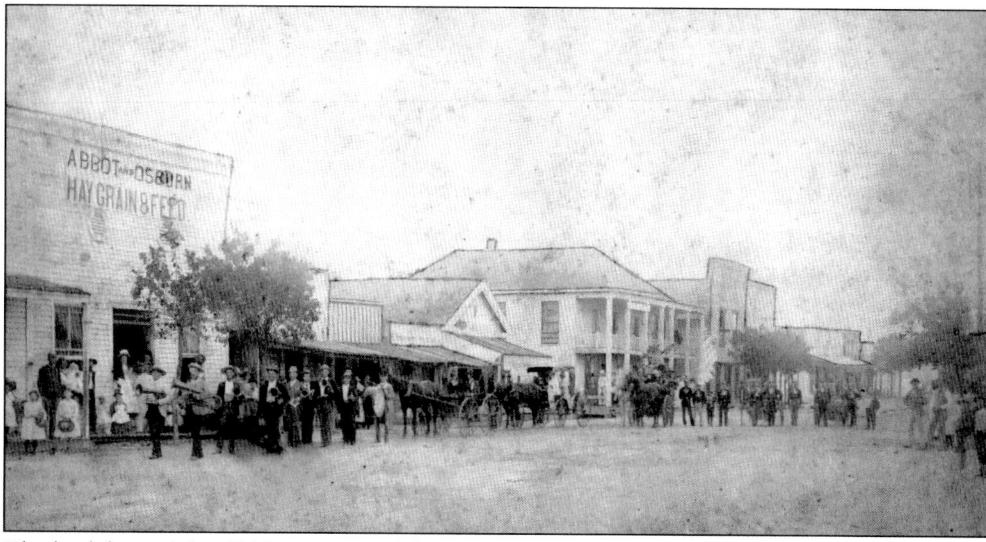

The backdrop of this 1893 patriotic celebration shows a section of the booming business district along the north side of Main Street, near Sixth Street. On the far left is the Abbott & Osborn Hay, Grain & Feed, owned by James O. Abbott and James M. Osborn. They also sold hardware and tinware. The large building in the center is the Lake City Hotel.

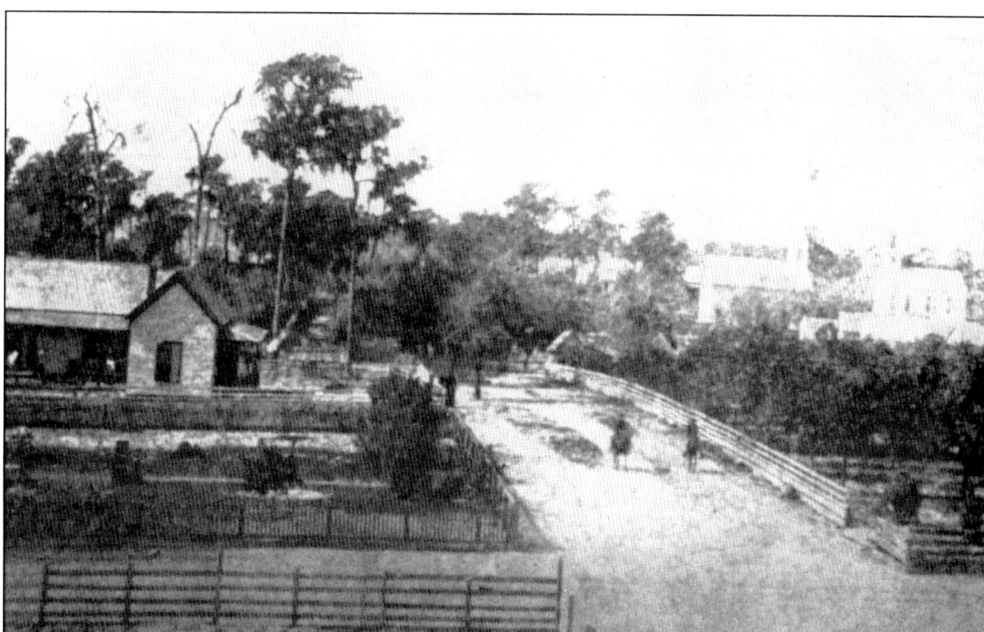

The neat and tidy road seen here in 1885 is Magnolia Street. On the right, looking west from Margaret Lea McCormack's Magnolia Hotel, are the Methodist and Presbyterian churches. The house was built around 1877 by Charles Lewis Thomas, originally of Clarksville, Tennessee, who was the founder of the *Leesburg Commercial* newspaper.

Two

The Lakefront City

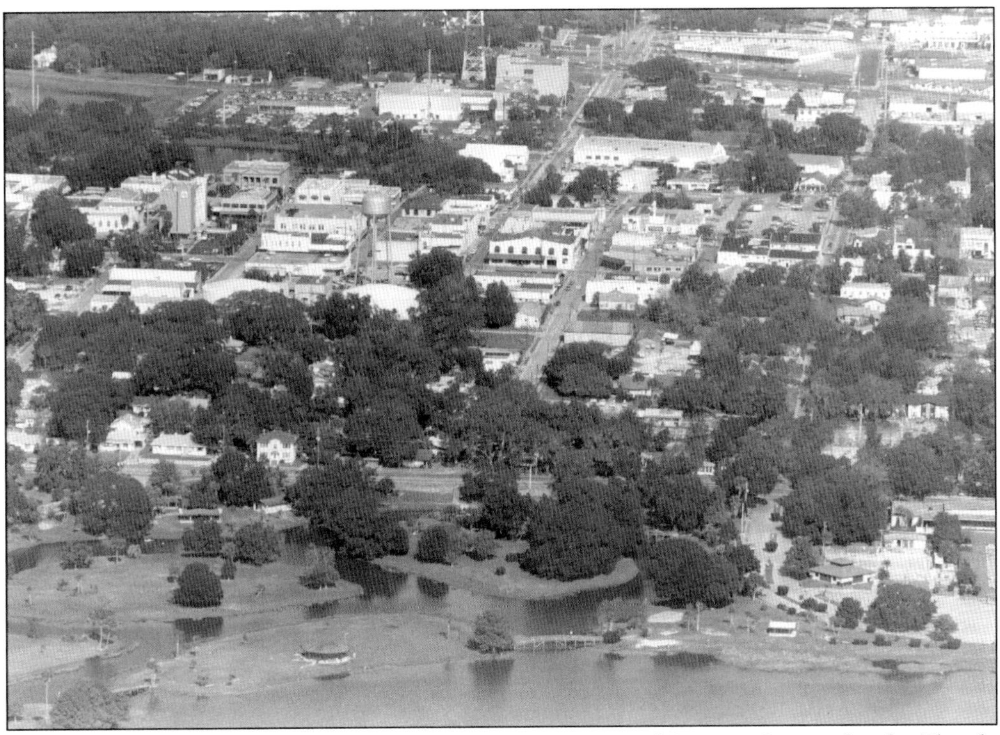

In 1868, Leesburg was named the temporary county seat of Sumter County by the Florida legislature until an election was held. The election was finally held in 1881, with Leesburg losing to Sumterville. On July 12, 1875, the citizens of Leesburg met and voted in favor of incorporation. On July 17, the first mayor, J.G. Wallace, was elected. In 1995, the city adopted the slogan The Lakefront City. This aerial photograph of Leesburg was taken in 1988.

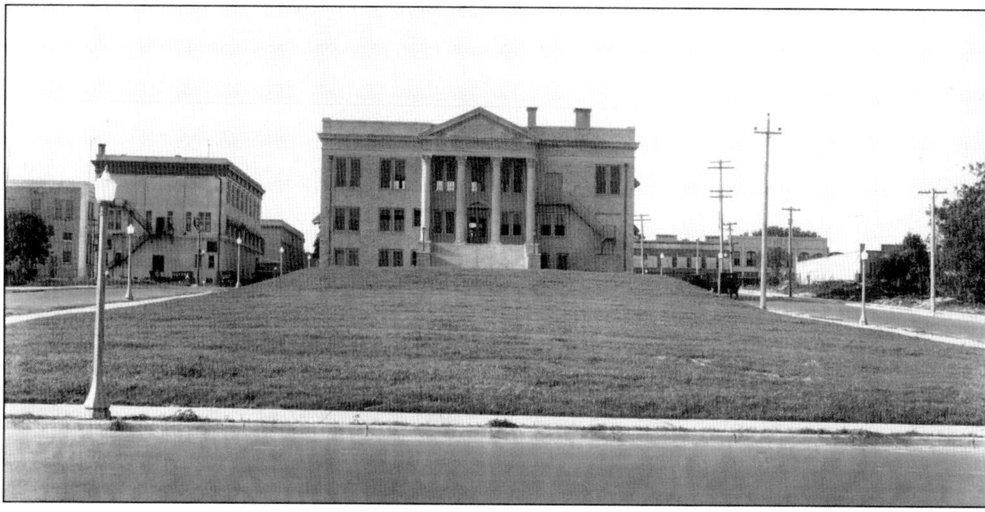

Since incorporating in 1875, the town council has met at several locations, including the Masonic lodge, on the northwest corner of Orange and Fifth Streets. In 1925, construction began on a more permanent city hall. It opened in 1926 and is still used by city officials today. This building originally housed the fire and police departments in the basement, along with the fire chief's quarters and the jail. In 1959, the police and fire departments relocated. City hall has gone through various phases of expansion and modernization over the years, and remains an architectural icon in downtown Leesburg. The photograph above shows the back of city hall after its completion, as well as the rear of the Masonic lodge and the bank building on the left. The 1930s photograph below shows the bay doors used by the fire department.

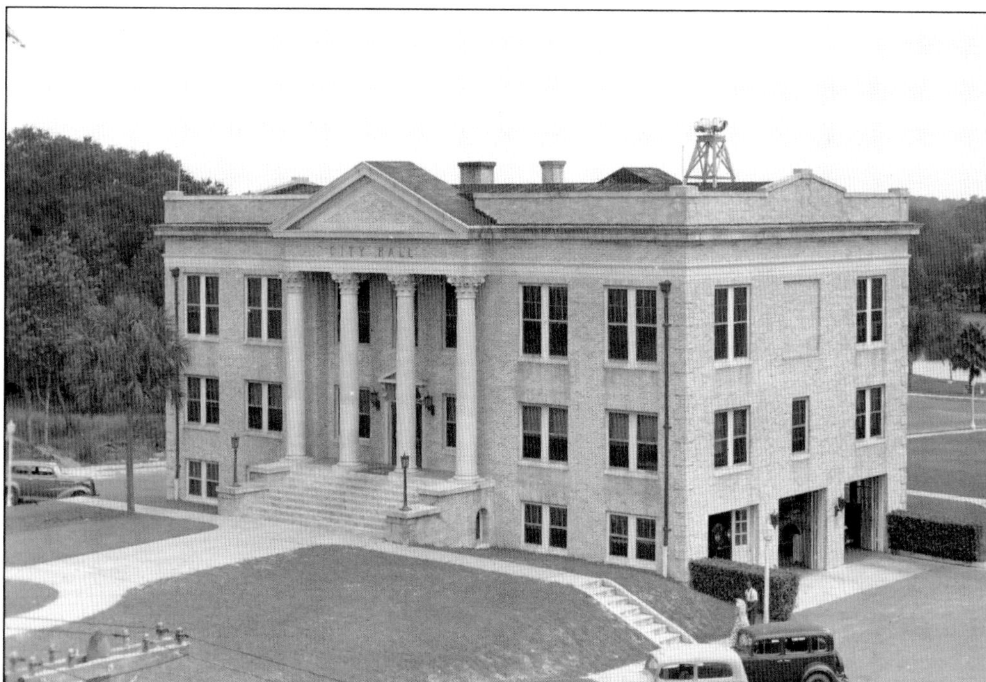

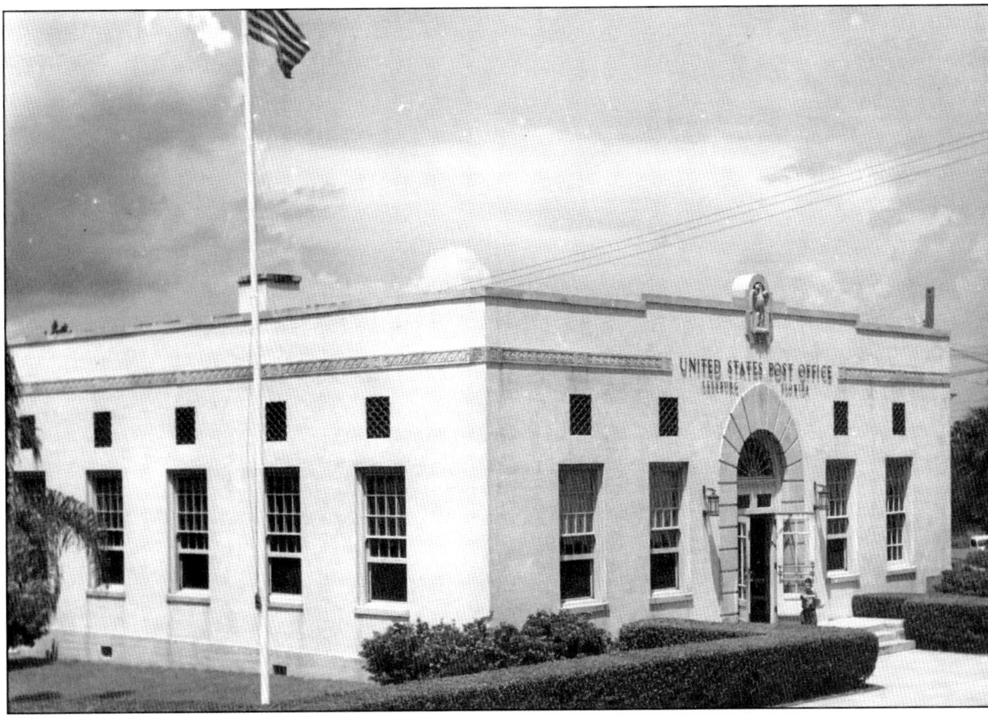

In the mid-1930s, the Works Progress Administration (WPA) was formed to help put America back to work during the Great Depression. Public roads and buildings were constructed throughout the country, including the federal building above in Leesburg in 1935. Soon after, the Leesburg post office moved into the building. Longtime US congressman Albert "Syd" Herlong Jr. was the postmaster at that time.

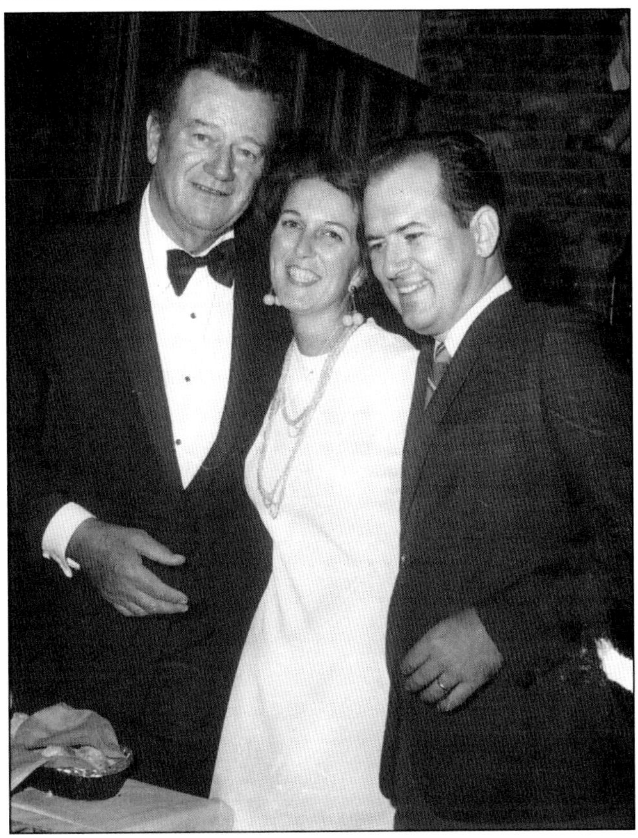

Bill Herlong was born in Leesburg in 1933. In 1968, he ran for US Congress and was narrowly defeated. From 1969 to 1974, he was the chairman of Florida's ASC Committee for the US Department of Agriculture. During this time, he and his wife, Margaret, were invited to dine with Pres. Richard Nixon at the White House, where they are pictured with movie legend John Wayne.

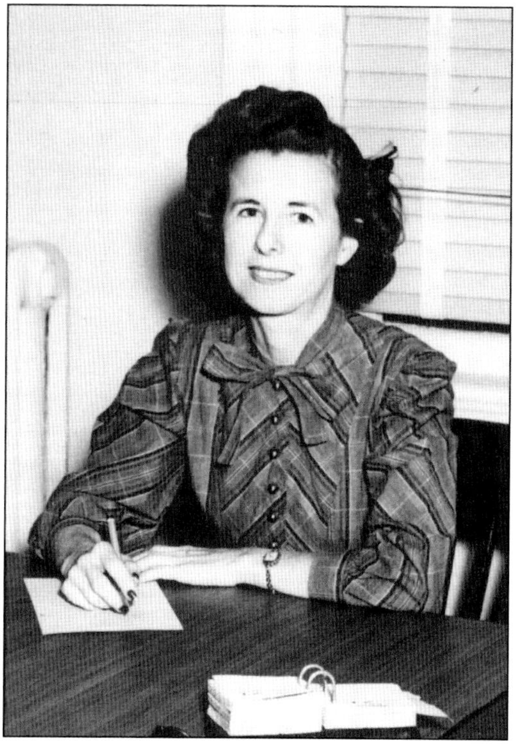

Sara Barcus, the daughter of Harry Edward and Olga McAlpin Barcus, became a city employee in 1936. She was the deputy city clerk until her retirement in January 1976. Sara began living with her mother at the Barcus family home, at 1434 West Main Street, in 1922, and remained there until her passing in April 2005.

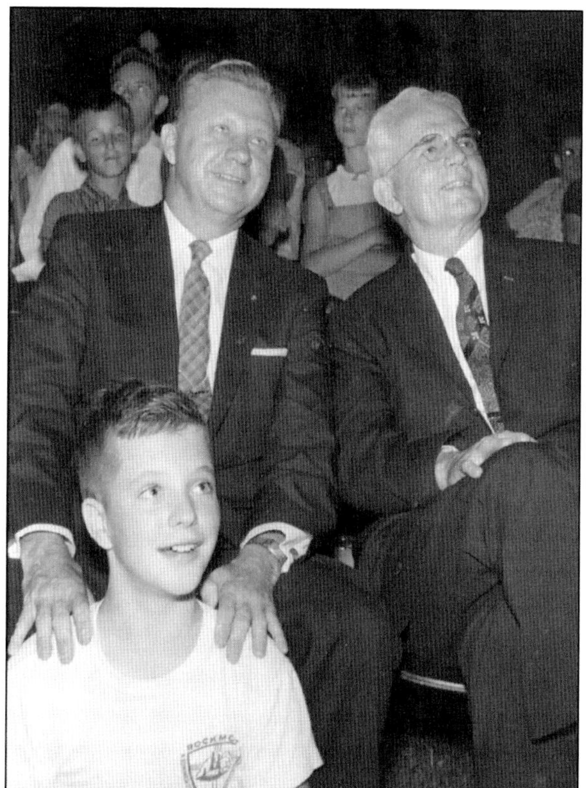

Banker James Carlisle Rogers (left) is seen here with his son James Jr. and Sen. Spessard Lindsay Holland, who was the governor of Florida from 1941 to 1945 and a US senator from 1945 to 1971. Holland wrote the following on the back of this photograph: "To my good friend Carlisle and his son Jim. With happy memories of Leesburg watermelons, lovely . . . old times and two good friends. Devotedly Spessard L. Holland, U. S. Senate Fla, Washington. Jan 4, 1970."

James Lee Hux was born in Lake County in 1871 and married Sarah Elizabeth Tison. His father, Thomas Asbury Hux, was a Confederate veteran. In 1923, James became Leesburg's police chief. Chief Hux's "End of Watch" came on February 13, 1924, when he was ambushed in the swamps of Eldorado while looking for the operators of an illegal moonshine still. He was Lake County's second law enforcement officer to be killed in the line of duty. (Courtesy of Judy Hux Rainey.)

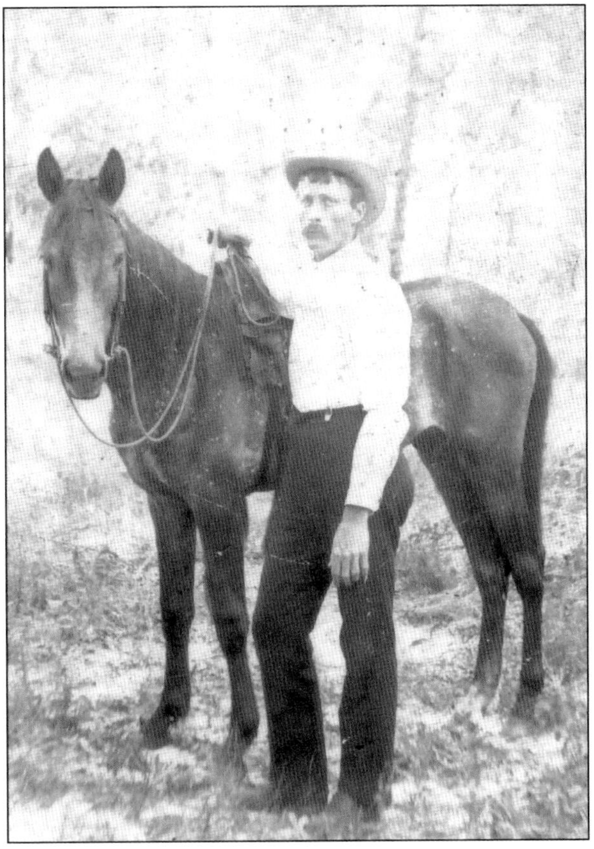

The Leesburg policemen in the late 1940s photograph below are, from left to right, Russell Lester "Cy" Wyckoff, Lester Clarence "Pop" French, Robert Lee Thomas, Chief William Leslie Fisher, James Richey, Harvey Tillman Hughes, and Joel Raymond Putnam. Fisher served as the chief of police from 1946 to 1968.

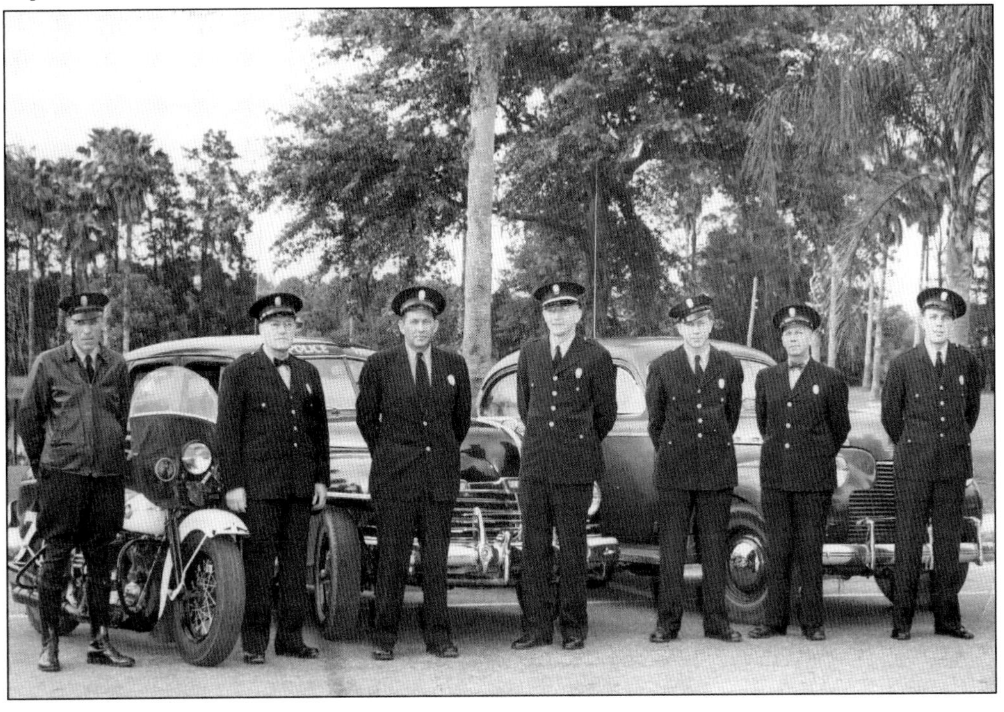

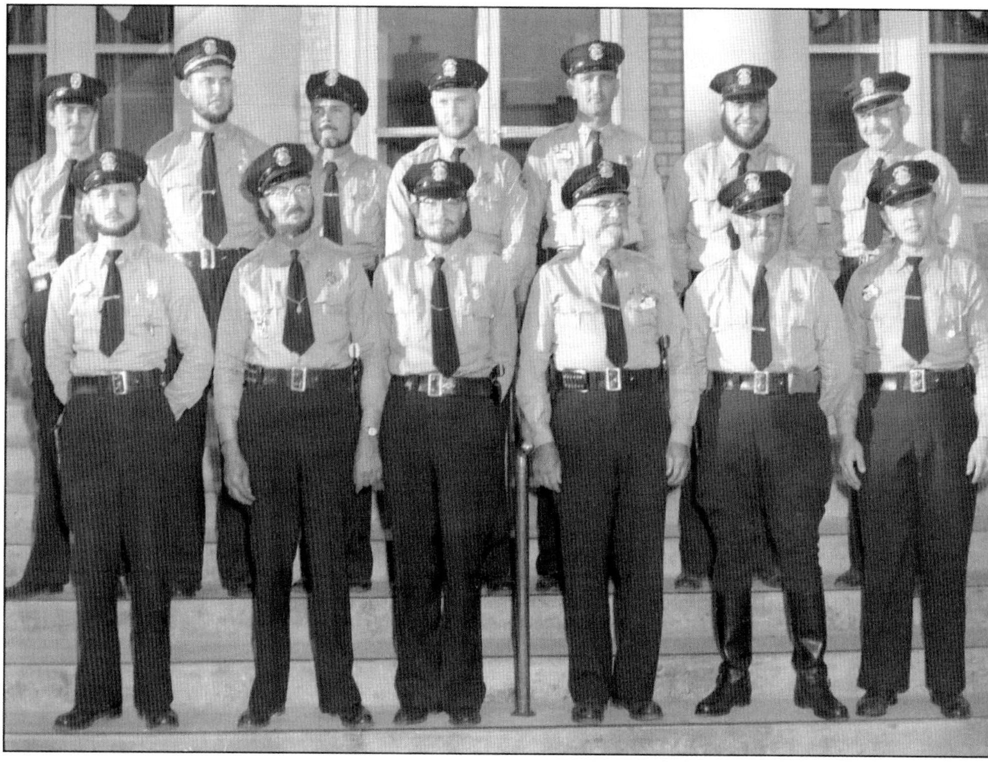

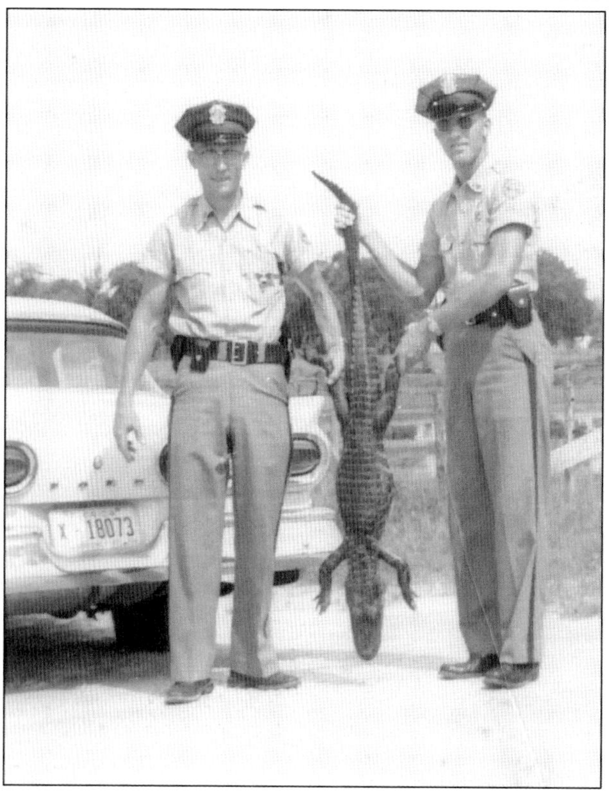

Ralph F. Perry (above, second row, second from left) joined the Leesburg police department as a patrolman in 1947, about 10 years before the photograph was taken. He served as chief of police from 1969 to 1982, succeeding William Fisher. During World War II, Perry served five years in the military police and one year as a criminal investigator in Hawaii. Note the similar beards that Perry and several of the officers are sporting for Leesburg's centennial.

In this 1958 photograph, Leesburg police officers Chester Rey Cocker (left) and Robert McClellan "Bob" Meeler Jr. hold a five-foot alligator they captured at the public marina. This juvenile alligator must not have given the officers much trouble, as the photograph shows that the gator's mouth and legs are not secured and there are no signs the animal was shot.

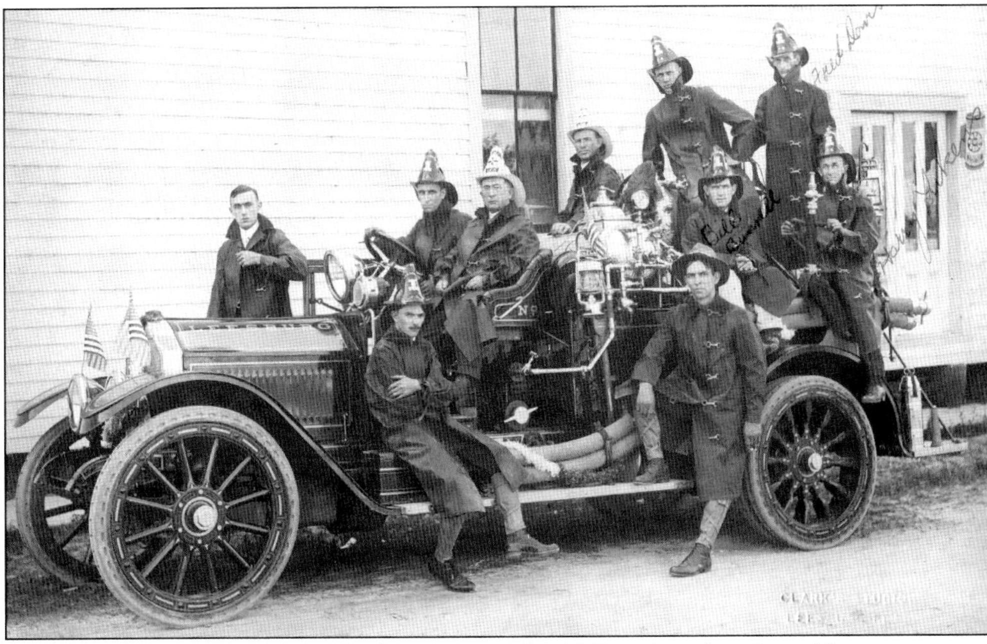

The Leesburg Fire Department had its roots in the 1860s, when friends and business owners lined up to form bucket brigades. By 1885, the town council moved forward in bringing "modern" firefighting to Leesburg. In 1886, town leaders had a Silsby steam fire engine built, and, in 1890, a fire bell was purchased from the Buckeye Foundry in Ohio. The contest held to name the steam fire engine was won by Georgia Dozier, the sister of the mayor, and the engine was dubbed the *Georgia D.* The photograph above shows the Leesburg Fire Department in 1918. The 1926 photograph below shows Leesburg city officials and firefighters on board the city's 1922 American LaFrance fire truck. This truck replaced the department's 1917 truck.

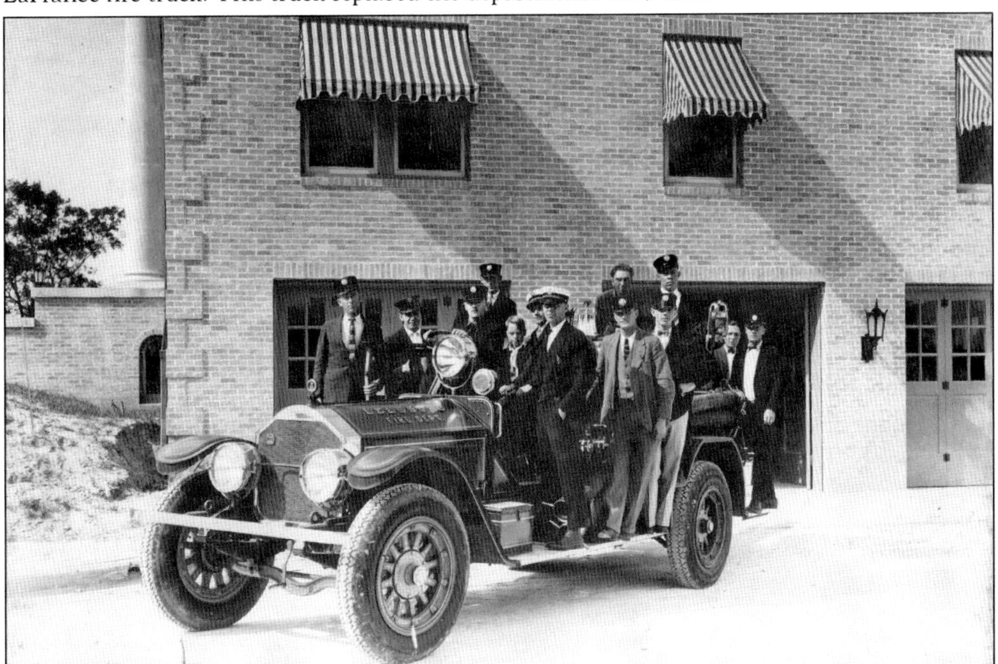

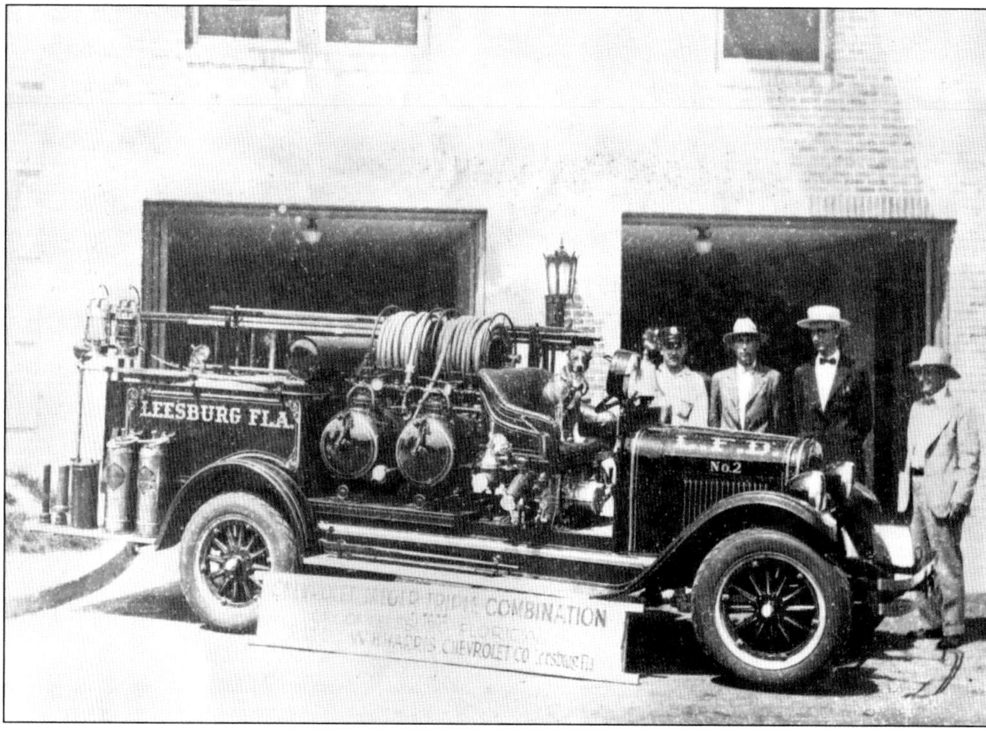

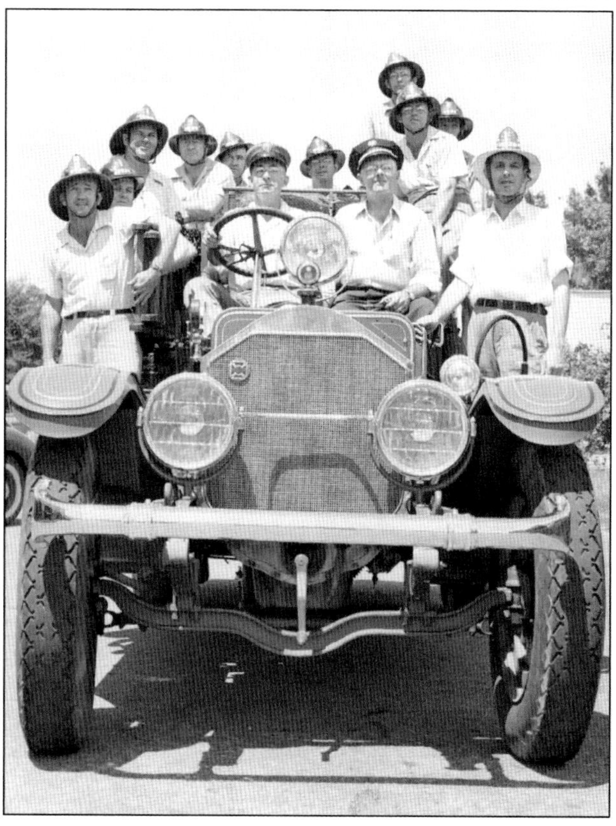

The sign leaning against the 1927 fire truck above reads, "Chevrolet Jaeger Triple Combination, City of Leesburg, Florida, Sold by W. H. Harris Chevrolet Co Leesburg Fla." The Jaeger Triple Combination truck was manufactured by the Jaeger Fire Equipment Company. It was made with a Chevrolet chassis and was praised by Jaeger as the first triple-combination-use truck. The department's formidable firefighting boxer commands the driver's seat.

Chief Robert Lee "Bunny" Stevens, holding his famous pipe, sits in the passenger seat of this Chevrolet-made 1927 fire truck in the 1960s. Chief Stevens served as the fire chief from 1937 until 1962. He started with the Leesburg Fire Department in 1922. He was married to Bertha Ellen "Nellie" Rast. This fire engine is still on display at a Leesburg firehouse.

Bruce Kirby polishes Leesburg's original 1890 fire bell. The 400-pound bronze bell was first mounted in the bell tower of a firehouse constructed by W.M. Trunnell, who built many Leesburg homes from 1880 to 1890. Later, the bell was moved to the town water tank, where it was used to signal war bond sales during World War II. Today, the bell is mounted in a place of honor at the fire station at Magnolia and Canal Streets.

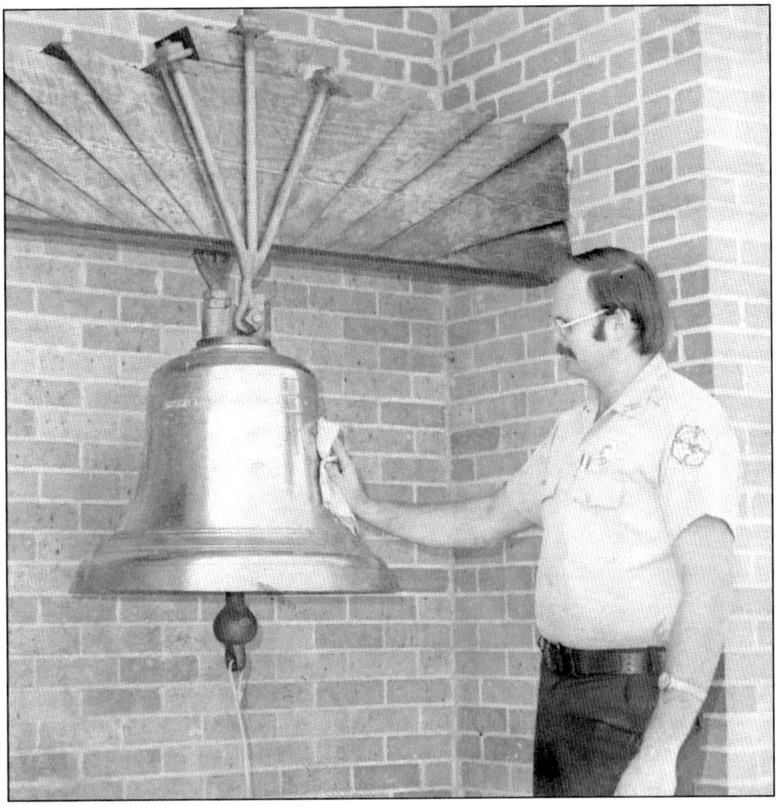

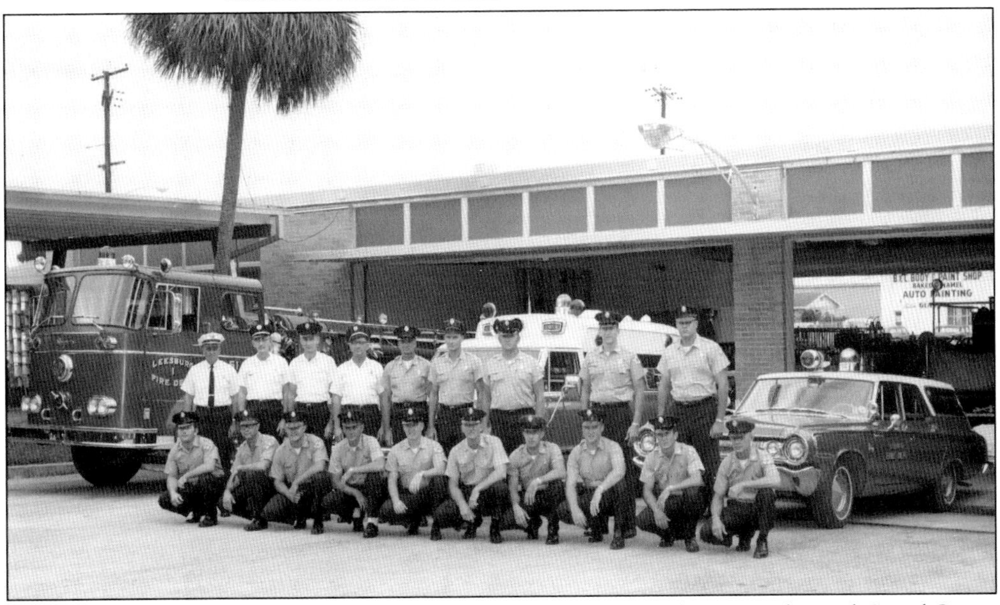

This 1971 Leesburg Fire Department photograph was taken at the Magnolia and Canal Street station. It includes, from left to right, (first row) Robert Jordan, unidentified, Ken Enloe, Robert Franklin, Al Ponds, Jim Yates, Tom Horton, Bill Reed, Doyle Harbison, and J.B. Hand; (second row) Chief Robert Taylor, Assistant Chief James Griner, Capt. Gene Twiss, Capt. Dale Hoornstra, Roy Snell, Clyde Twiss, Byron Works, Jim Engle, and Terry Seawell.

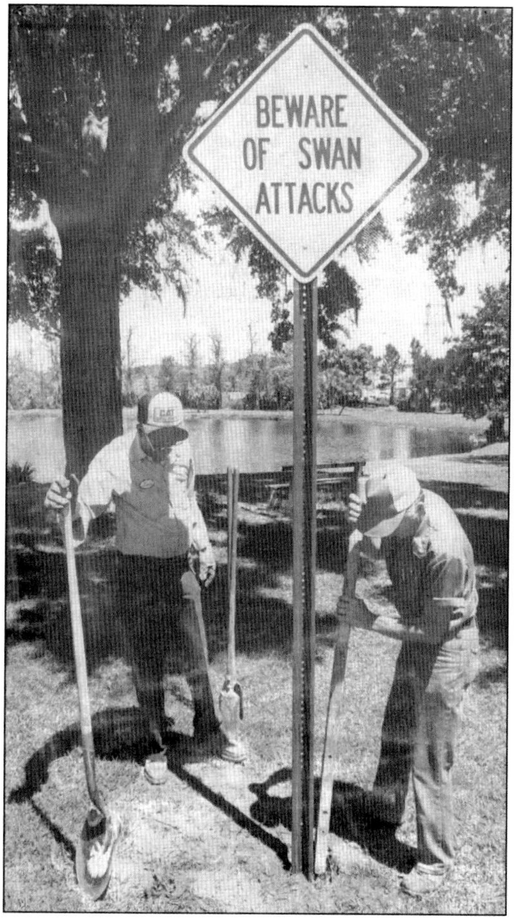

The work to create Fountain Lake Park began shortly after the city acquired the land in 1926. The park, located on the north side of city hall, went by several different names in its early history. It was known as City Hall Park, City Pond, and Swan Lake. In the 1950s, swans began to call the park home. The swans were quite aggressive, especially during the mating season. While nesting, the cobs became very protective of their territory. City workers were attacked while mowing, and one woman ran out of her shoes making her escape from an attack. At left, city workers Monroe Lawrence (left) and B.L. Castle install a "Beware of Swan Attacks" sign at the park. Below, in 1976, to celebrate America's bicentennial, a time capsule containing a variety of memorabilia was buried in Fountain Lake Park.

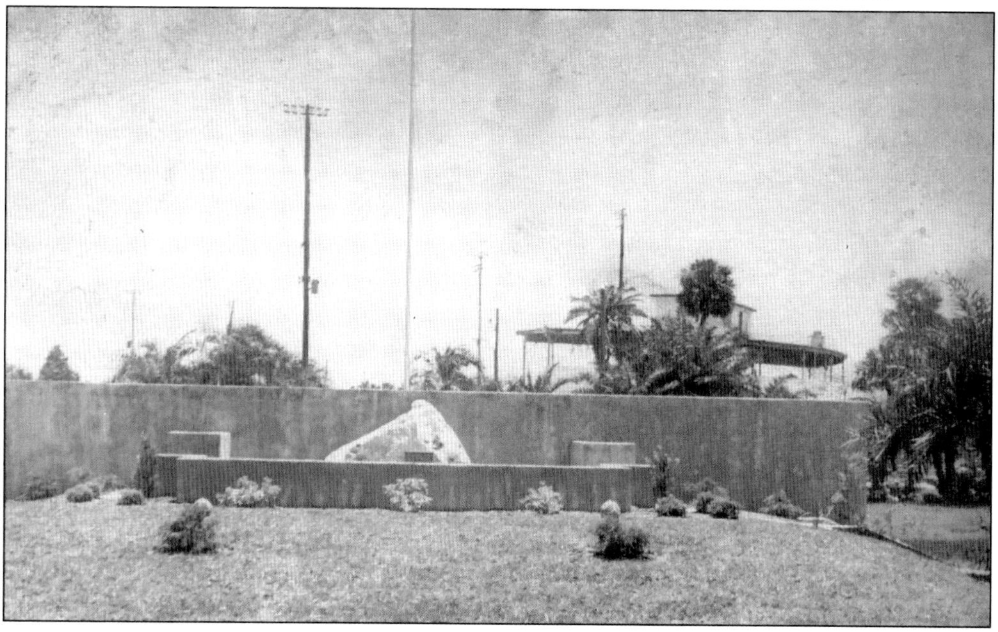

Three

Leesburg Legends

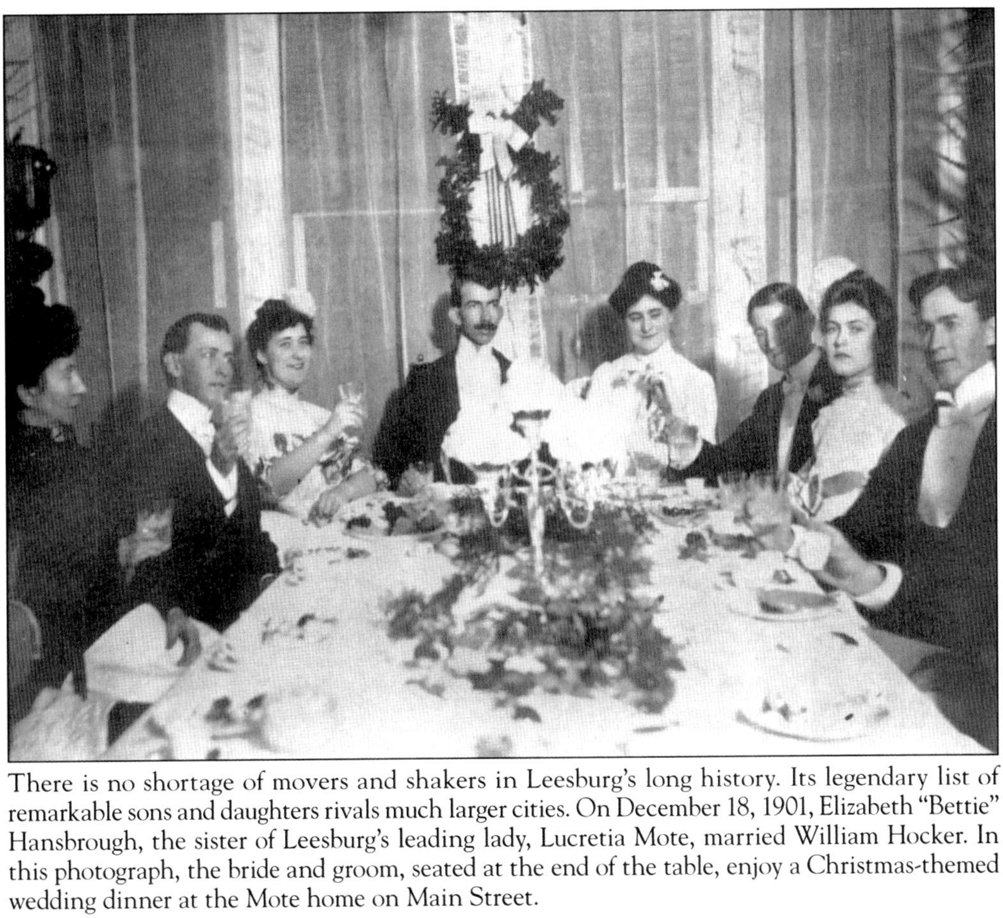

There is no shortage of movers and shakers in Leesburg's long history. Its legendary list of remarkable sons and daughters rivals much larger cities. On December 18, 1901, Elizabeth "Bettie" Hansbrough, the sister of Leesburg's leading lady, Lucretia Mote, married William Hocker. In this photograph, the bride and groom, seated at the end of the table, enjoy a Christmas-themed wedding dinner at the Mote home on Main Street.

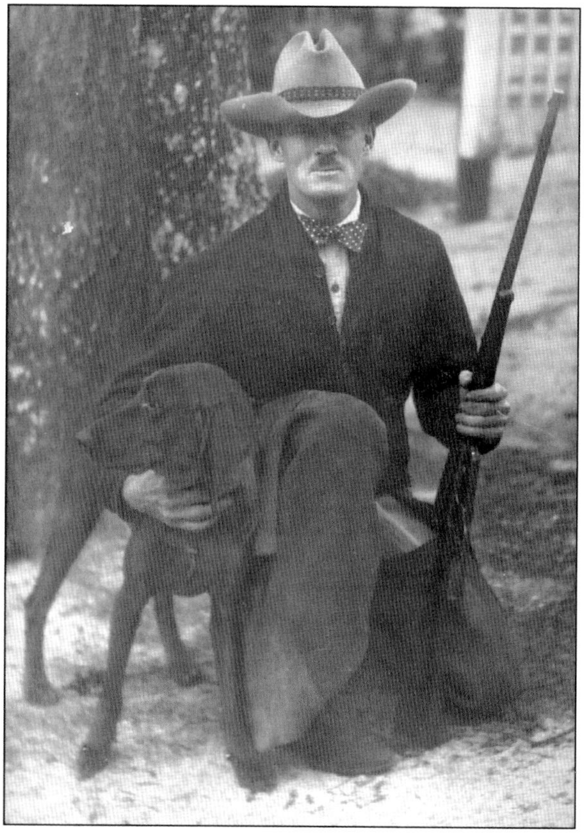

David McCheyne Newell was born in Chicago and moved to Leesburg in 1912. He was a novelist, children's story writer, and illustrator. He wrote and illustrated art for many publications, including the *Saturday Evening Post*, The *New York Herald-Tribune*, *Boy's Life*, and *Field and Stream*, of which he was the editor. A naturalist and hunter, Newell hosted a nature and hunting show on television in the 1950s.

John Jacob Stoer, pictured with his hunting dogs, came to Leesburg between 1910 and 1920 with his wife, Margaretta Kunigunde Mugele. Stoer, whose parents were Bavarian immigrants, was born in 1854 in Pittsburgh, Pennsylvania. He married Margaretta, also from Pittsburgh, in 1879. Stoer was a liquor dealer, a lumber merchant, and a paint manufacturer.

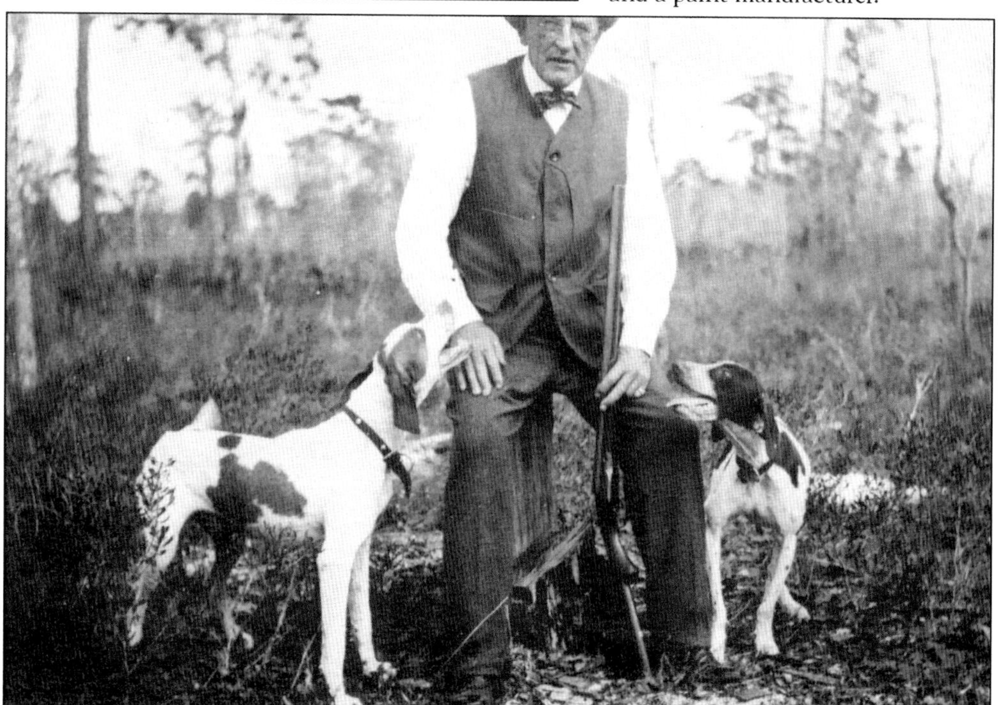

Isabella May Haynes Keeling (far right) operated a popular boardinghouse on Main Street from the 1890s until the 1930s. She was the oldest daughter of Capt. Melton Haynes. From left to right are Isabella May's sisters Sarah "Sallie" Haynes, Minnie Haynes Smith, and their mother, Sarah Isabella Vaught Haynes. Isabella May and Sallie were charter members of Leesburg Chapter 84 Order of the Eastern Star, which was chartered on April 15, 1914.

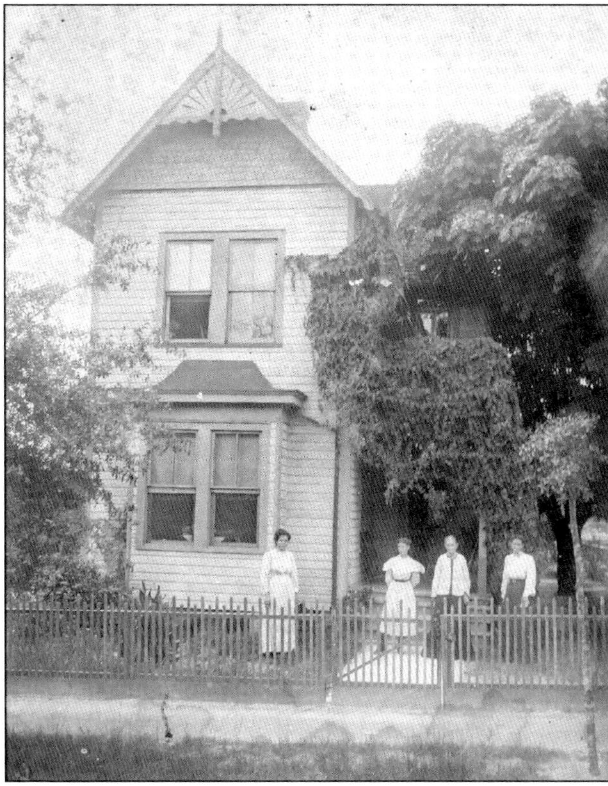

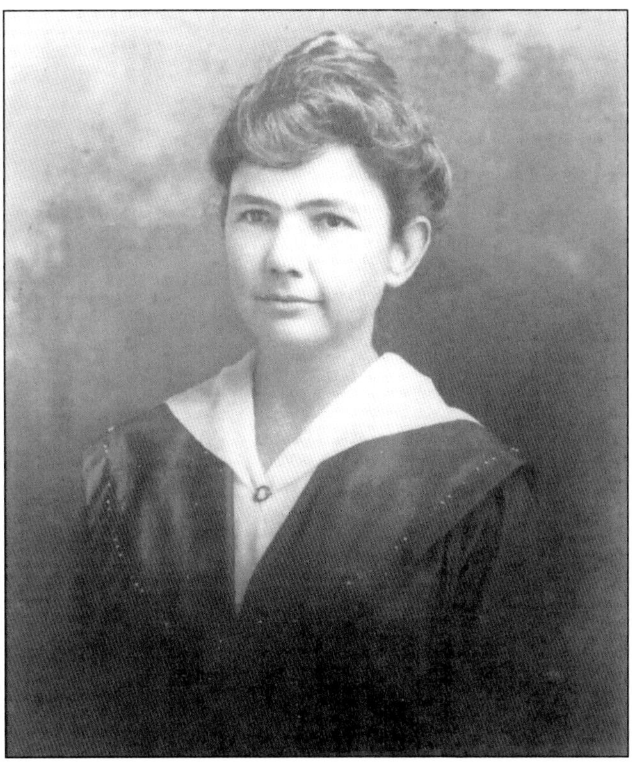

Mabel Haynes, seen here in 1900 at age 20, was the daughter of Volney and Carrie Lovell Haynes and the granddaughter of Capt. Melton Haynes. Known as Miss Mabel by everyone, she never married, but kept very busy working with her mother at their boardinghouse. Mabel died on April 6, 1970, and is buried in Lone Oak Cemetery. She donated her home to Morrison Methodist Church. (Courtesy of the Lovell family collection.)

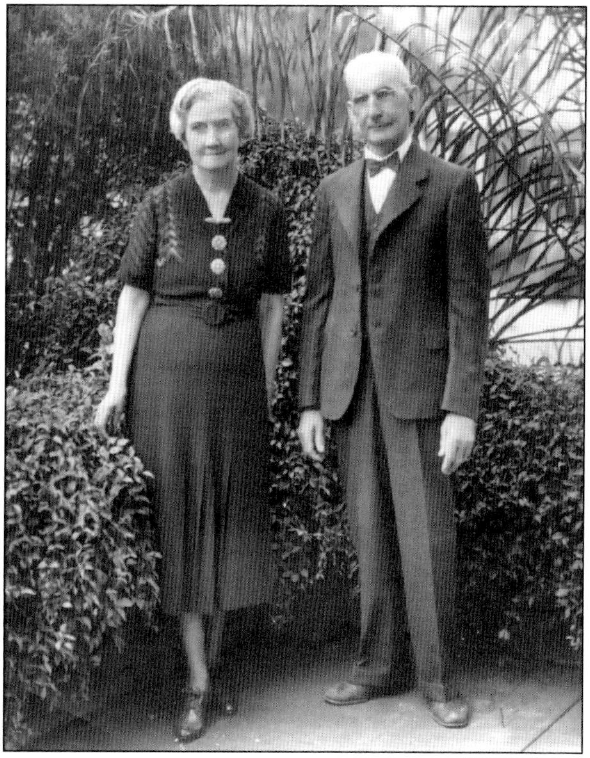

Arthur Hugh Bourlay and Florence May Lee Bourlay are seen here. Florence May was the daughter of George Marion Lee and the granddaughter of Evander Lee. The Bourlays purchased property south of Lake Griffin that was originally homesteaded by Thomas Robertson, and later by James Fussell and Evander Lee. The Bourlay family owned the land for over 100 years. Arthur Bourlay III donated the land in 1999, creating Bourlay Historic Nature Park.

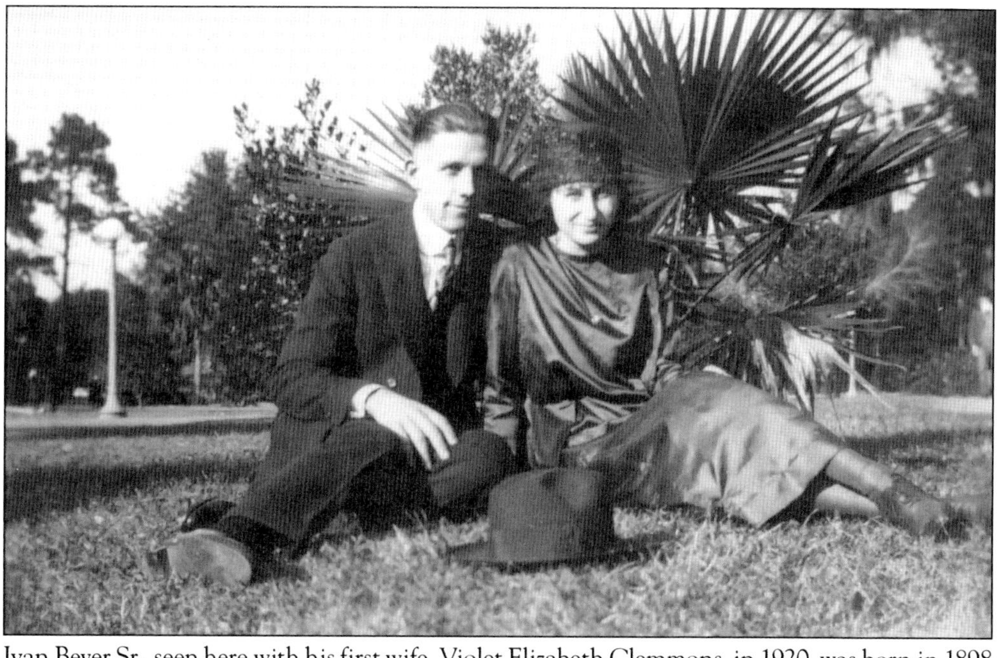

Ivan Beyer Sr., seen here with his first wife, Violet Elizabeth Clemmons, in 1920, was born in 1898 in Illinois to John William Beyers and Cecelia Florine Thomas Beyers. Ivan came to Leesburg in 1916 and worked for B.D. Harris in 1918, the same year he opened his first funeral home in Umatilla. He went on to open a funeral home in Leesburg in 1931, in the Jonathan Yates Clark house on Main Street.

George Rast (left) and Robert "Bunny" Stevens are seen at right in the 1920s. Rast was born in Orange Springs, Florida, in 1904. He was a longtime banker, retiring in 1969 as a vice president of the First National Bank after a 46-year career. A community leader, Rast was a charter member of the Leesburg Lions Club in 1935, headed Leesburg's watermelon festivals in the early 1950s, served as the general chairman for the city's centennial celebration in 1957, and headed the Leesburg Heritage Society for many years after it was formed in 1976. Rast and his wife, Mildred, were one of only a few centenarian couples in the country, though Mildred passed away three months after her 100th birthday. George lived to be 102, passing away in 2006. He is seen below on the far right, serving on the 1948 Chamber of Commerce Beauty Contest committee.

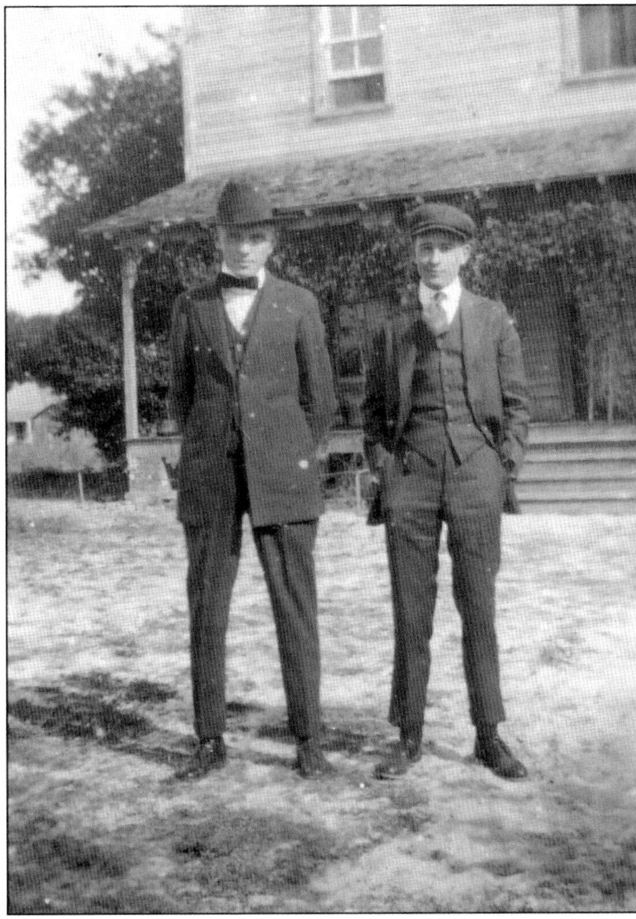

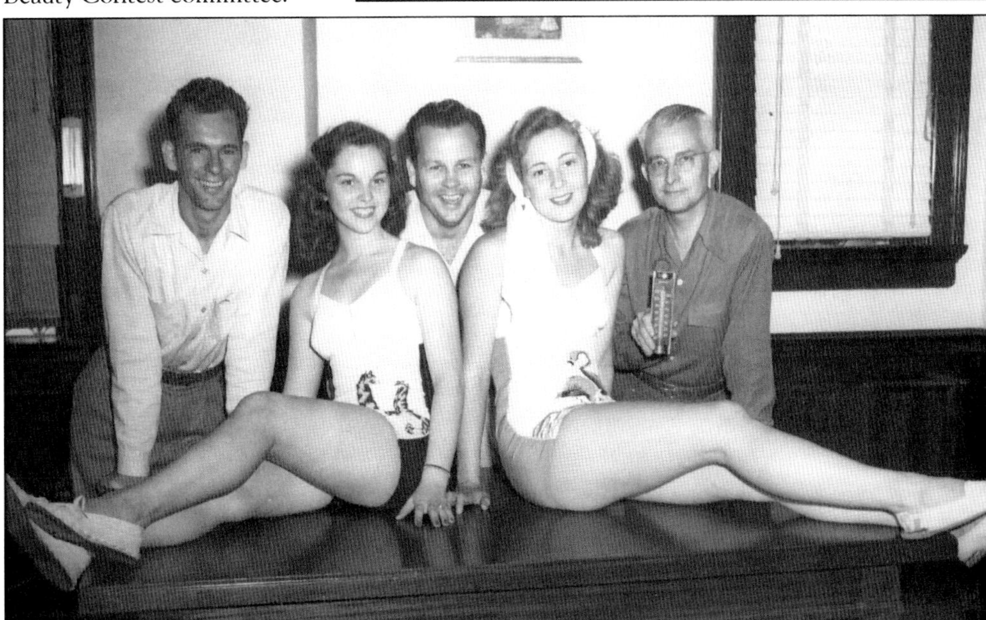

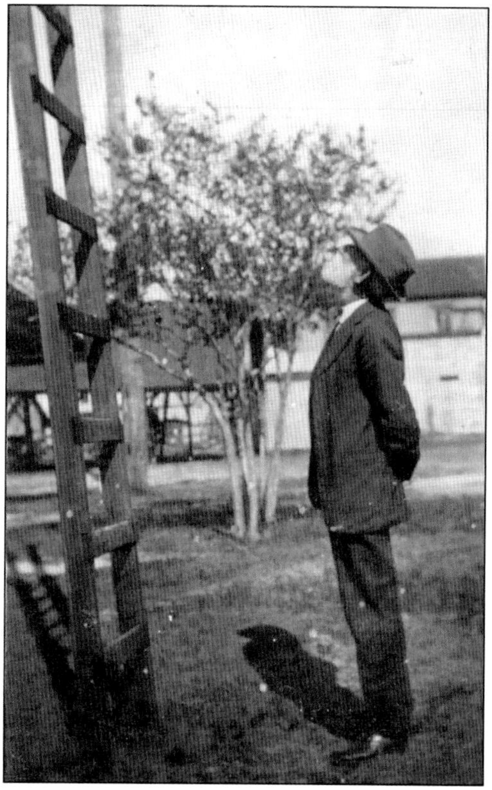

Leesburg's first telephone exchange was built by Dr. Peter W. Butler around 1900. The exchange was located in the old city library, on Orange Street. Dr. Butler is seen here overseeing some construction work. In 1918, with the telephone exchange having about 250 customers, Butler sold his interests to Otto Wettstein Jr., who created the Florida Telephone Corporation in 1925.

In 1942, Jacquelyn Hester became the first woman to be employed as an international radio telegraph operator in commercial aviation. Of the four applicants for the Pan American Airways job in Miami, she was the only one to make the grade. Though coded messages usually ran less than 50 words, the first one she received was 207 words. "Jacky," born in 1924, was the oldest daughter of Earle and Katherine Ross Hester.

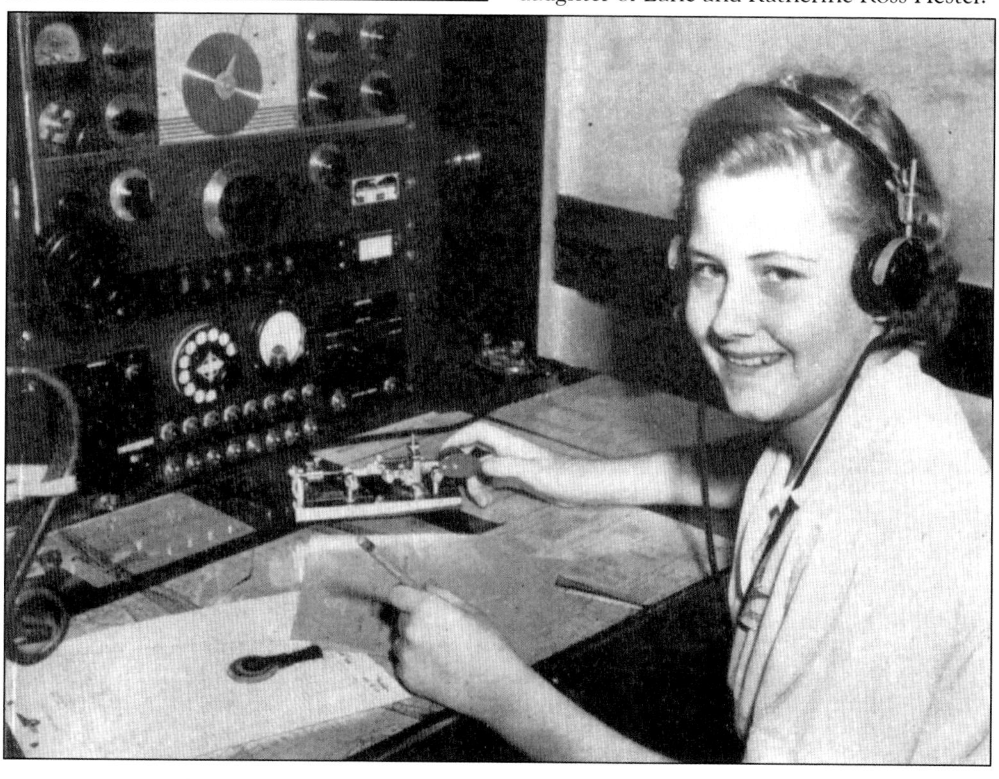

Jonathan Yates Clark (right), seen here with Govan George Ware, was born in Chicago in 1872. He became one of Chicago's largest contractors, building many of the city's famous buildings, including the Art Institute on Michigan Avenue. He moved to Fruitland Park in 1902 and then to Leesburg in 1906, where he established a light and water plant. He was married to Mae Knight and passed away in Leesburg in 1928.

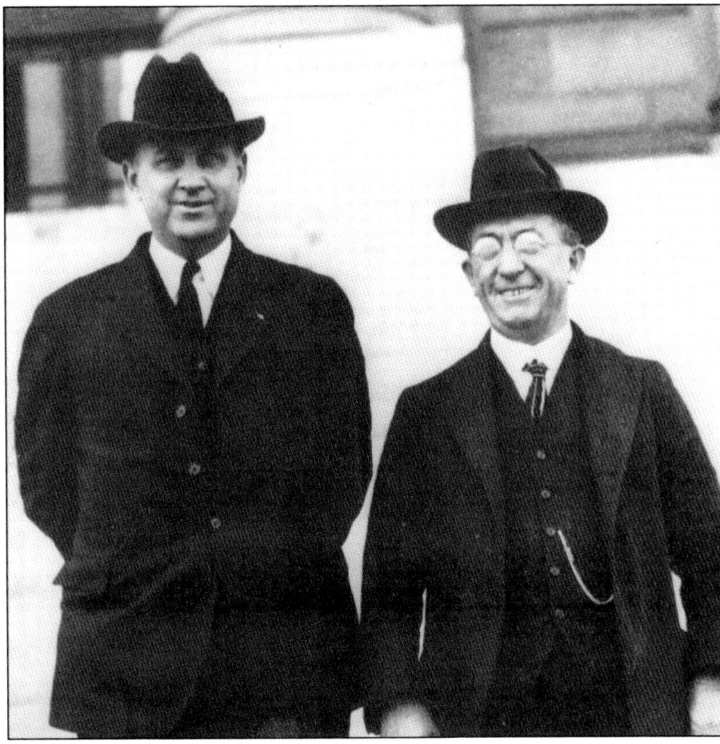

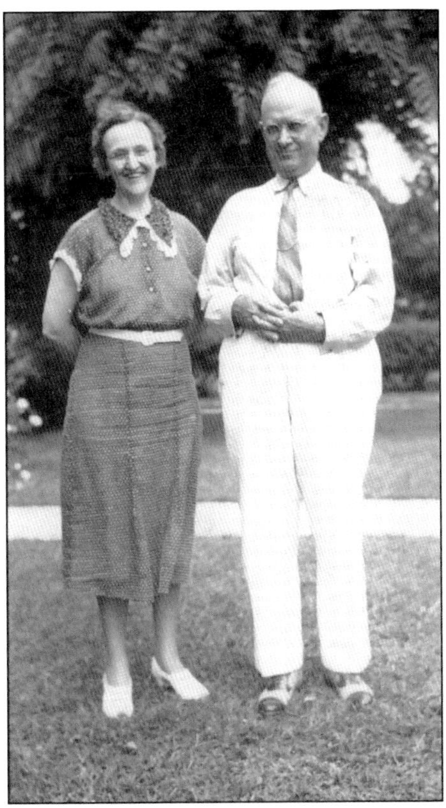

Govan George Ware, seen here with his wife, Clara Freeman, was a native Floridian, born in Bradford County in 1885. In 1909, he became a bank cashier and went on to be the president of the First National Bank of Leesburg. He was known as Mr. Leesburg. He served as the president of the Leesburg Commercial Publishing & Printing Company, the Crystal River Rock Company, and the Silver Lake Country Club.

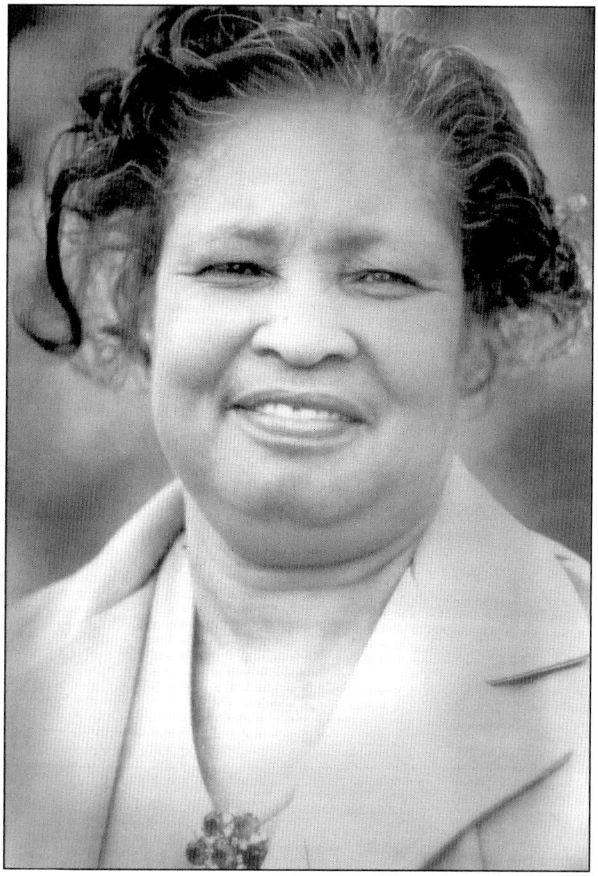

Margaret Cason Ward was a renowned Leesburg educator and community activist. She was born in 1924 and moved to Leesburg in 1947 from Madison, Florida. She was the founder and CEO of the Dabney Manatee Heritage Group and was the first African American inducted into the Lake County Women's Hall of Fame. Ward was a certified reading specialist for the Lake County School District and a member of St. Paul A.M.E. Church. She passed away in 2011.

Below, Annie DeLoss Robertson Hester (right), her husband, Frederick Cummins, and their children have their photograph taken in front of their home at 1317 West Main Street in 1916. The couple was married on September 19, 1894. From left to right are Frederick Cummins Jr., Mary Anna, Frederick Cummins Sr., Allifair "Fairy," and Annie. The woman and child on the side porch in left background are unidentified.

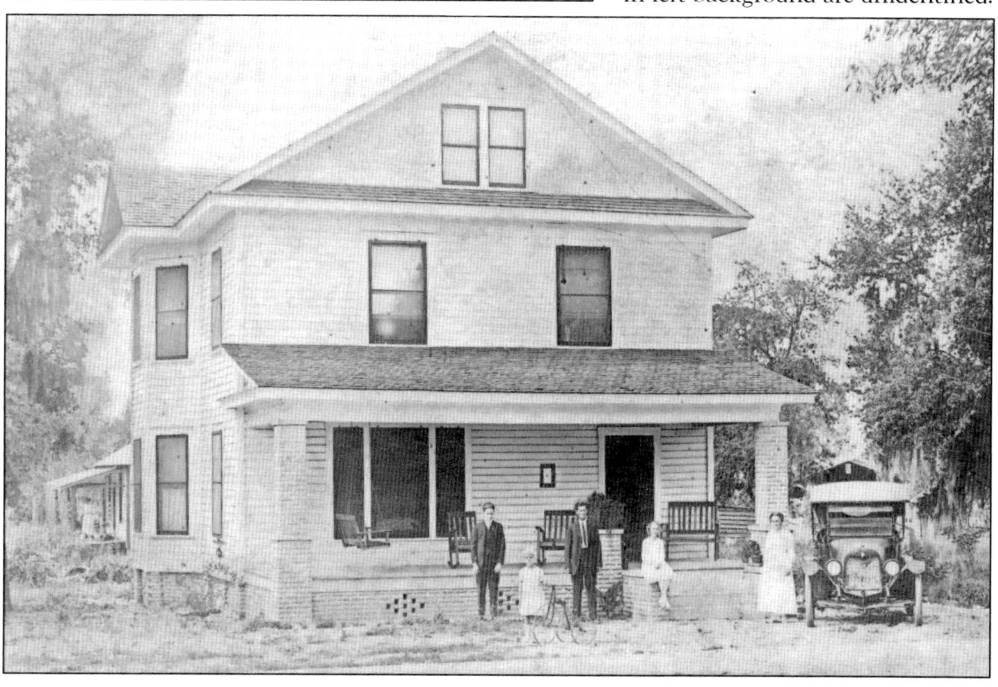

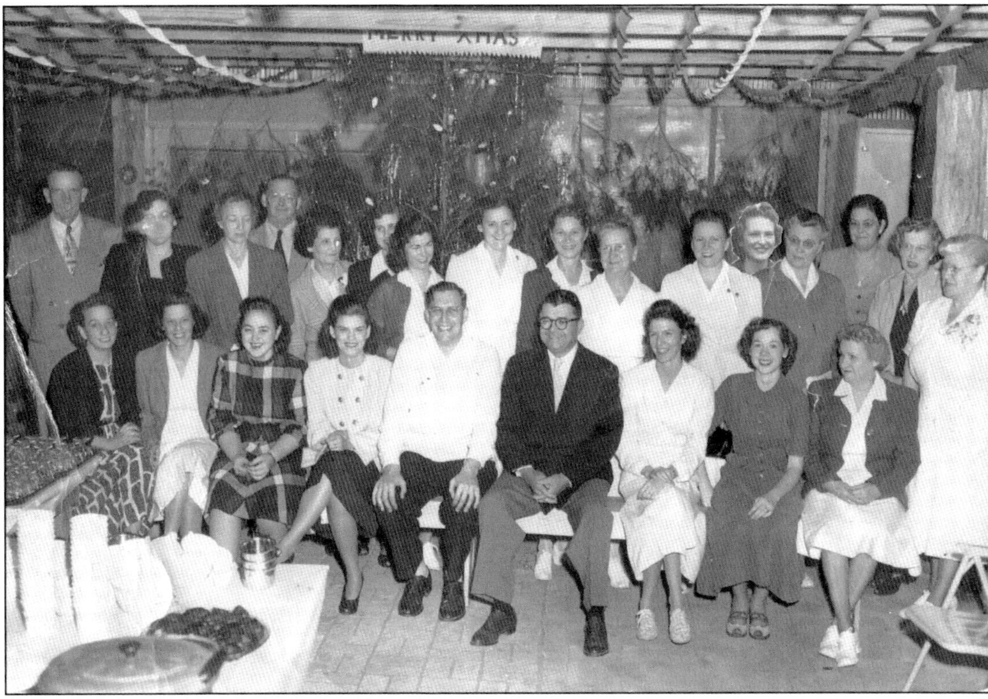

Dr. Howard Grey Holland (above, seated, in black jacket) came to Leesburg in 1925 and opened a hospital in the old John Love home (below) on West Main Street. Dr. Holland was one of Leesburg's most well-known doctors and surgeons. He named his hospital Theresa Holland Hospital. Born in Headland, Alabama, on August 8, 1896, Dr. Holland married Valeta May Grant in Jackson County, Florida, on September 11, 1916. Valeta May was born in Headland as well, in 1895. In 1940, Dr. Holland made extensive additions to the hospital, and, in 1947, a clinic, office space, nurses' quarters, and more rooms were built next door. He passed away in 1954.

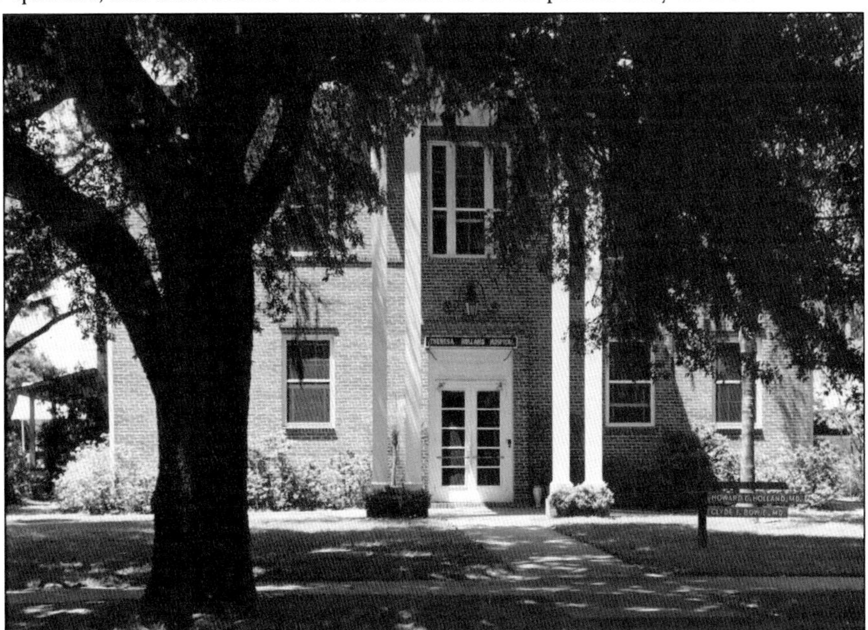

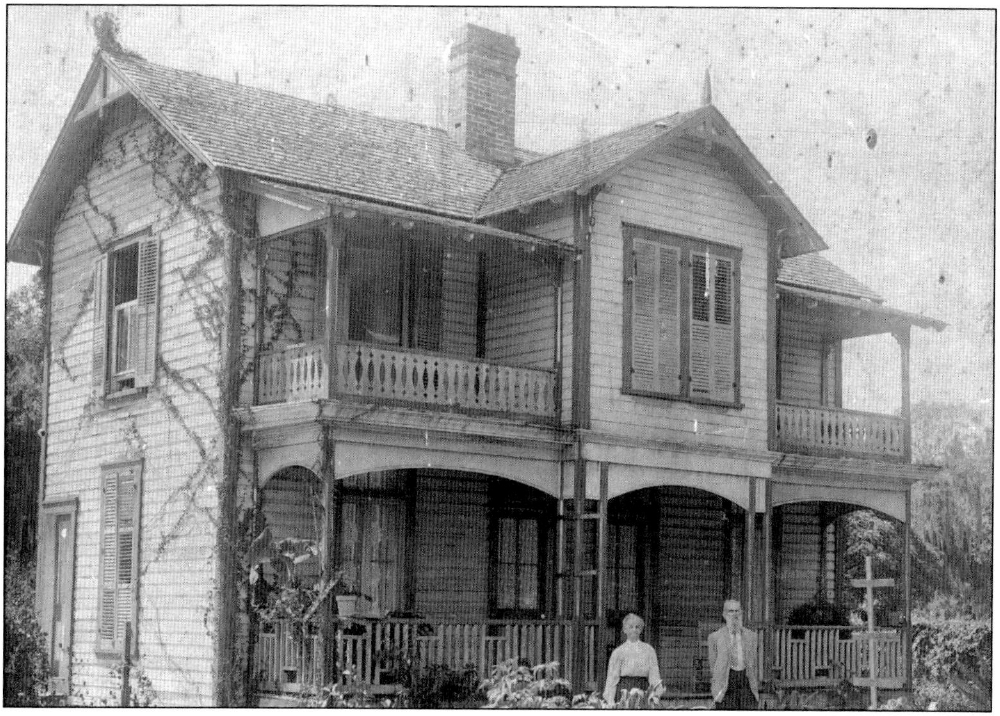

Asa Sleeth Hardman and his third wife, Samantha Jane Horn Ryan, are seen here at their home at 6 Lilly Street around 1915. Asa was born in Freeport, Indiana, in 1839. He was an artilleryman in the War Between the States and fought at the Battle of Gettysburg. He was the postmaster in Leesburg in 1892, and served as the justice of the peace for Lake County from 1913 to 1917.

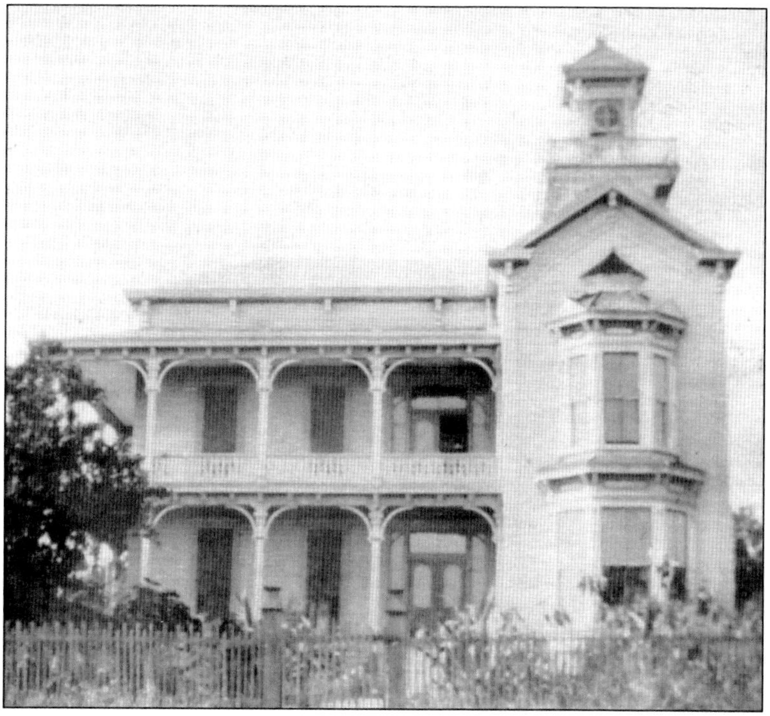

This photograph of the Dr. Arthur Abrehart Stivender house was taken on November 25, 1917. Construction on the home began in 1885, but it was not completed until 1888. Stivender, a very successful orange grower, developed his famous wild grove along the shore of Lake Harris on the Eldorado-Sunnyside peninsula. The house is still standing.

Edward and Lucretia Mote's home on Main Street was built in 1892 and cost $9,000 to construct. In 1908, Bishop Henry Clay Morrison bought the house as a retirement residence. In 1918, the home was sold to John and May James Morris. A member of the Morris family lived there for the next 70 years. On September 1, 1990, it was relocated to Magnolia Street.

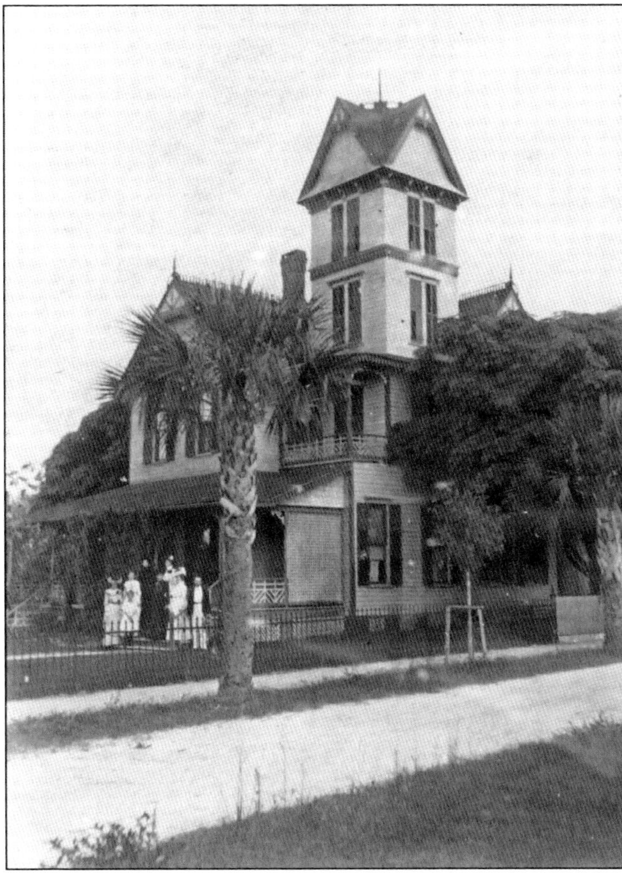

Leesburg's first twins, Pearl and Ruby Stallings, are pictured around 1905 at the Stallings home at 107 North Twelfth Street. They were born on January 16, 1895, to Jesse Lane and Lenora Mary Matthews Stallings. Lenora's father, David Matthews, homesteaded on Picciola Island on Lake Griffin when he arrived in Florida in 1874. Pearl died in 1987, but Ruby lived to only 16, passing away in 1911.

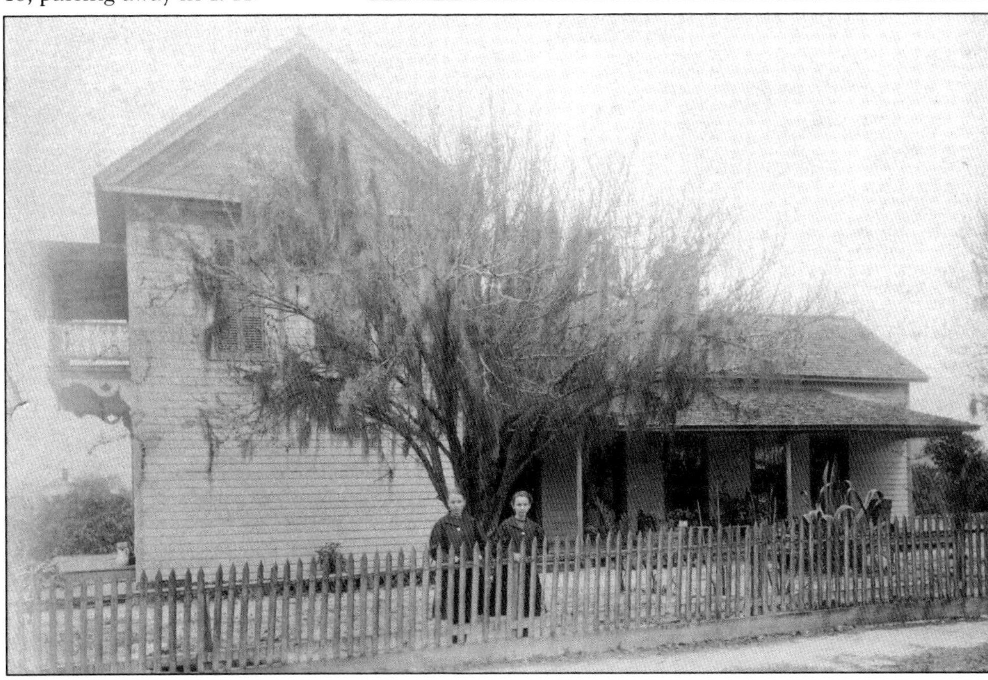

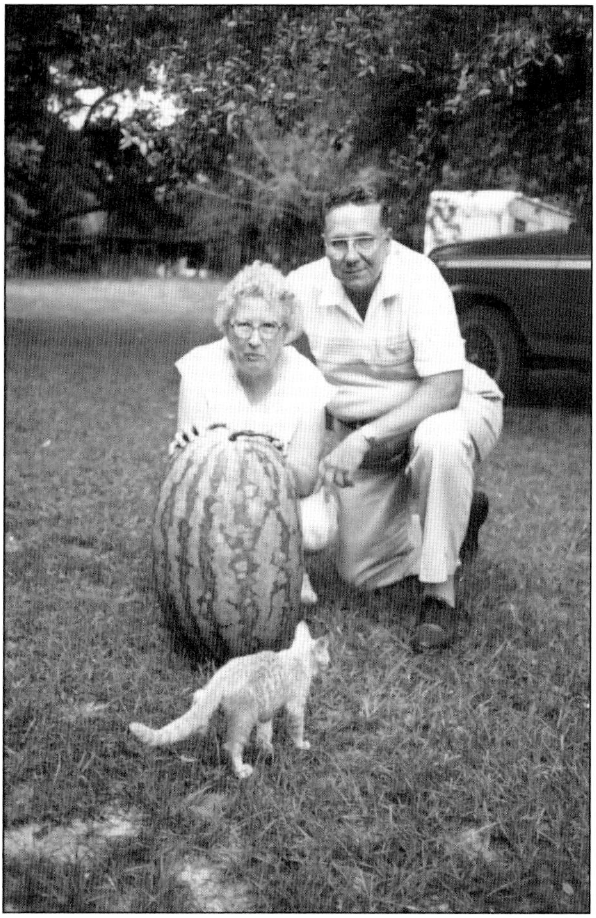

Gordon and Peggy Dorris are seen here with an 85-pound watermelon they raised in 1987. They were experts at growing very large watermelons. Gordon said that watermelons were in the family blood, and, after working in the office all week, he liked to get on his old tractor, chew a little tobacco, and raise watermelons.

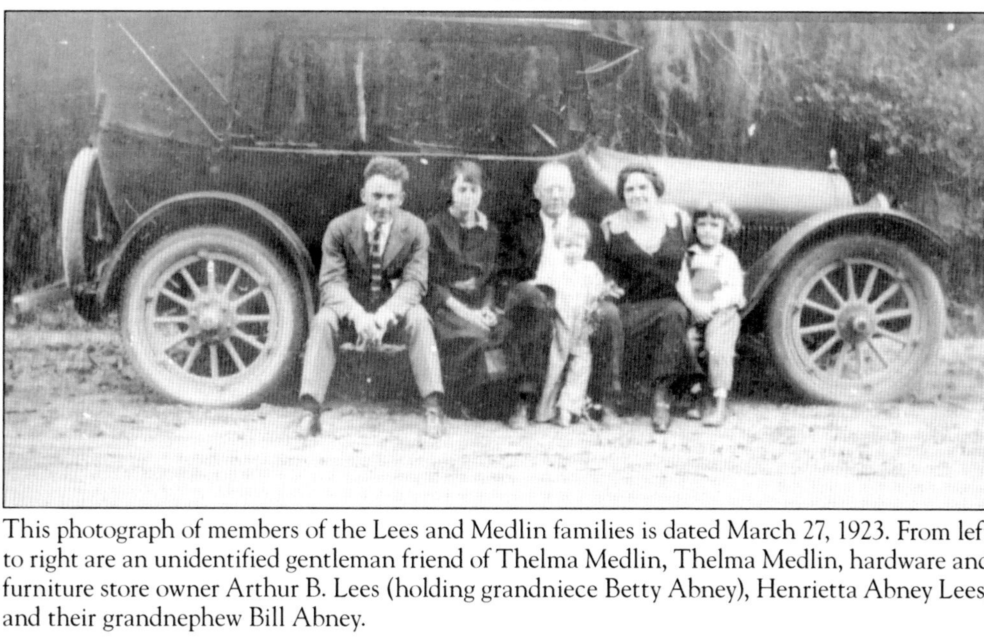

This photograph of members of the Lees and Medlin families is dated March 27, 1923. From left to right are an unidentified gentleman friend of Thelma Medlin, Thelma Medlin, hardware and furniture store owner Arthur B. Lees (holding grandniece Betty Abney), Henrietta Abney Lees, and their grandnephew Bill Abney.

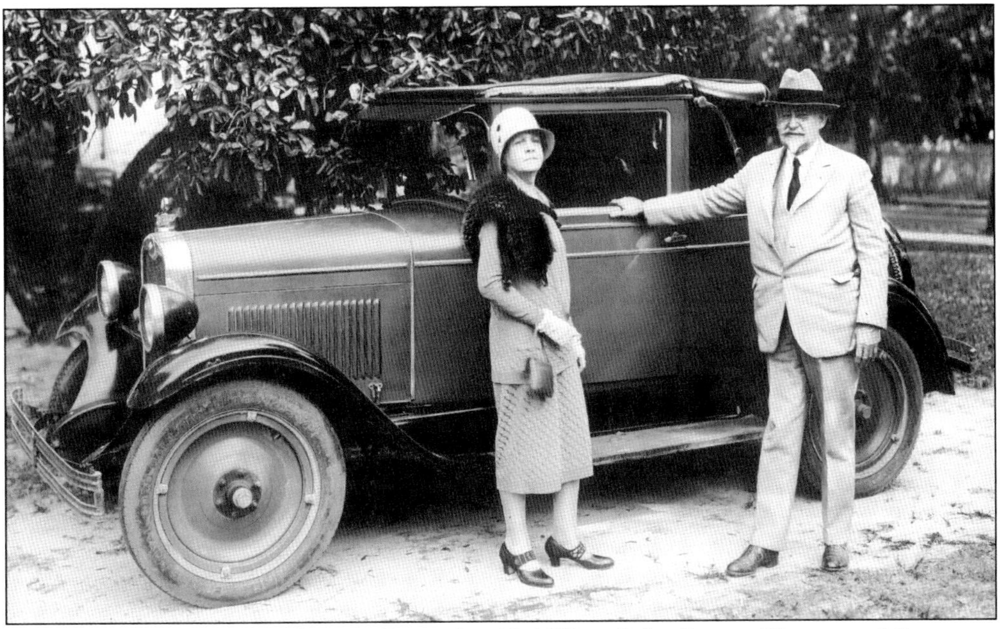

Thomas Newton Lynch was born on December 13, 1875, in Giles County, Tennessee. His parents were Irish immigrants. He married Virginia Lee Bailey in Lake County on September 7, 1921. Thomas was a paving and road contractor, and later a general contractor in Leesburg. He passed away in 1950. Thomas and Virginia had four children: Helen Virginia, Thomas Newton Jr., Betty Sue, and Margaret Frances.

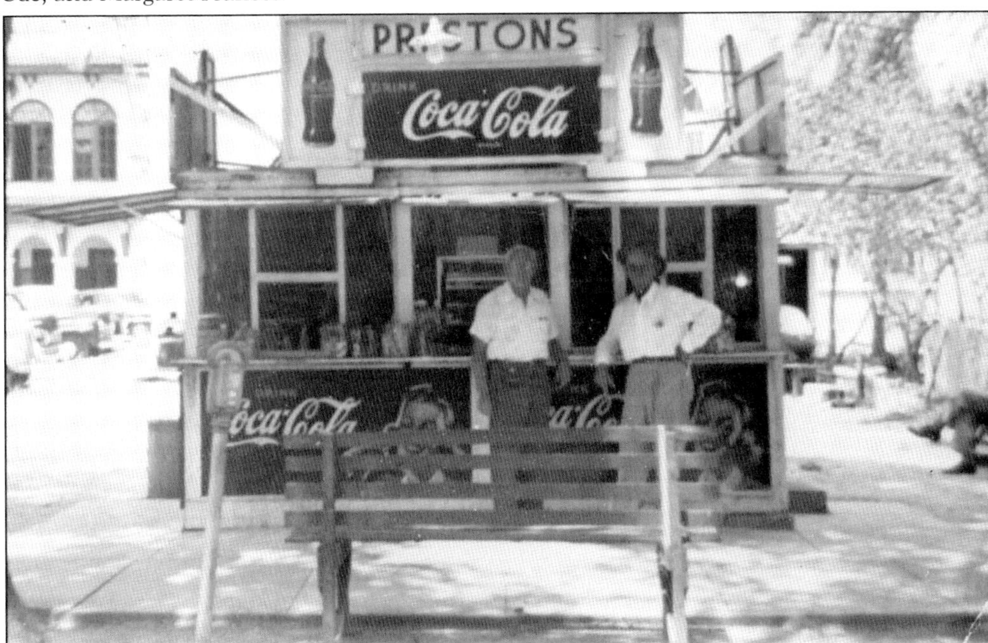

Glenn "Pop" Preston (left) and Thomas Lynch Sr. stand in front of Preston's snack bar on Main Street in the 1950s. Preston and his wife, Daisy Grace Cooper, lived in Tampa before moving to Leesburg around 1940. Preston was a candy maker famous for his big peppermint squares and horehound candy, which he sold at his hot dog stand.

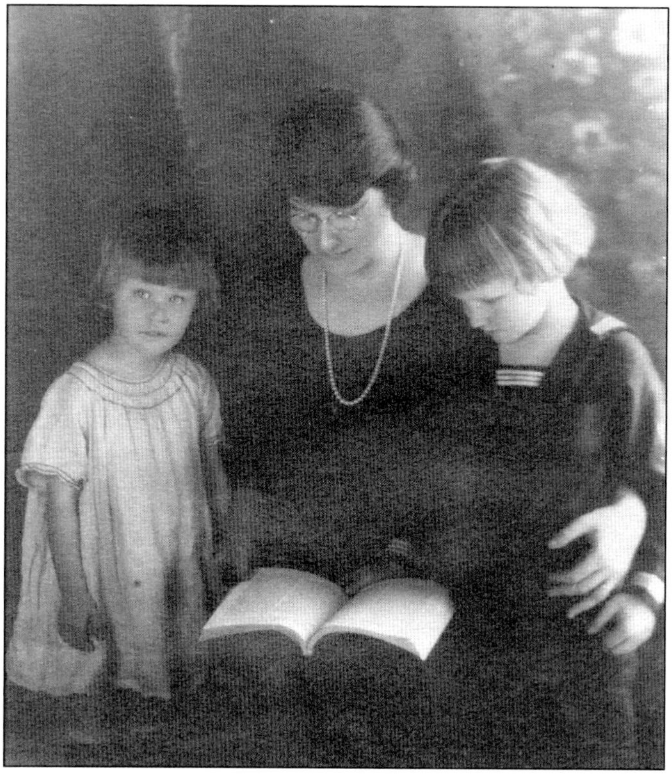

Elisabeth Watts Hunter Geiger, seen here with her grandchildren Billy and Betty, was born in Sumter County on January 30, 1898. She was a popular writer for the *Leesburg Commercial*, and was considered the city's first local historian. Her first marriage was to William Azariah Abney. They had two children, William Herbert and Elisabeth. She had one child, Jeanne, with her second husband, Claude E. Geiger.

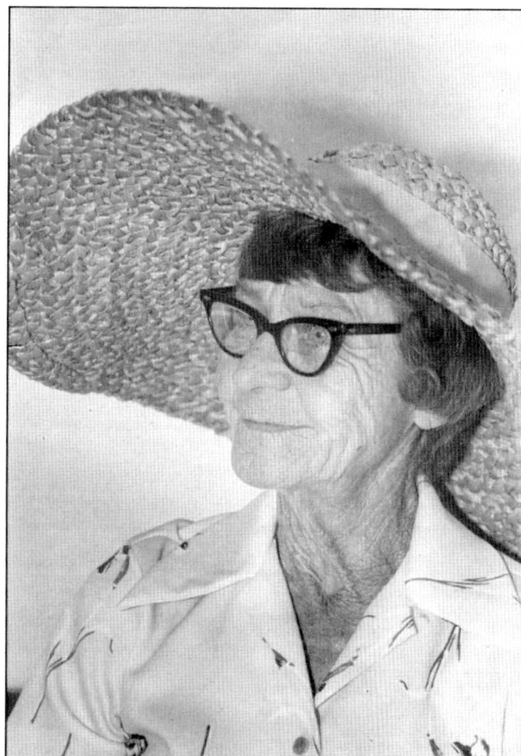

Journalist Norma Carroll Canaday Hendricks was born in Leesburg in 1911. Known for her heart, humor, and outrageous hats, Hendricks was the *Leesburg Commercial's* most popular columnist. She joined the *Commercial* in 1951. In 1962, she was the first woman elected to Leesburg's city commission, and in 1965, she became the city's first female mayor. She wrote for the *Orlando Sentinel* in the late 1960s, but returned to the *Commercial* in 1975 and worked there until she died in 1990.

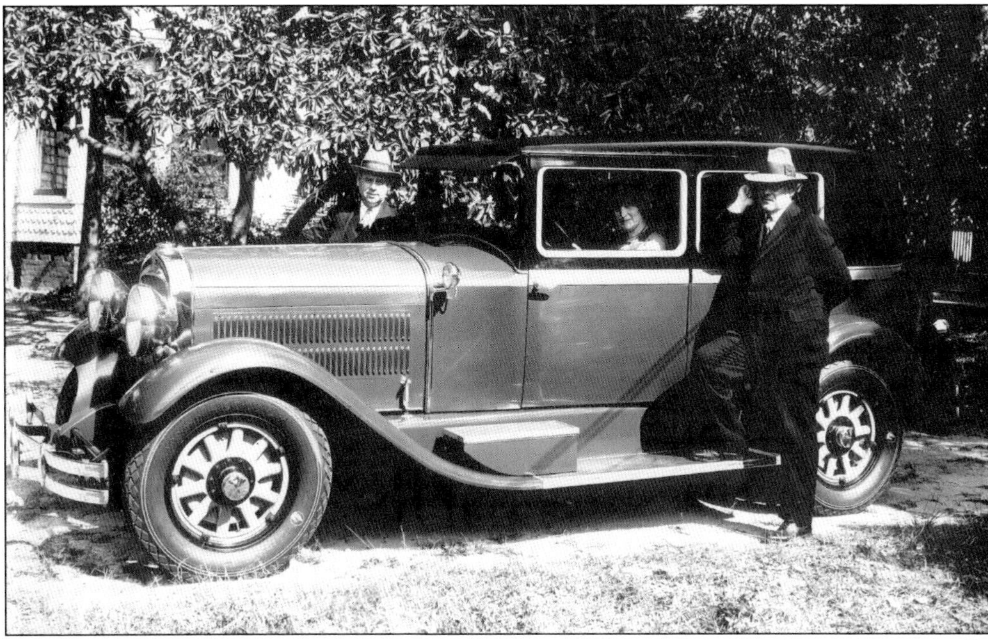

Seen here on February 8, 1929, are, from left to right, Fred Ezra Briles, Kathryn Marie Costello, and John Clarence Costello. In 1924, Fred Briles owned Briles Service and Storage at 631–633 West Main Street. In 1939, he opened the Briles Motor Company. Born in 1891, Briles was a sergeant in the Army during World War I. He was married to Caroline Adah Pahl.

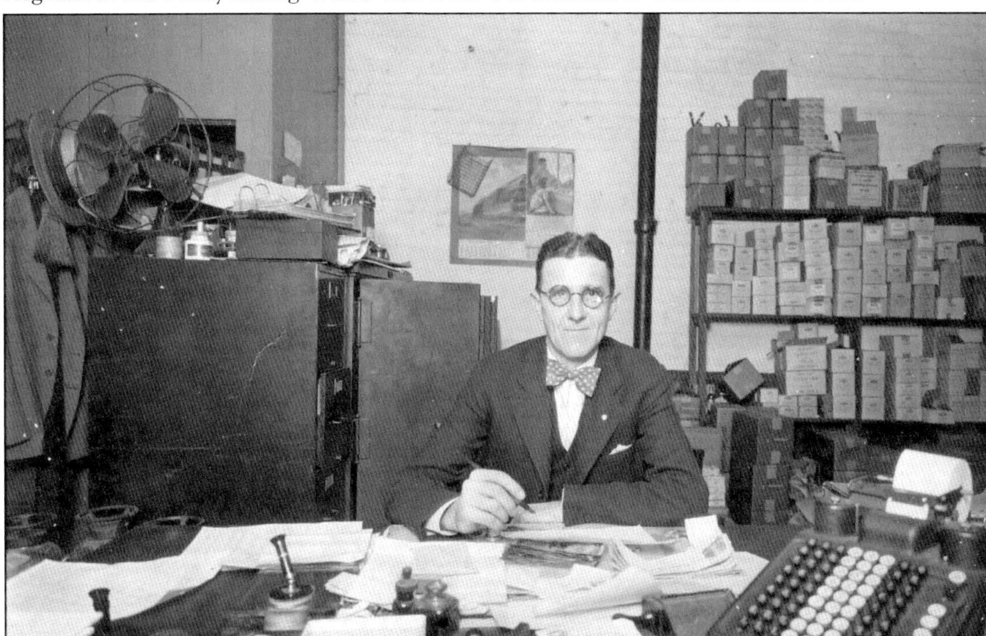

James Locke Williams Sr. was born on September 1, 1891, in Monroe County, North Carolina. He was a resident of Leesburg beginning in 1910. In 1920, he worked as a bookkeeper for the Williams Company, a wholesale grocer. In 1930, he became the manager. By 1940, he was an insurance salesman. This photograph shows Williams in his office on South Second Street.

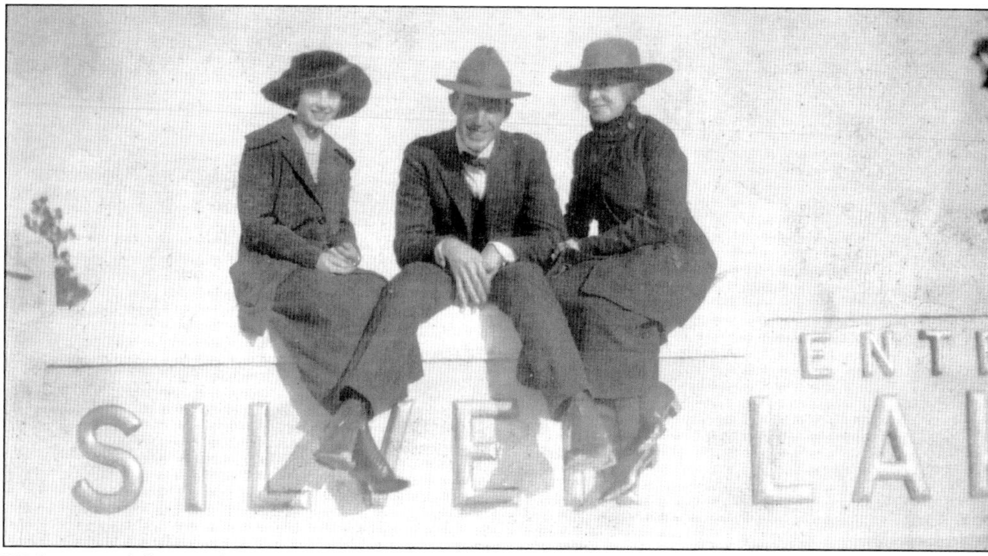

Welcoming folks to Silver Lake in this early 1920s photograph are, from left to right, Willeen Porter, Maurice Abney McCormack, and Vida Eva Oder McCormack. Maurice and Vida McCormack were recently married when this photograph was taken. Maurice, born in 1888 to Charles B. and Cora M. Abney McCormack, served as a private in World War I.

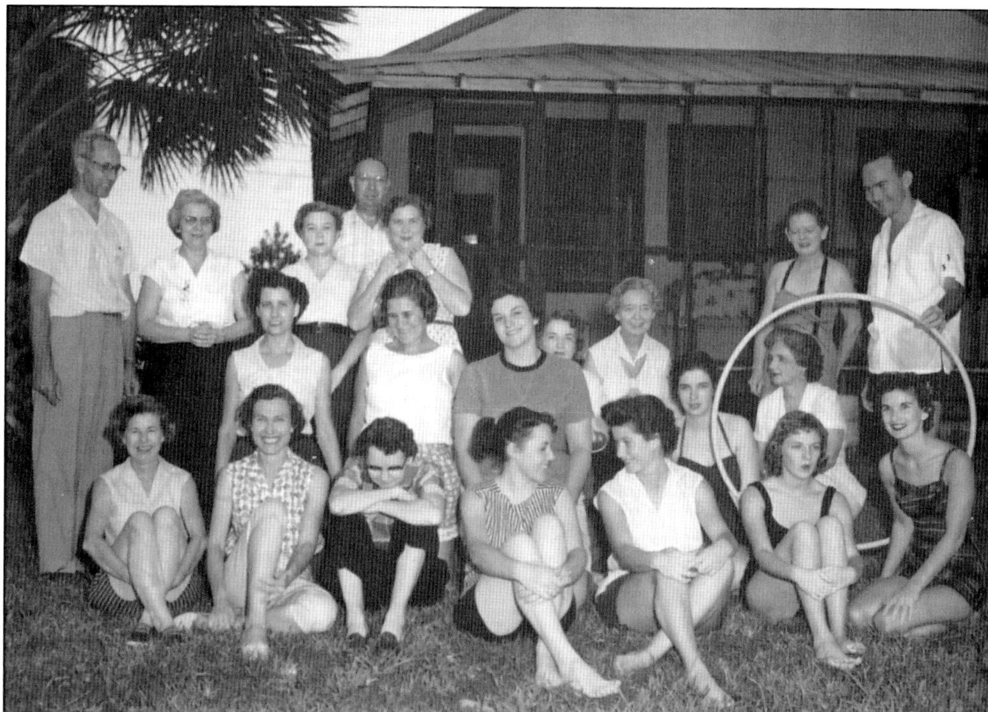

This 1958 photograph was taken at the old Stivender house in Lake Weir. From left to right are (first row) Sara Barcus, Fay Rodriquez, Bea Taylor, Rosalie Rabun, Barbara Jones, Sandy Irwin Jasmanski, and Margie Pickett; (second row) Carolyn Glover, Louise Hoornstra, Helen Payne Carr, Myrtle Patterson, Jean Acton, Jane Garner, and Dorothy Little; (third row) R.K. Evans, Eva Butler, Beulah Sanchez, Pat Thomas, Mable Sattler Kennedy, Virginia Pierce, and Frank Stivender.

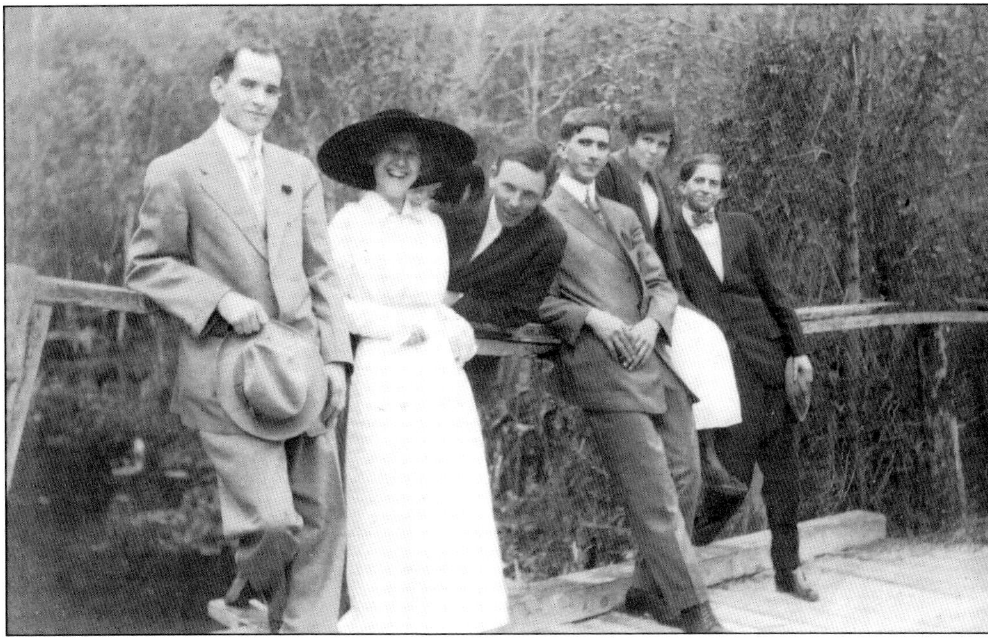

John Lee (far right) enjoys a Sunday out with friends in the early 1900s. Lee, of Leesburg's namesake family, was the son of John Chester and Marion Walker Lee. John Chester Lee served several terms on the city council and was the chairman of the board of trade. Like other members of the Lee family, he engaged in the dry goods business, as well as orange growing and farming. John's close friends Sebastian Bergmaier and Frank Bourlay are on the far left and fourth from left, respectively.

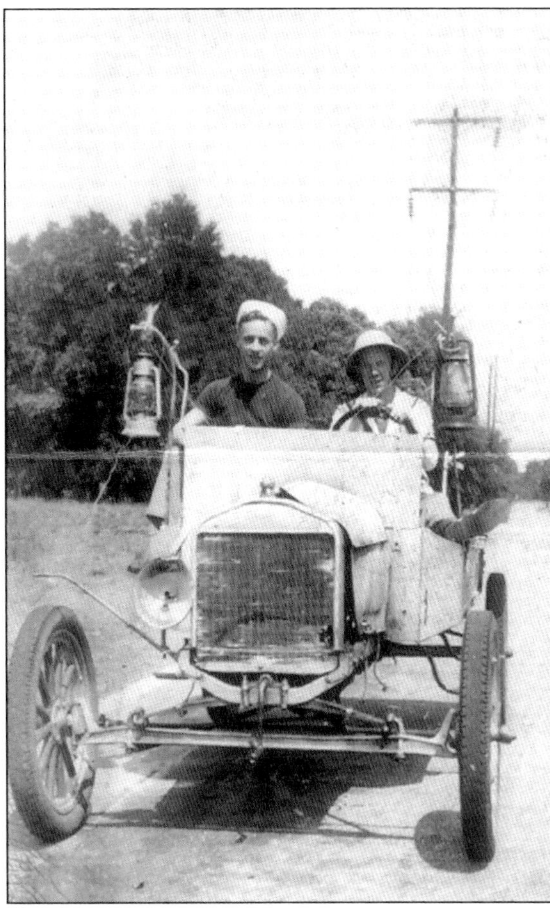

Robert McCollum Cottrell drives his first automobile along South Ninth Street near his birthplace in 1941. He was born on December 22, 1922, and passed away on September 8, 2012. Riding with him is Edwin Clyde "Pogie" Dusenbury, who was born on October 23, 1922, and passed away in 1999. Cottrell rebuilt this 1909 hand-crank-start auto. One headlight was missing and the other was broken, so he mounted lanterns on each side.

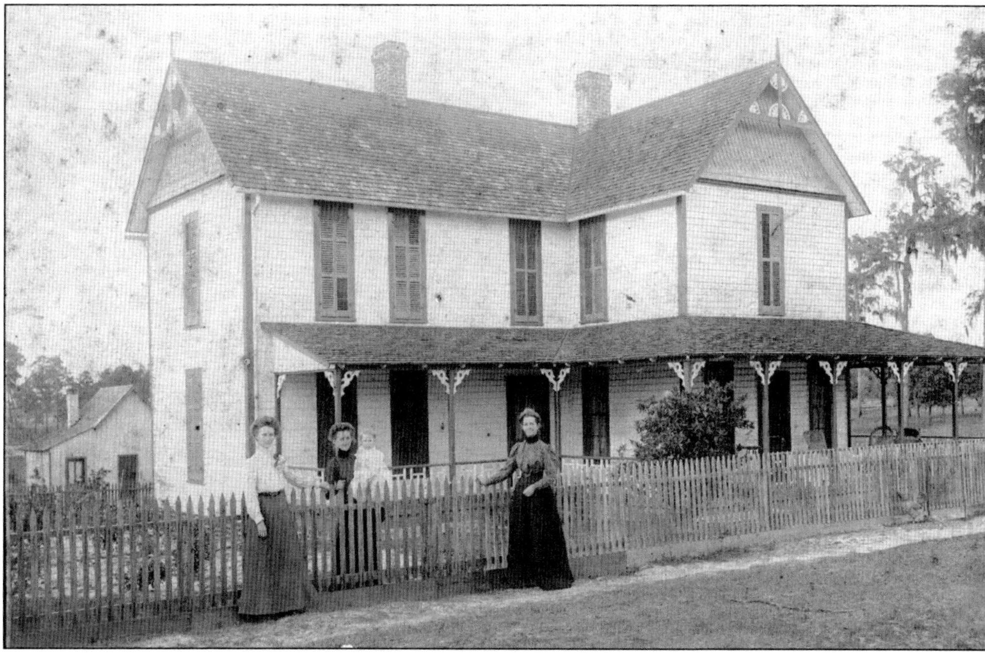

Susan Ann Kennedy is on the far left with unidentified family members at the Kennedy house on Line Street in 1902. Susan and her husband, John, whom she married on February 18, 1896, owned a grocery store on Main Street. Her parents were Needham Calvin Lee and Commans Fontaine Bouknight Lee, and her grandfather was Calvin Lee, who gave Leesburg its name. Susan Ann Kennedy passed away in April 1960.

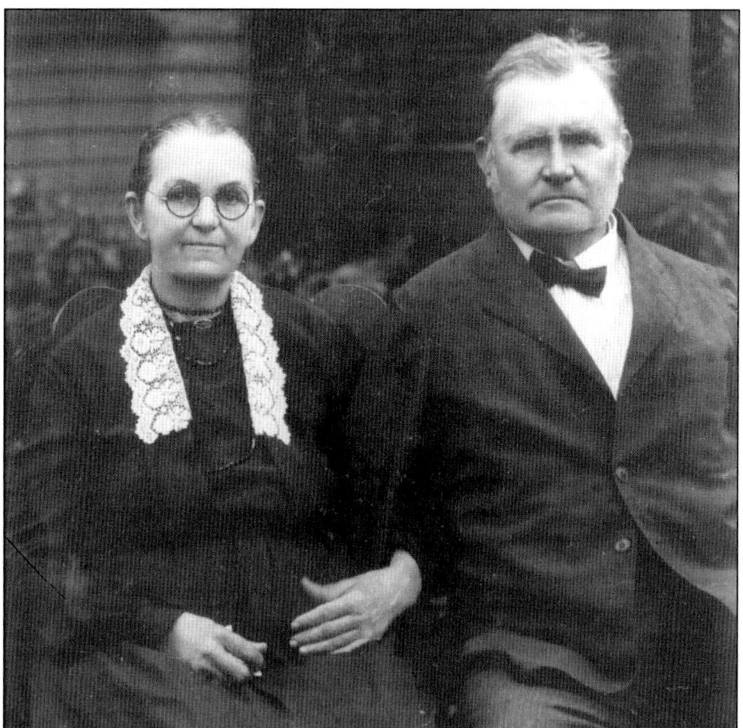

Dora Elizabeth Gafford Bozeman takes the arm of her husband, William Franklin Bozeman, in the early 1900s. William, born in 1852, was a farmer in Sumter County, near Center Hill, in 1900. In 1910, he became a fruit broker in Leesburg; in 1920, he was a retail merchant of seeds and feed; and in 1930, he worked as a market garden farmer. The Bozemans had twelve children, six boys and six girls, with six born in Alabama and six in Florida.

Four

"Thy Halls Are Filled with Memories All Golden"

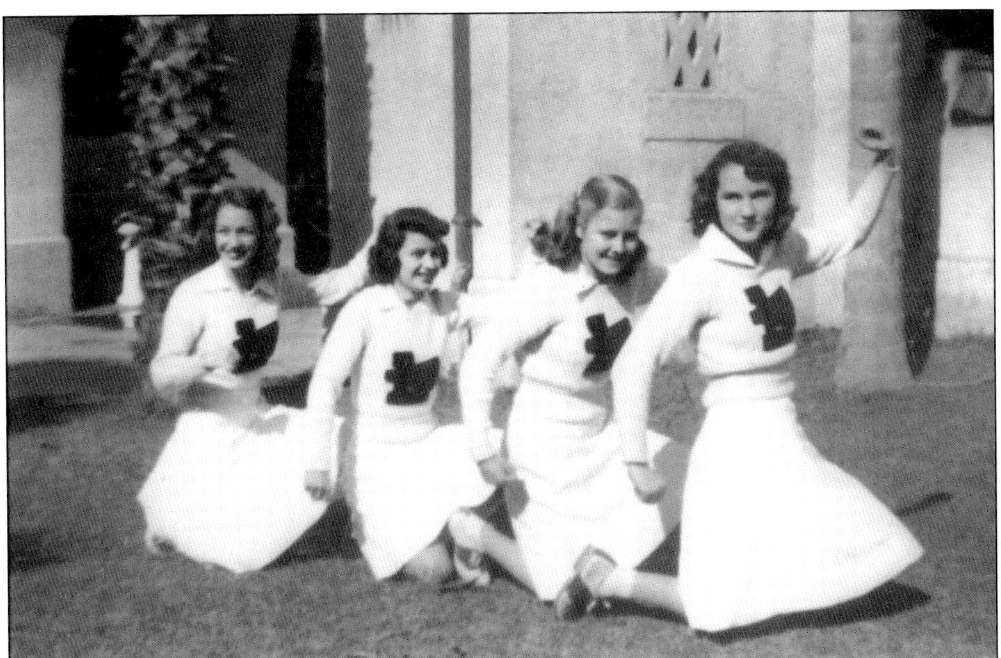

"Dear Leesburg High, our hearts to thee are holden / With loyal love, for each familiar scene / Thy halls are filled with memories all golden / The days we spent so happy in thee!" These are the words to Leesburg High School's alma mater song, written by Paul Searcy, class of 1942, to the music of "Finlandia" by Jean Sibelius. The 1941 Leesburg High cheerleaders seen here are, from left to right, Jackie Lott, Lois Howey, Jacky Hester, and Mary Jean Floyd.

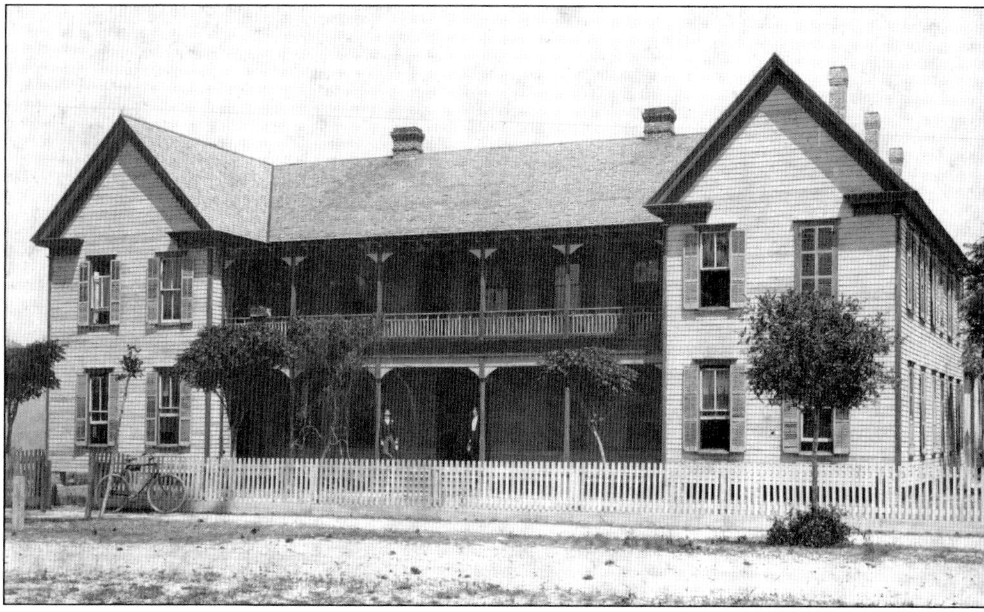

Florida Southern College, located in Lakeland, had its roots in Leesburg in 1886. In the late 1880s, the school went by a different name: Florida Conference College. This photograph shows the girls' dormitory, built in 1889. *Daily Commercial* columnist Elisabeth Geiger wrote that this dormitory was "one of the handsomest in the state." It later became the Heights Hotel and is currently the Colonial Apartments.

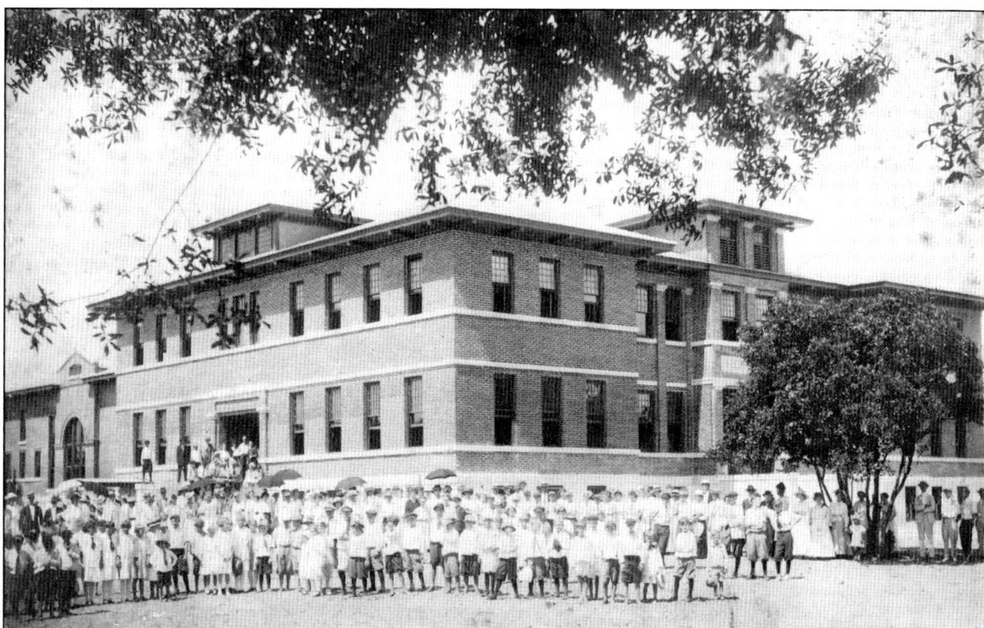

In 1914, the cornerstone for Lee School was laid. Located on North Lee Street, the school was built on a six-acre grove purchased from John Love; it opened in 1915. This photograph from around 1920 includes the entire school body and their teachers. Lee School was expanded in 1923 and a dedication was held, with William Henry Fahs giving the keynote address. The school was listed in the National Register of Historic Places in 1995.

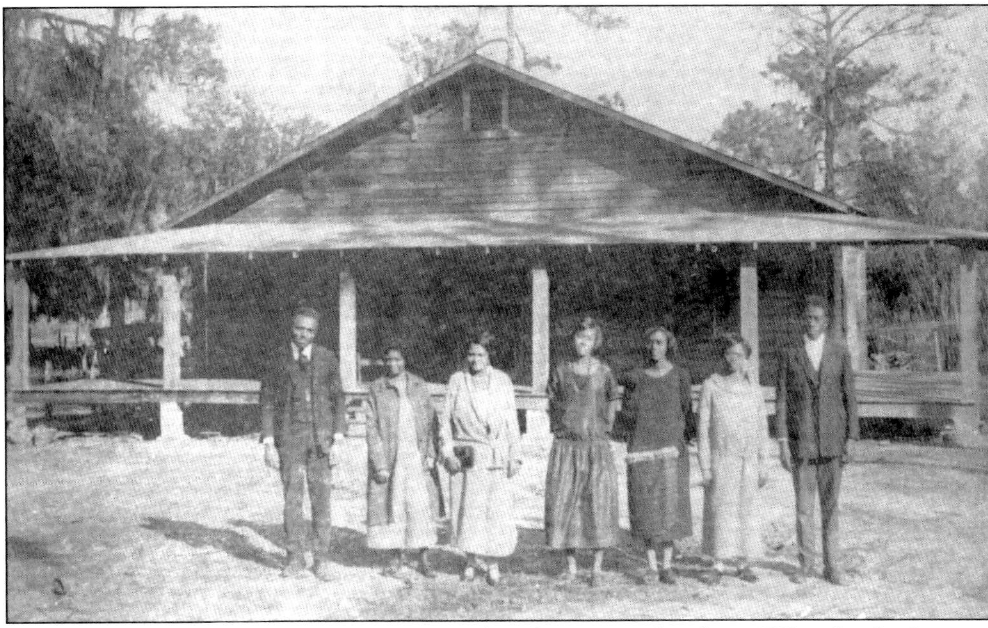

The first school for African Americans in Leesburg began in a church in 1878 under the direction of Rev. S.A. Williams. John M. Dabney was the school's teacher, and he became the principal in 1882. In 1921, after years of moving between different locations, five acres of land were purchased to build a permanent school. In 1922, the Lake County Training School (LCTS) was constructed and opened. D.H. Moore, the Lake County school board superintendent, appointed Henry McCrary as the school's principal. LCTS opened with less than 100 students and a five-member faculty. From 1925 to 1940, John Wesley Johnson served as the principal. Under his administration, the school became an accredited four-year high school. In May 1930, the first senior class graduated. Carver Heights High School replaced LCTS in 1954. The photograph above shows the LCTS faculty in 1925; the vocational agriculture class of 1922 is seen below.

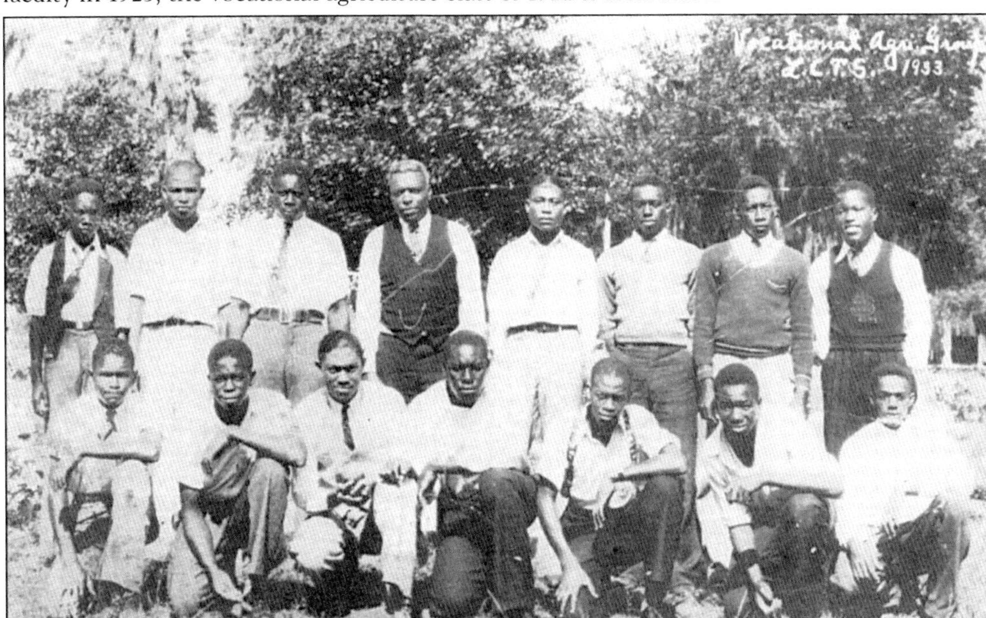

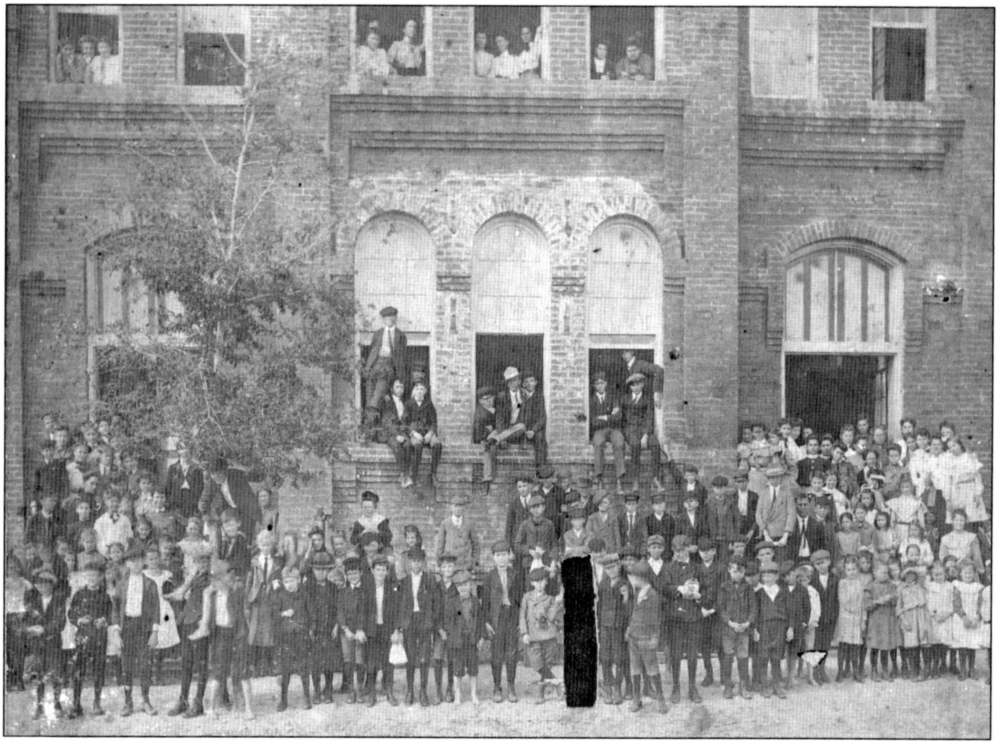

Leesburg officials issued bonds in 1892 to pay for the purchase of a building from the Methodist Conference College, located on Thirteenth Street. It was to be used as a permanent location for a school. Under the direction of professor J.H. Fulks, who lived in Center Hill, the building and a large lot were purchased for $4,000. He organized the school to include two high school teachers and three grade school teachers. Nelle Skeen, who taught at this school in 1914, had great respect for Fulks. She described the professor as a learned and shrewd man. All grade levels were taught at this first school. It was used until 1915, when the new Lee School opened. The 1905 photograph above shows the upper grades of Leesburg's first school. The lower grades are seen below in the early 1900s.

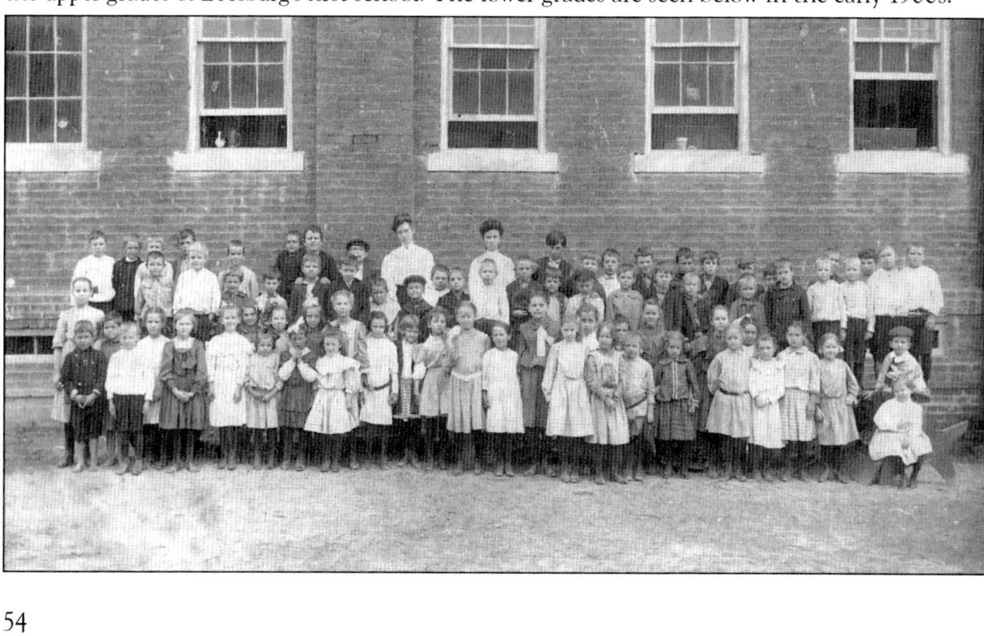

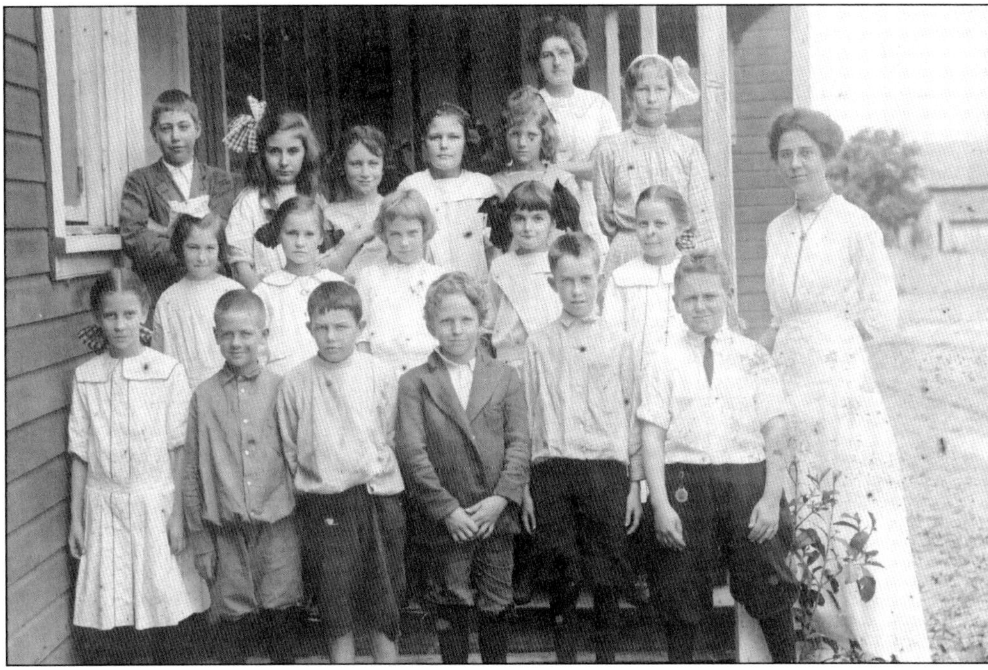

The Lee School fourth grade class of 1912–1913 included, from left to right, (first row) Eunice Grady, Maitland Schaeffer, Jamie Mahoney, Allan Entz, Spencer Carney, and Maurice Stafford; (second row) Virginia Morrison, Mattie Von Whatley, Belle Vinson, Flora Stevens, and Evelyn Grady; (third row) Joel McClendon, Alice Huebner, Mary Wilson, Inder Greer, Mary Richey, and Etha Stuckey. The teachers are Ruth Williams (right) and Pearl Johnson (back).

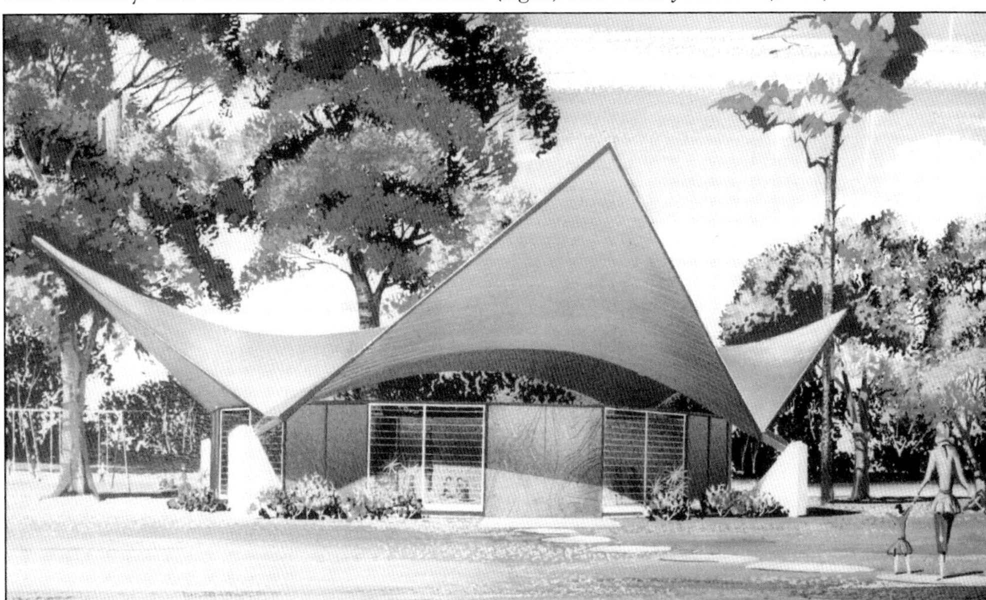

This artist's rendering depicts the kindergarten that was built at 608 South Ninth Street in the early 1960s. Ted Prosser financed and owned the building, which he rented to Mary Whitehead Jones, the kindergarten teacher. She said the children loved the building's unusual shape. They pretended they were in a circus tent or on a spaceship exploring the galaxy.

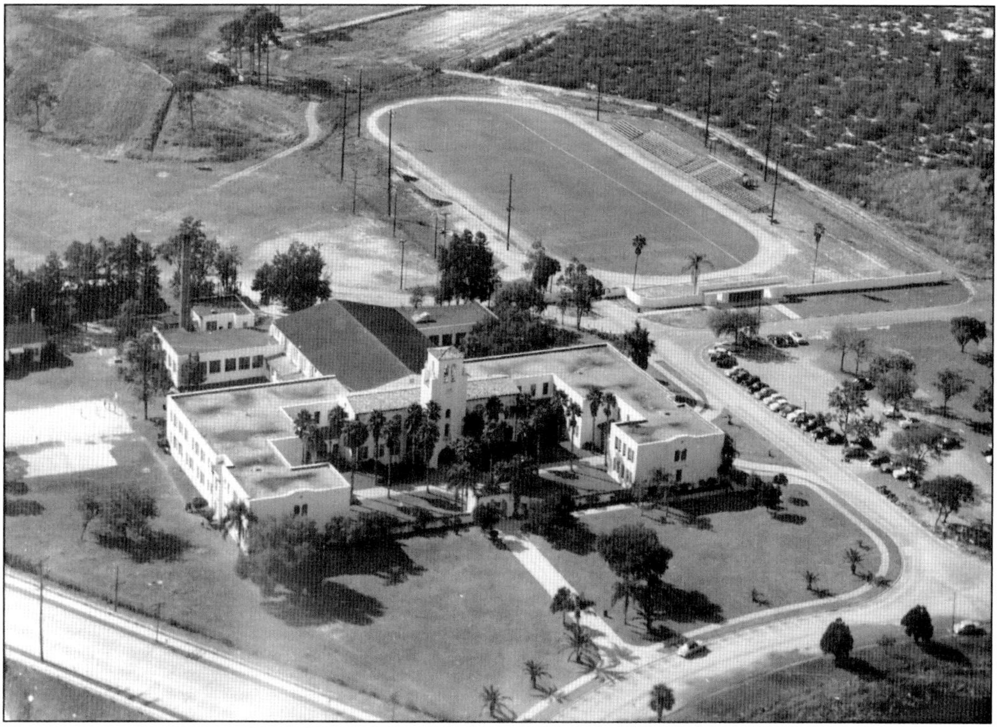

In 1927, construction of Leesburg High School began on a 10-acre tract donated to the city by former major league baseball pitcher Lee Meadows. The cornerstone was laid on September 29, 1927, and the building was ready for the beginning of the new school year by September 1928. William B. Treloar was appointed the first principal. This aerial photograph of Leesburg High School was taken in the 1950s.

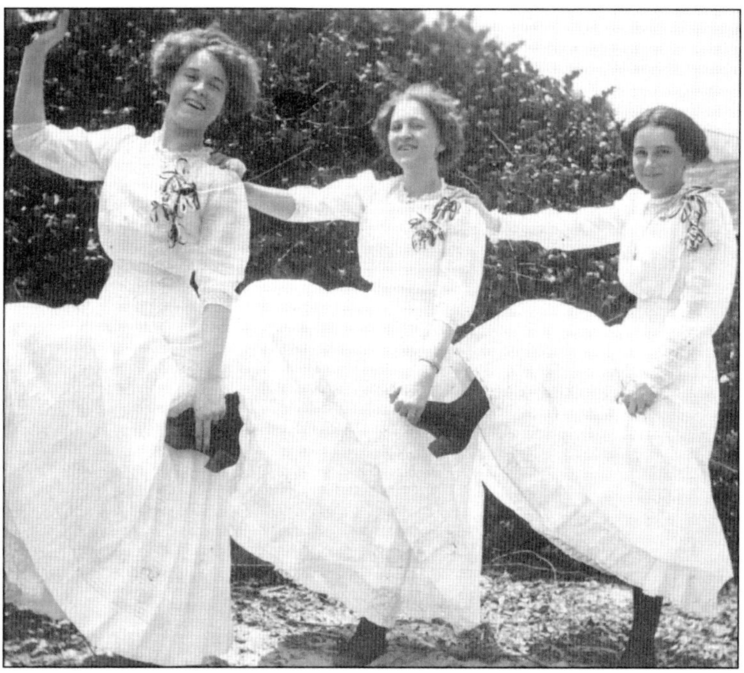

Lucie J. Kramer (center) enjoys post-graduation ceremonies with two friends in 1910. She was born in Leesburg in 1892 to Fred and Adelherd Kramer, and married A.V. Miller in 1911. From 1921 to 1936, she was a Leesburg school teacher. An active member of the community, she was a member of the Leesburg Women's Club and the Leesburg Garden Club. She passed away on October 28, 1988.

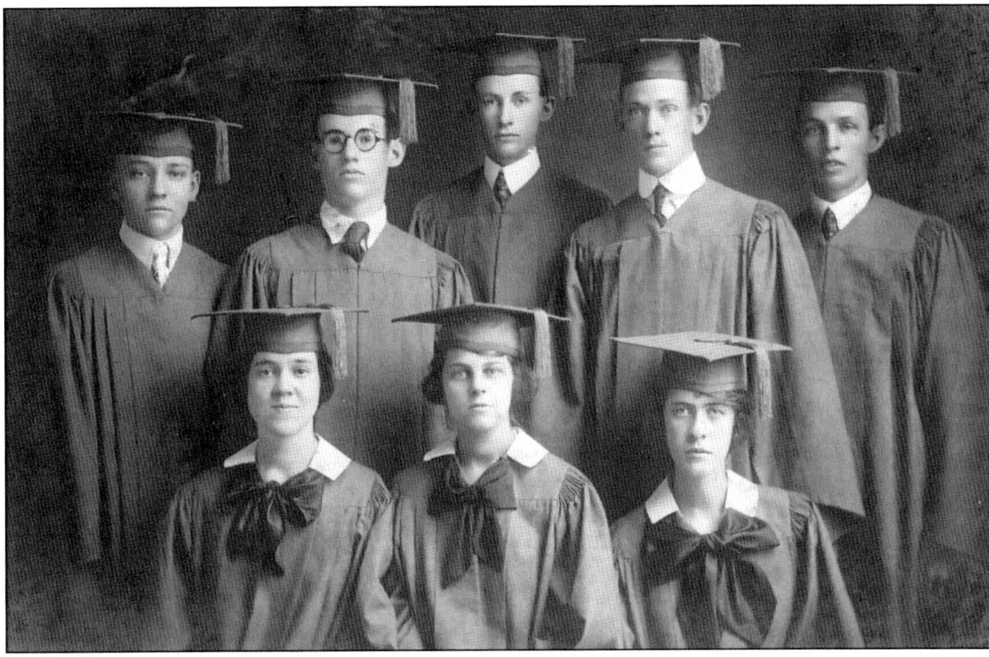

The May 17, 1920, graduating class of Leesburg High School included, from left to right, (first row) Jane Williams (class president), Thelma Medlin (secretary), and Frances Mahoney; (second row) John Allison (vice president), Phillip Newell, Kent Walker, Alex Alsobrook, and Anderson Potter (treasurer). Lee School continued as an elementary school after Leesburg High School opened in 1928, and served in that capacity until 1974, when it became Lee Adult High School.

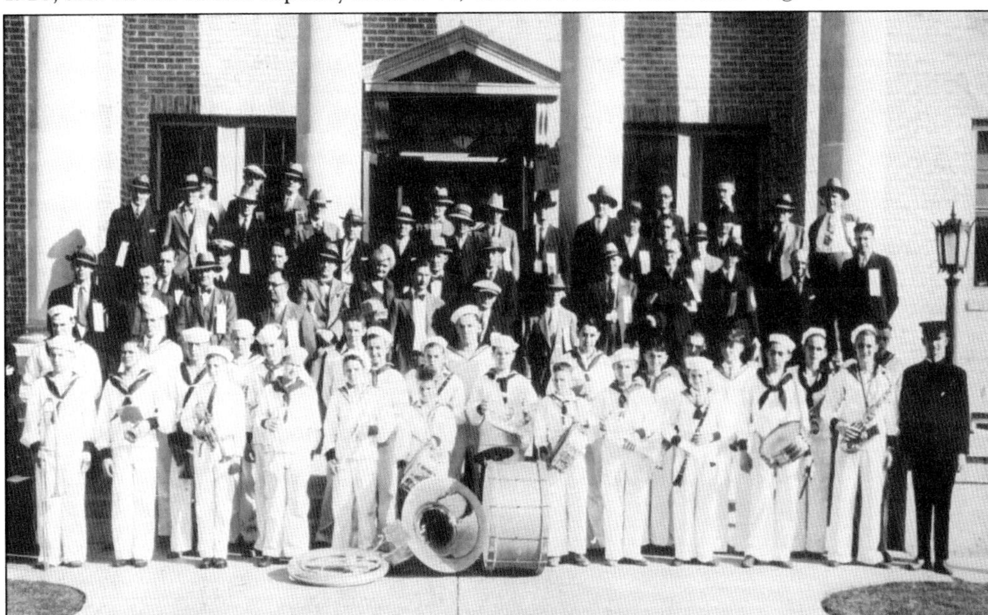

The Leesburg High School marching band, the Believers in Leesburg, are seen here at city hall in 1929. Performing for a patriotic celebration, the boys are dressed in Navy seaman uniforms, commonly referred to as the Cracker Jack uniform. The lone woman in the photograph is Margaret McCormack (center left), better known as Mrs. Maggie, the owner of the Magnolia Hotel.

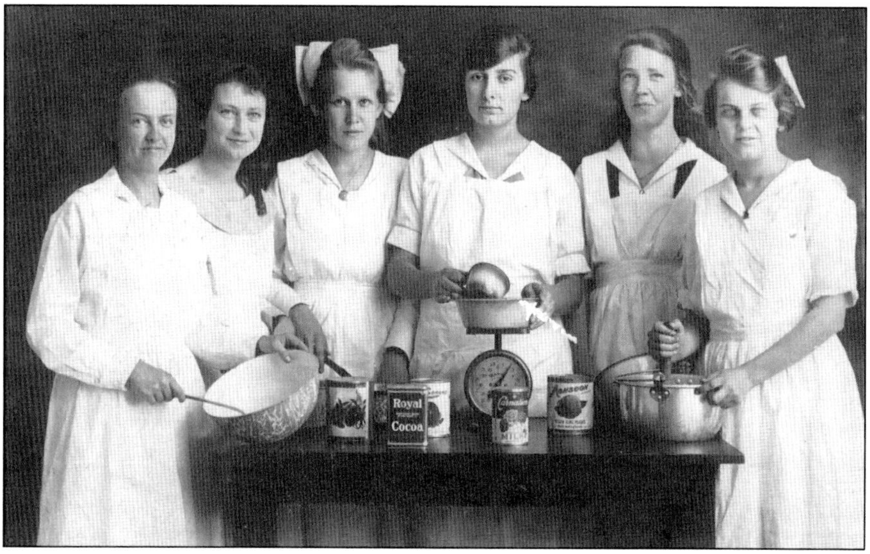

The juniors and sophomores in Leesburg High School's domestic science class in 1919 (above) were, from left to right, Mary Helen Cox, Mary Katherine Wilson, Margaret L. English, Alice E. Huebner, Lucy E. Williams, and Irene Thelma Medlin. Domestic science class was provided to educate young women about running their future households. The class of 1921 is seen below having their school picture taken in 1919. "Carpe Diem," from the Latin poem by Horace, translates to "Seize the Day." This photograph does not identify every student by row, but the sophomore roll for 1919 included Bartley Corley, Mary Helen Cox, Edwin Eigle, Allan Entz, John Fahs, Alice Huebner, William Hunter, James Mahoney, David Matthews, Harold Peters, Maurice Stafford, Lucy Williams, L.B. Walling, Iris Walling, Mary Wilson, and Nelson Oberholtzer. John Fahs (third row, third from left) married Mary Katherine Wilson (third row, left).

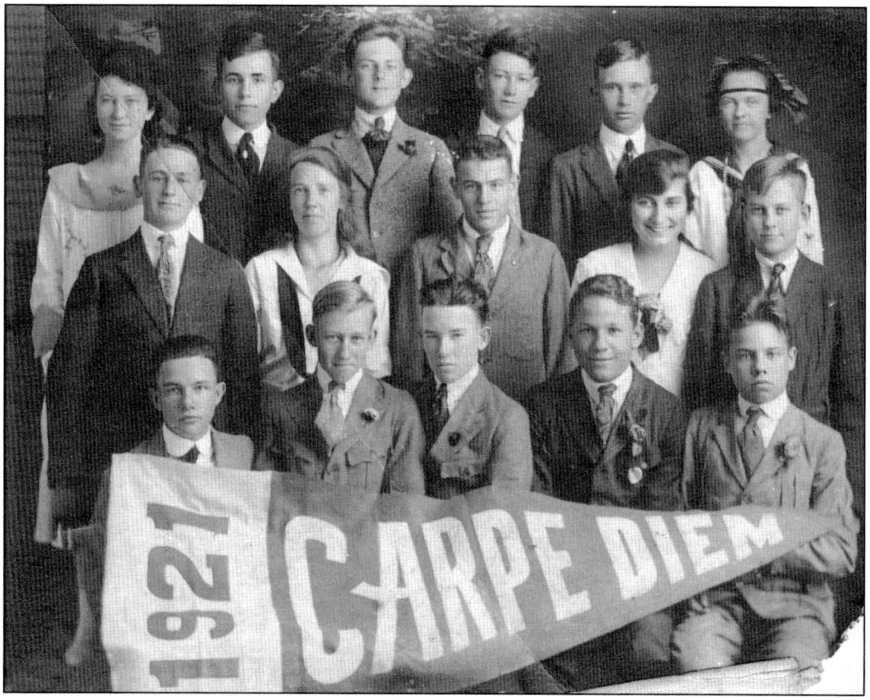

The Leesburg High School teachers seen here around 1940 are, from left to right, (first row) Ellah Kramer, Cordia A. Swaverly, Lucille Miller McDowell, and Nelle C. Skeen; (second row) Leila V. Holman, Evelyn Bowden Wickham, Faye Blackman Oberholtzer, and Pauline Sanders Stalker; (third row) Ossie Davis, Myra Goodwin Sanders, and Milbry Smith; (fourth row) Claire O. Lee, music teacher Margaret Hayes, Gladys Davis, Betty Hampton Bigger, and Lyndelle Hoover.

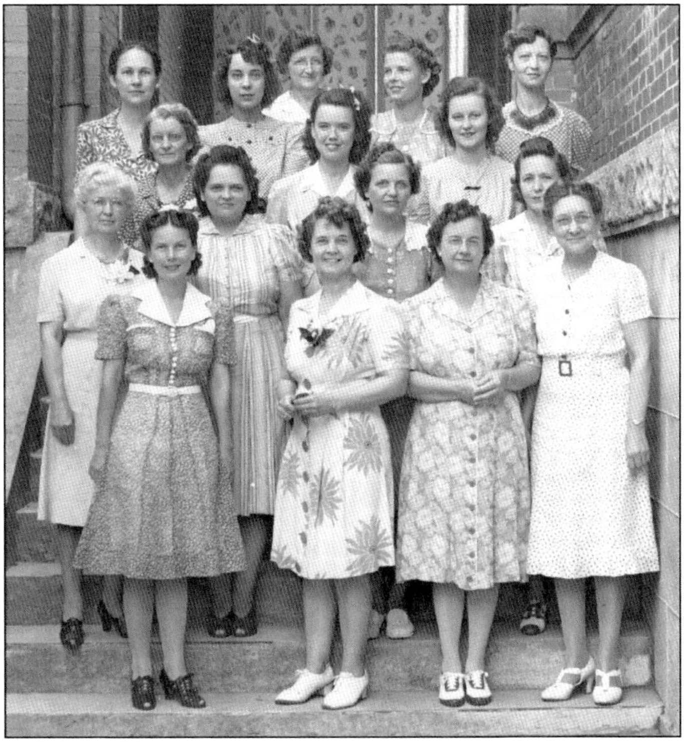

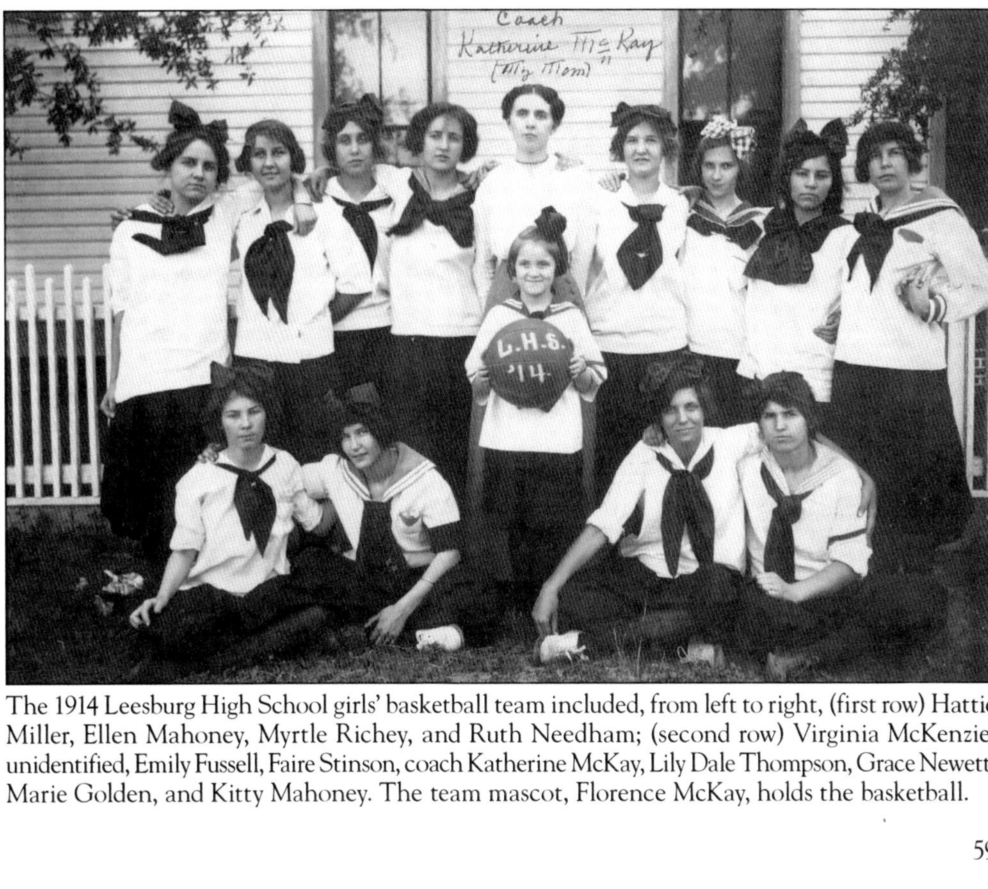

The 1914 Leesburg High School girls' basketball team included, from left to right, (first row) Hattie Miller, Ellen Mahoney, Myrtle Richey, and Ruth Needham; (second row) Virginia McKenzie, unidentified, Emily Fussell, Faire Stinson, coach Katherine McKay, Lily Dale Thompson, Grace Newett, Marie Golden, and Kitty Mahoney. The team mascot, Florence McKay, holds the basketball.

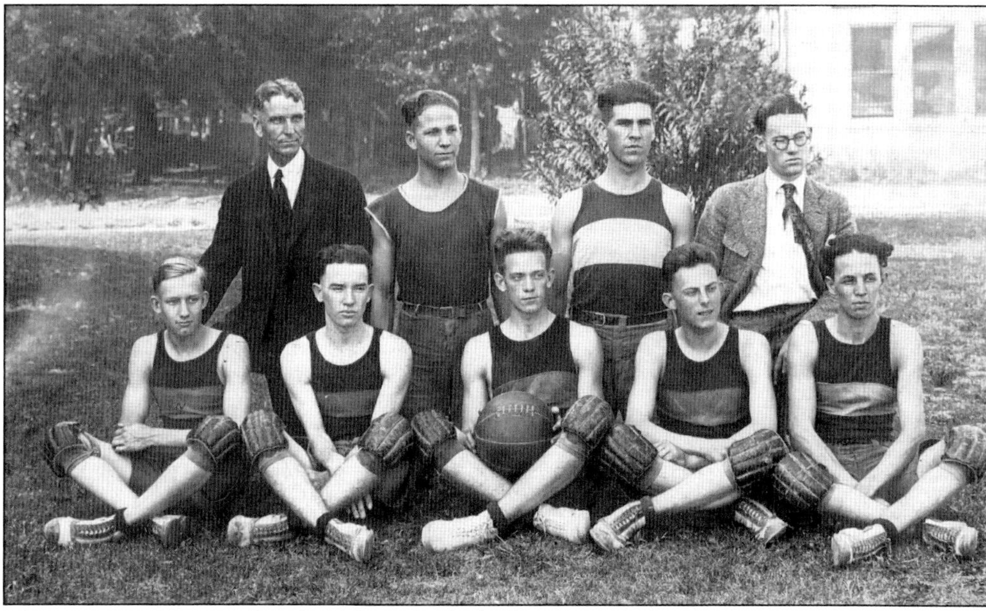

The 1920 Leesburg High School boys' basketball team included, from left to right, (first row) Nelson Oberholtzer, Billy Hunter, Alex Alsobrook, John Fahs, and Anderson Potter; (second row) coach Jimison F. Skeen, Allan Entz, Ezra Raasch, and manager Philip Newell. Coach Skeen was married to educator Nelle Conley Skeen, whose teaching career in Leesburg spanned four decades. Skeen Elementary was named in her honor.

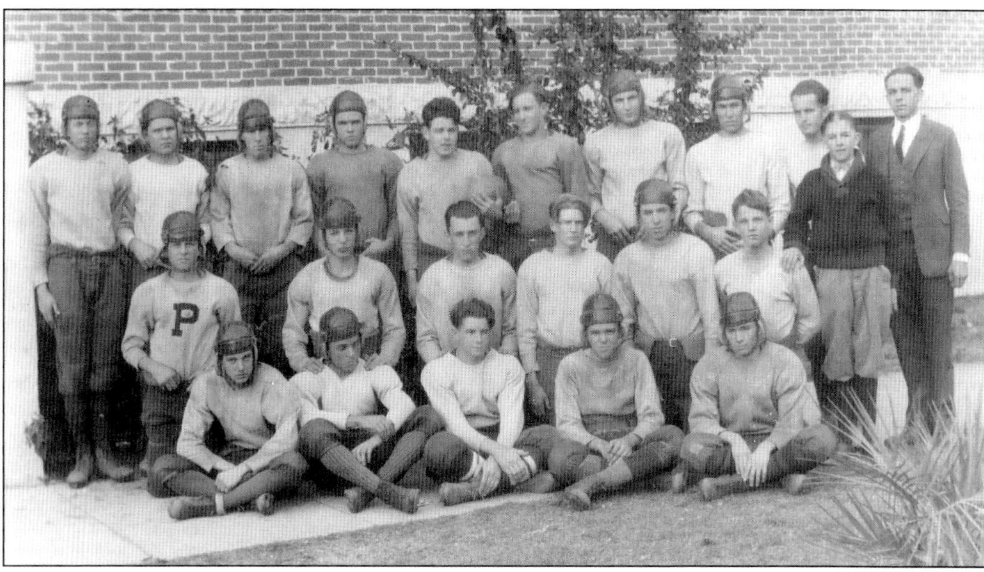

The 1924 Leesburg High School football team included, from left to right, (first row) William Morris, Everett Burgdoff, Clifford Flood, Eugene Morris, and Otis Butler; (second row) Drennen Brown, Guy Boyer, Franklin Ezell, William Morrow, Donald McCann, and Marvin Entz; (third row) J.D. Cox, Sanford Wicks, Robert Morrison, Buster Porter, David Browder, Sydney Herlong, Harold Wicks, Kenneth Thompson, and Felix Green. The team went 1-6 that year.

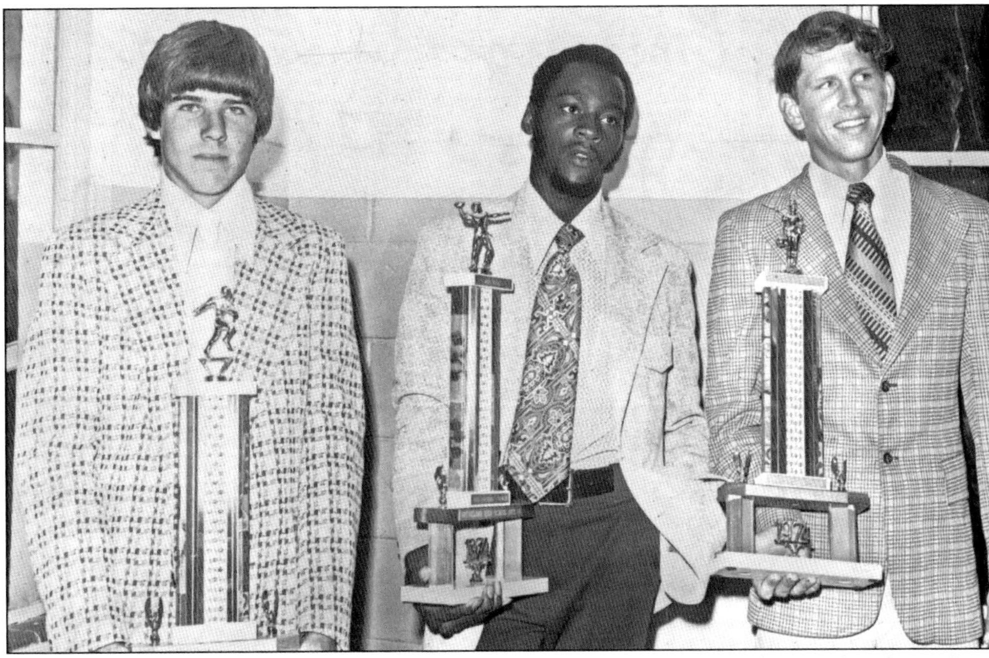

In 1974, three players on the Leesburg High School football team were honored with trophies. They are, from left to right, Joseph "Joey" Tottle, most valuable player; Amos Evans, most valuable lineman; and Denny Summersville, most dedicated player. This photograph was published in the *Leesburg Daily Commercial* on June 5, 1974.

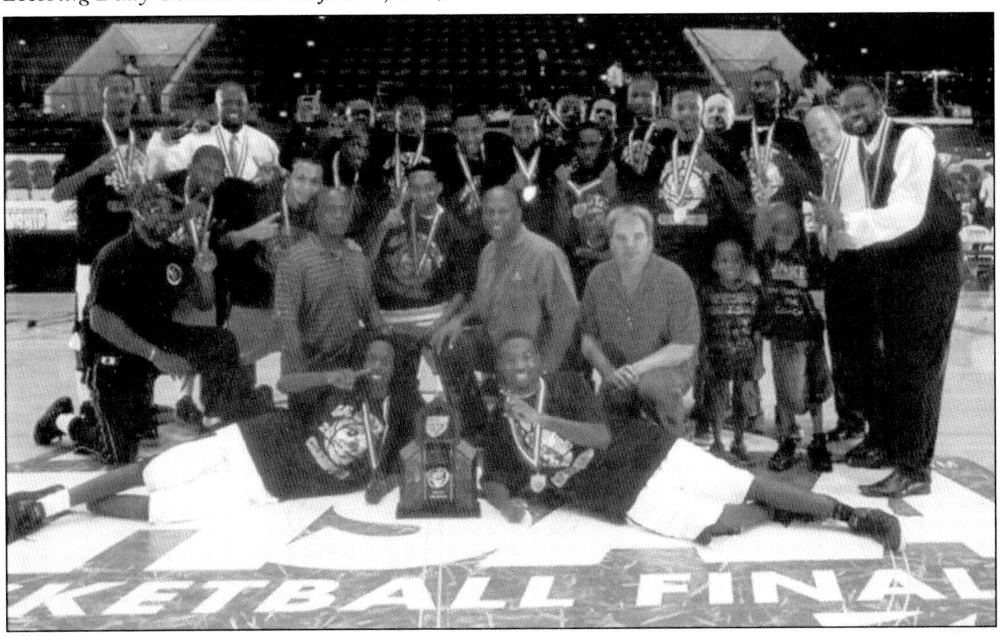

On March 5, 2011, Leesburg High School won the class 4A state basketball title. The Yellow Jackets, under head coach Marcel Thomas, defeated Cardinal Gibbons High School of Fort Lauderdale 66-58 at the Lakeland Center. Junior point guard Joe Toolie had 18 points, 4 assists, and 4 rebounds to lead a balanced team effort. The Yellow Jackets finished the season with a 28-4 record. It was Leesburg's second state title; the first was in 1977. (Courtesy of Gerald Lacey.)

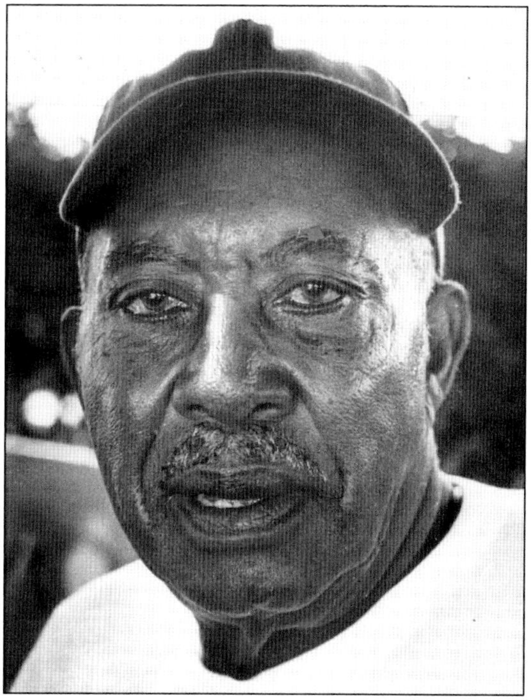

Joe Rimes, a World War II veteran and farmer, was born in Columbia County, Florida, in 1906. He married Acordy St. Clair in 1926. In 1959, after he retired, Rimes sold 11 acres of his farm to Lake County to build a school. He donated an additional acre to be used for a playground. The new school, named for Joe and Acordy Rimes, opened for classes in August 1961.

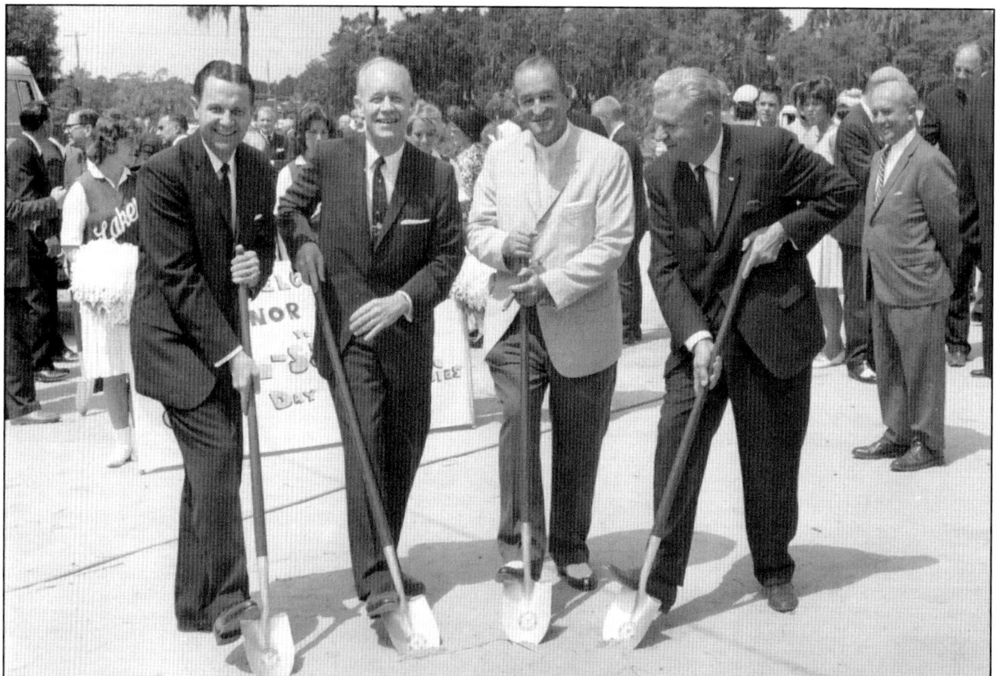

Lake-Sumter Junior College was established by the Florida legislature in 1961. On September 5, 1962, classes began in a temporary facility. On May 18, 1964, a ground-breaking ceremony was held for the college's permanent campus. From left to right are college president Dr. Paul P. Williams, Gov. Cecil Farris Bryant, Rep. E.C. Rowell, and J. Carlisle Rogers. In November 2012, the college changed its name to Lake-Sumter State College. (Courtesy of R.G. Teese.)

Five

The Liturgy in Leesburg

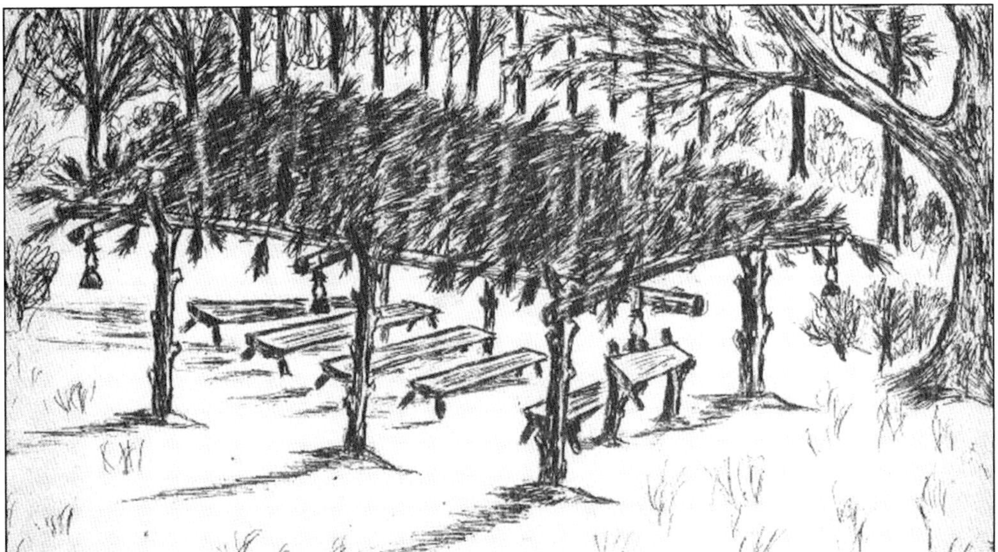

Leesburg's early settlers came from areas where church played a very important role in daily life. From the 1840s to 1859, Leesburg's first place of worship was an arbor made of pine poles and covered with cabbage palmetto leaves, depicted here in an artist's rendering. It was located on the south shore of Lake Griffin, where Thomas Robertson first settled in 1843. In 1859, a small log cabin church was built at what is now Lone Oak Cemetery. (Courtesy of the Leesburg Sesquicentennial Committee.)

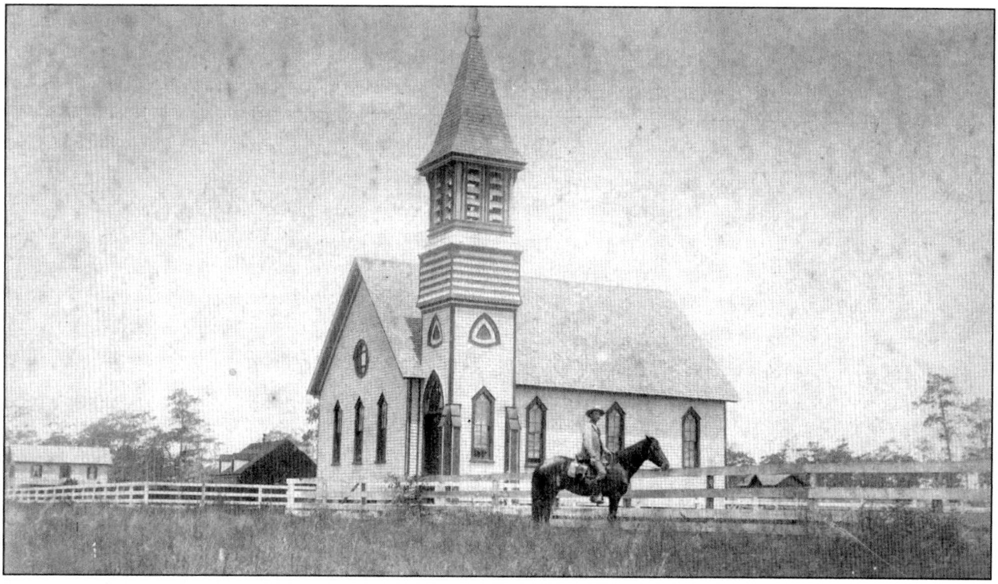

In 1887, the Methodist church was the first church organized in Okahumpka, near Leesburg. Seen here is Edmund Snyder of Germantown, Pennsylvania, who served as the first pastor. He was solely responsible for the funds for building this church, raising the money in the north. This original church is no longer standing.

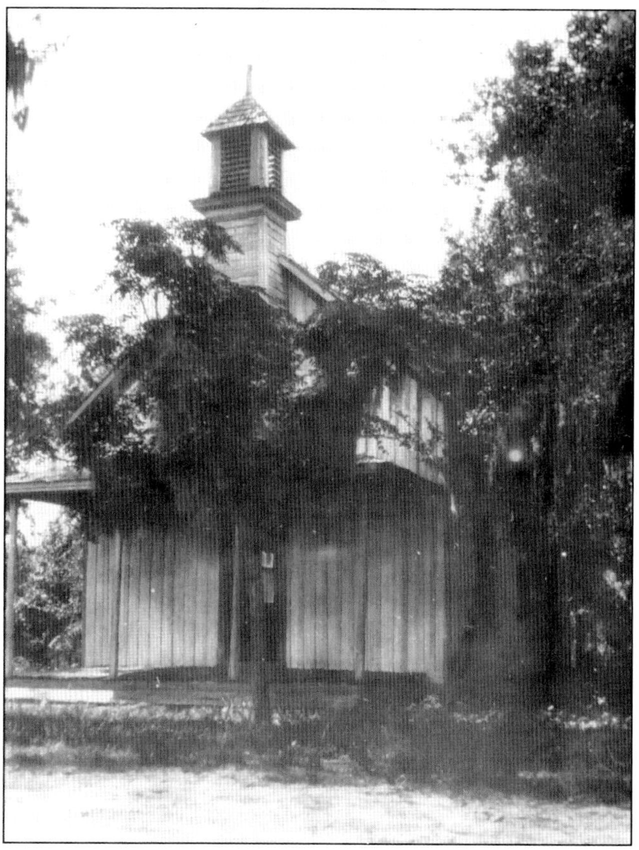

The Richmond Chapel is seen here in 1926. It is no longer standing, and there is no record of the chapel's existence since 1939. The Richmond Cemetery, which was behind the original chapel, is located on County Road 48 between Okahumpka and Yalaha.

St. James Episcopal Church was organized in 1885. The church functioned as a mission under the Diocese of South Florida from 1885 to 1938, when it became a parish. The church, seen here before a fire in the late 1940s, was a white, Gothic-style frame building. A bell, forged in England in 1858, was placed in the belfry in 1889.

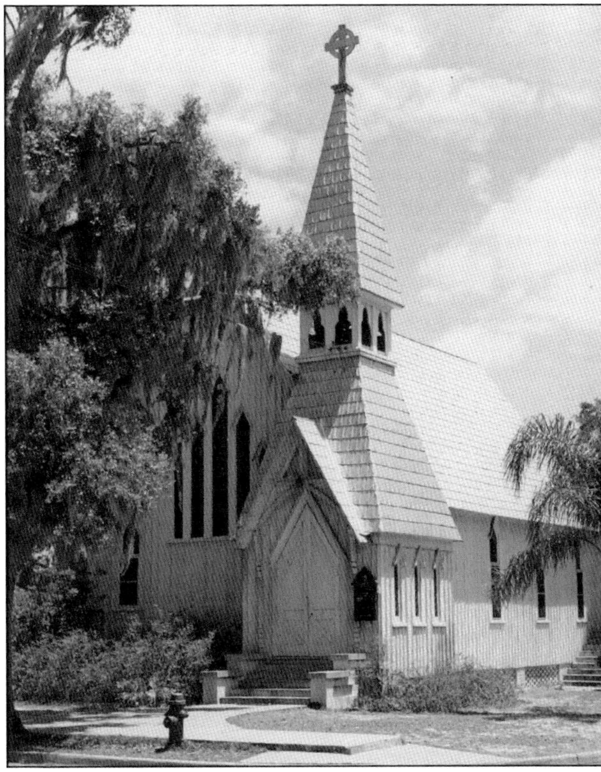

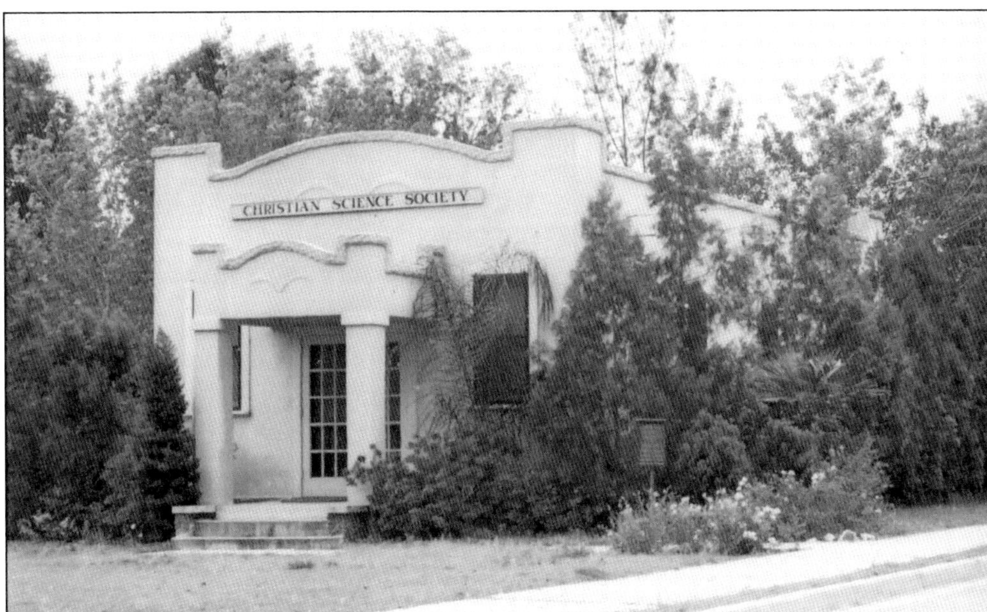

The Christian Science Society church was on Line and Thirteenth Streets. The rectangular stucco building was constructed in July 1928 and dedicated in September 1929. Constituted on January 25, 1923, and incorporated in January 1925, the First Church of Christ, Scientist, first held services at the Leesburg Women's Club at 107 South Sixth Street. This church building is still standing.

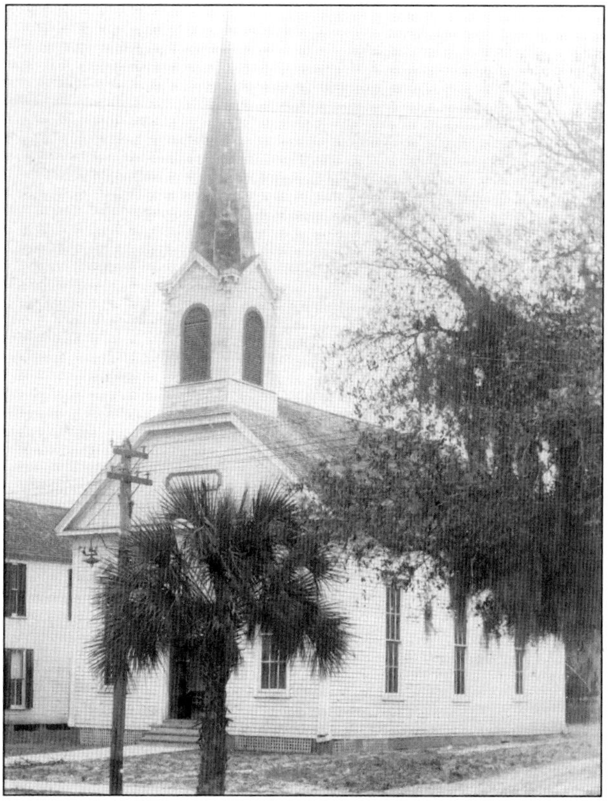

The First Methodist Church (left) was the first edifice on Main Street. It was a wooden structure built in 1883. In 1888, the parsonage was built. It burned down in 1927 and was replaced that same year. In 1906, the church was damaged by fire, but repairs were completed in time for the congregation to move back in 1907 to celebrate their 50th anniversary. In 1921, the wooden church was moved to the back of the church property so a new church (below) could be built. It was completed in 1924 and named Morrison Memorial Methodist Church in honor of Bishop Henry Clay Morrison. With his wife, Mary Elizabeth Stoner, Morrison moved to Leesburg in 1908. They bought the Mote home as a retirement residence and lived there until 1918, when they sold it to John and May Morris. Bishop Morrison passed away in 1921.

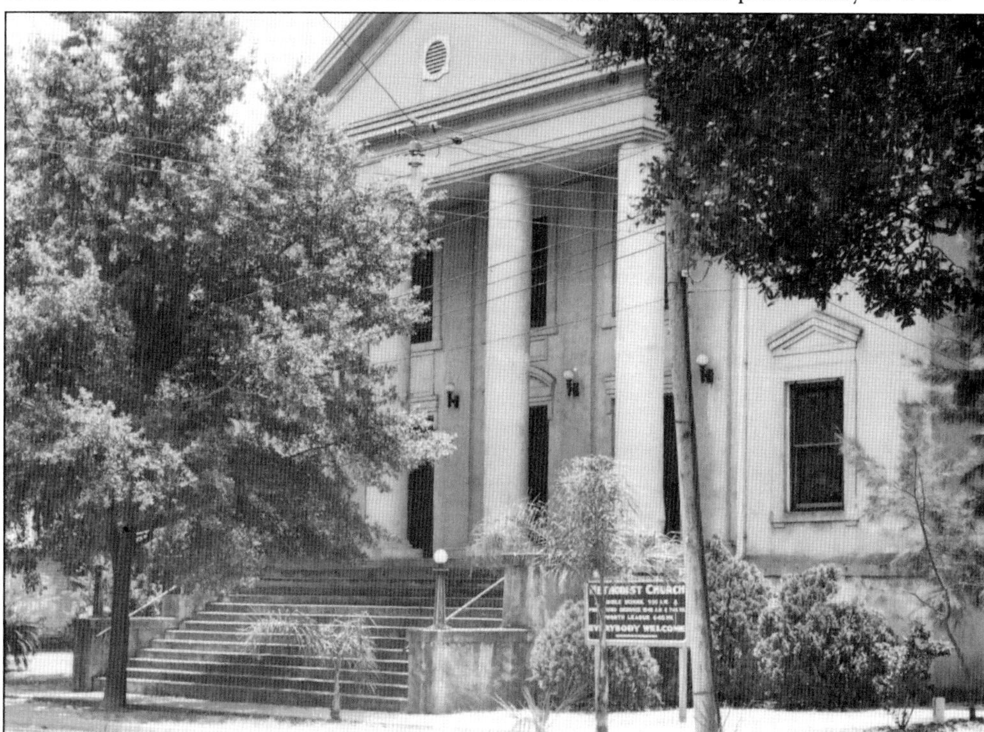

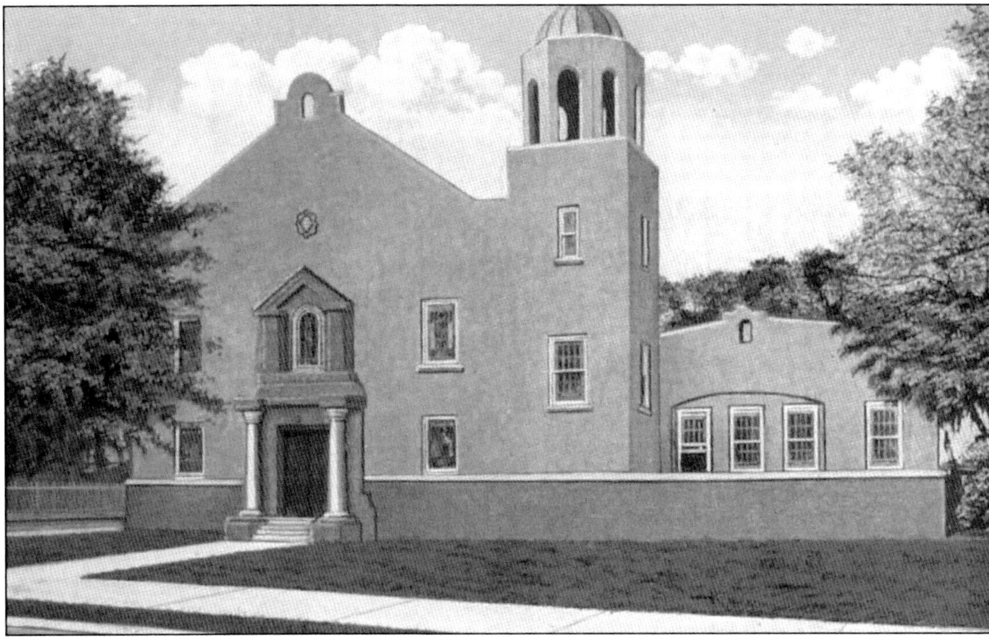

In 1884, this stucco, Spanish mission–style Presbyterian church was built at the corner of Perkins and Main Streets on an acre of land donated by John Love. The church featured seven memorial windows of art glass. In 1923–1924 it was remodeled, and in 1926, a pipe organ was installed and dedicated to the memory of Rev. William H. Fahs. The organ was moved to the new sanctuary on Vine Street in 1956.

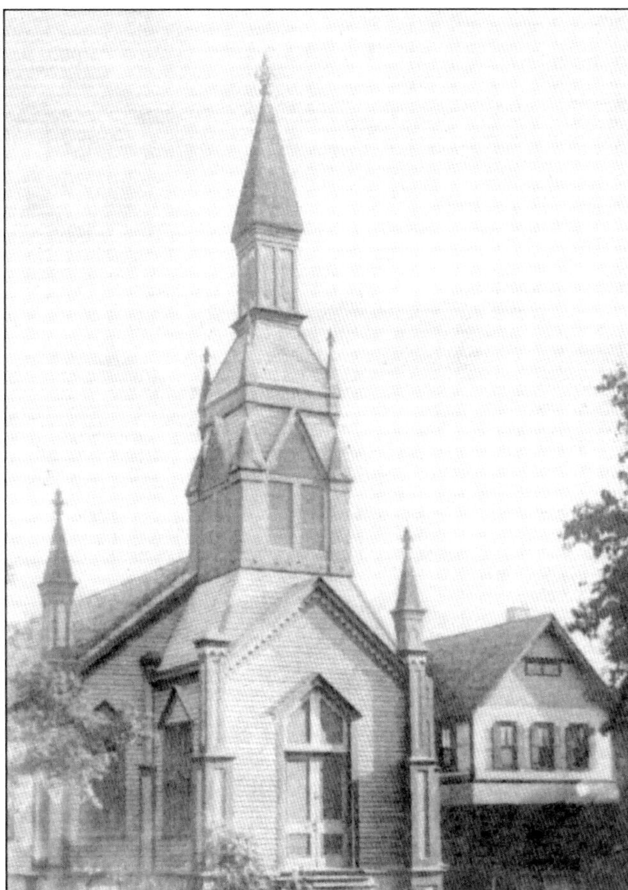

Lone Oak Baptist Church was organized around 1870 and held services in the Lone Oak Community Church. Rev. W.J. Hughes was the church's leader. In 1883, a one-room building was built on the corner of Twelfth and Main Streets. In 1886, the church, seen here, was rebuilt, and Sunday school rooms were added. This building was used until 1927, when a new Georgian-style church was built on Thirteenth Street.

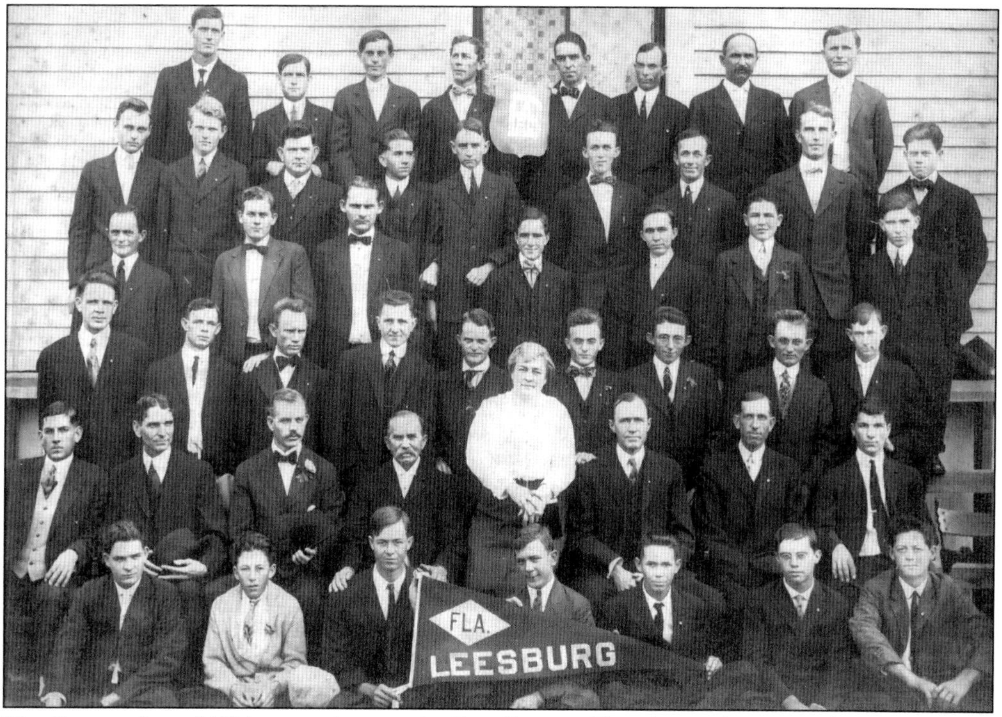

The Baraca class of 1914 is seen here at the First Baptist Church. At that time, the Baraca class, an interdenominational Bible study class, was taught only to young men. Lucretia Mote (second row, center) was the teacher. Notables include Jimison Skeen (second row, second from left) and the school's principal, F.D. Graves (second row, third from left). The name Baraca comes from the Hebrew word meaning blessedness or happiness.

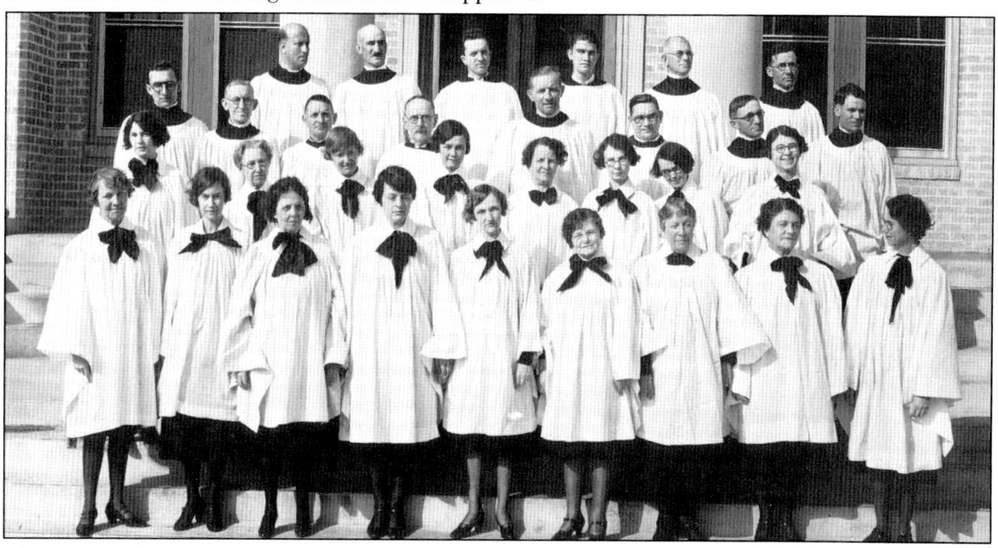

This group photograph of the Leesburg Choral Club was taken in February 1929. The club was organized in the 1920s by music lovers in the Leesburg area. They built an extensive library of musical scores through the years, including two Gilbert and Sullivan operettas and many Christmas and Easter numbers. Though they disbanded around 1960, former members of the club donated the old club's library to Lake-Sumter Junior College in May 1963.

Six

LEESBURGERS IN PARADISE

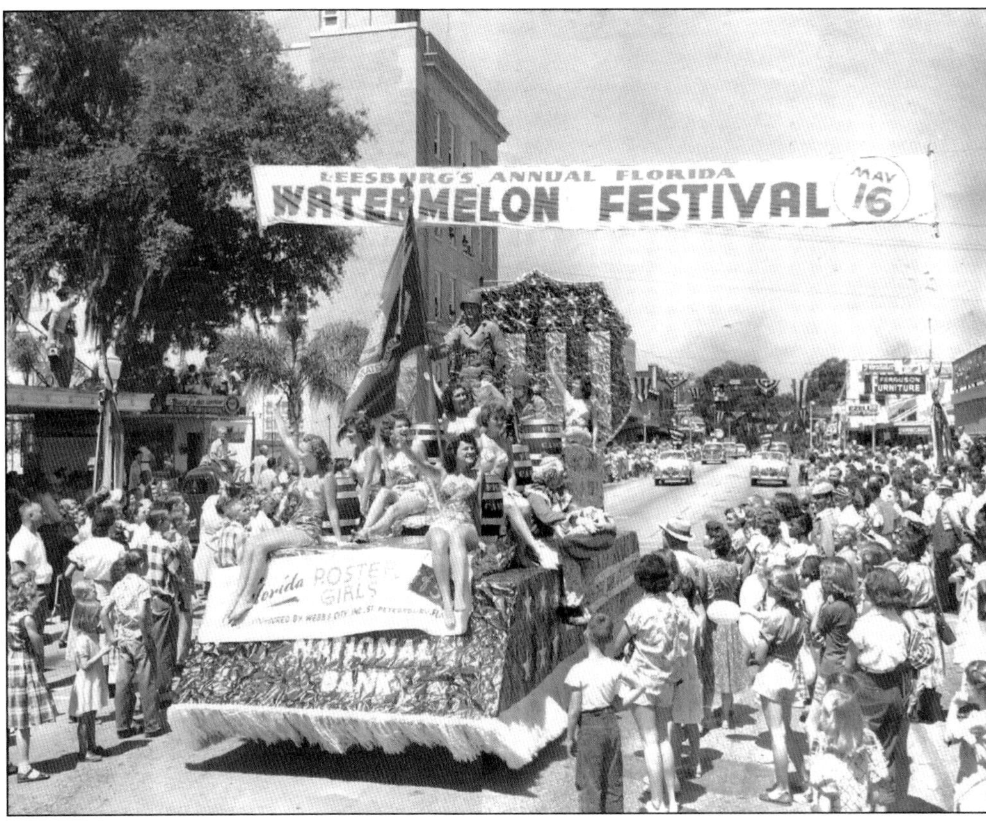

Since the late 1800s, Leesburg has been a city that celebrates and competes. The National Fresh Water Bass Tournament, the Fun and Art Festival, Mardi Gras, Bikefest, the centennial and sesquicentennial celebrations, and the legendary Watermelon Festival have all lured visitors and tourists to Leesburg. In the 1950s, the Watermelon Festival drew crowds of 20,000, as seen in this photograph of the May 16, 1951, parade on Main Street.

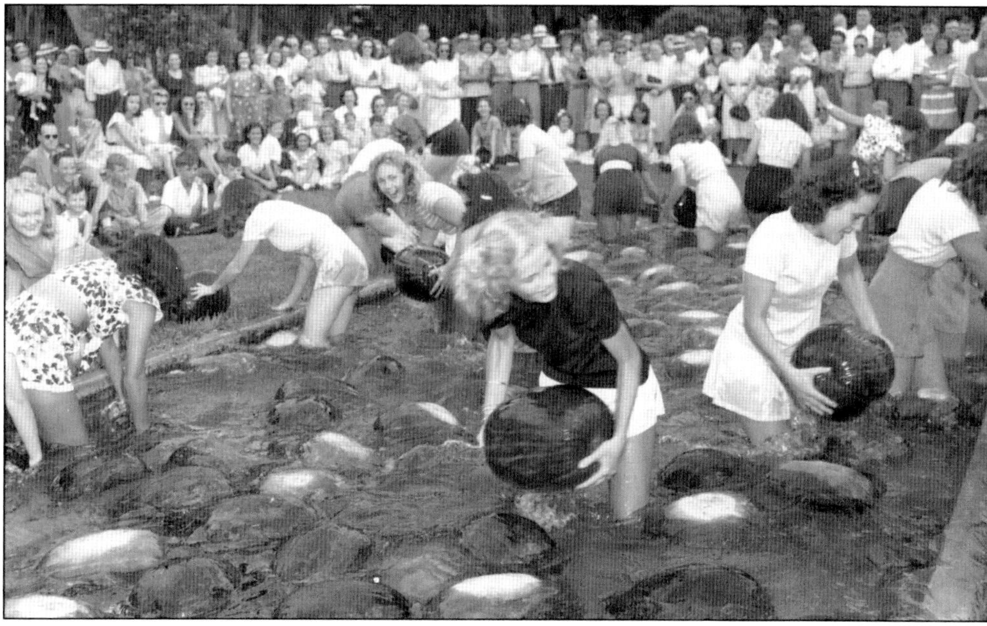

Leesburg was once declared the Watermelon Capital of the World. Watermelon growing in Leesburg began in 1894 when produce buyer G.W. Franklin shipped the first load of watermelons out of Florida from Leesburg. Leesburg's first Watermelon Festival was held on June 5, 1930, with 5,000 people attending. The festival was immensely popular, but was suspended in 1939 due to World War II—it returned in 1946. Festival highlights included a beauty contest, band concerts, celebrity speakers, fireworks, the crowning of the watermelon queen, and presentation of awards. Above, contestants choose a watermelon for the eating contest from the wading pool where the melons were kept cool. Below, the contestants in the 1947 watermelon-eating contest were, from left to right, Joanne Ferguson, Anne Louise Fletcher, two unidentified, Pat Hunt, and Pris Stevens.

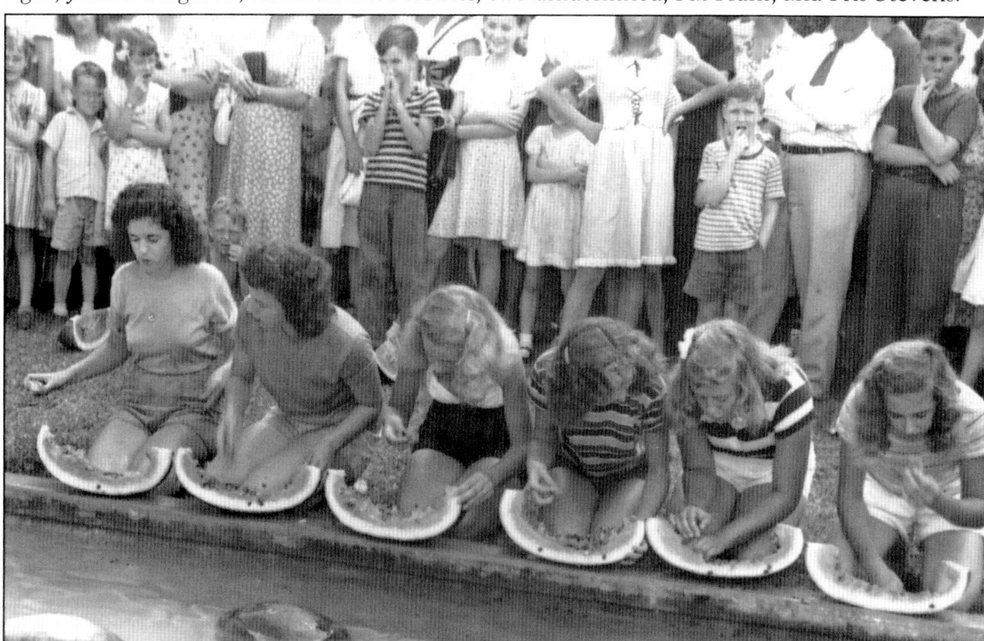

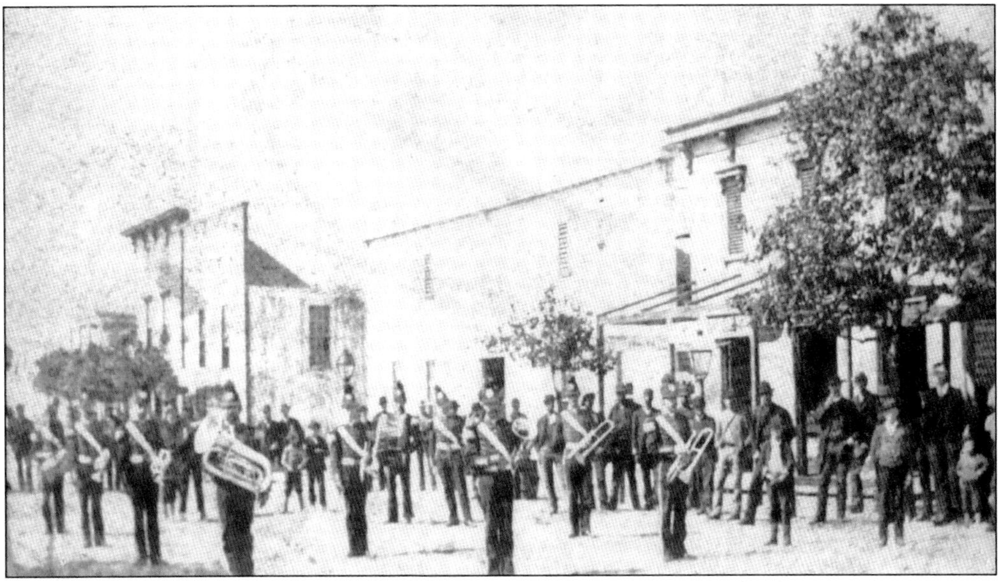

The Leesburg Cornet Band, in full parade dress, prepares to march along Main Street in the late 1880s. The band was made up of members from the local community, including businessmen, farmers, and carriage makers. Many of the brass band's early members were veterans of the War Between the States.

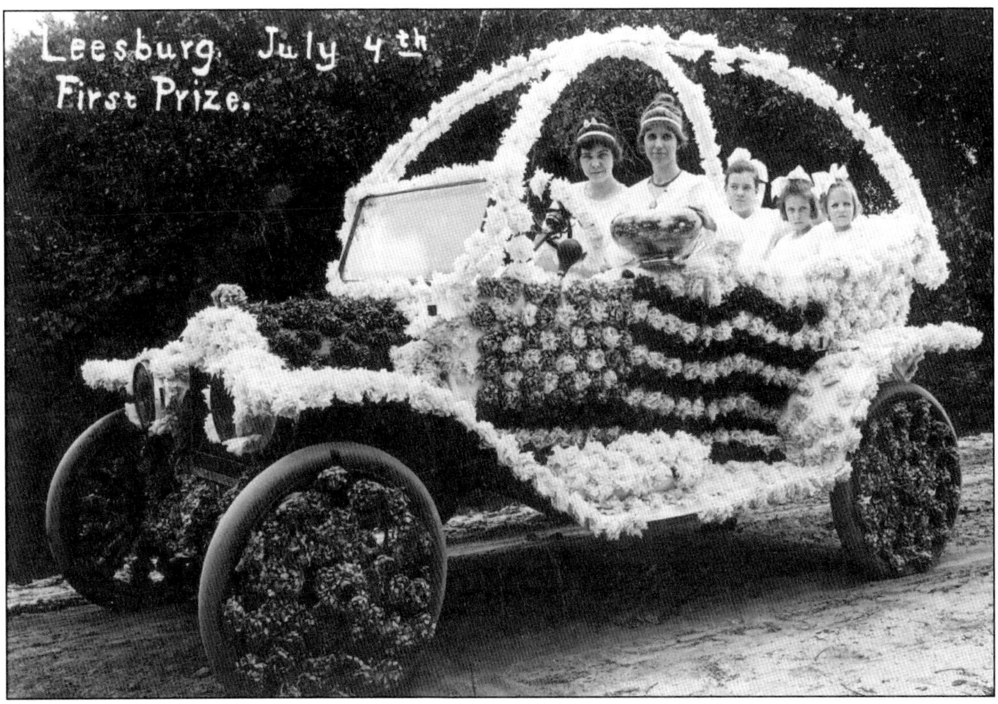

In 1914, Ivy Clough Johnson (second from left) won first prize for best decorated automobile in Leesburg's Fourth of July parade. She was married to successful Leesburg businessman Lewis Miles Johnson, who was prominent in the Lake County school system, having served as a member and chairman of the Lake County school board from 1908 to 1920. He was also Leesburg's city clerk and treasurer from 1906 to 1916.

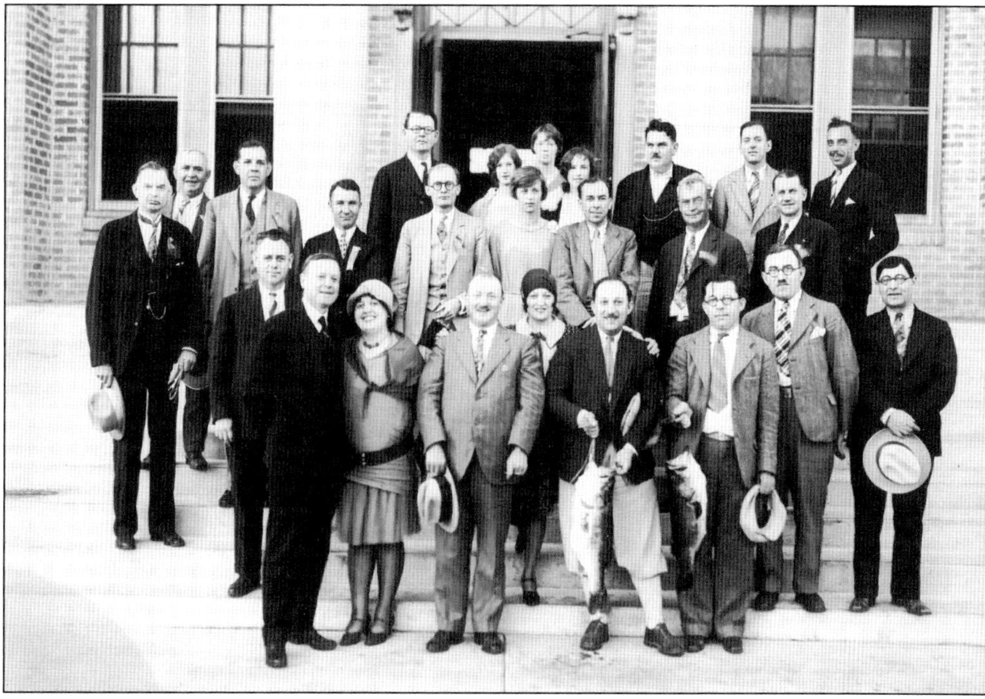

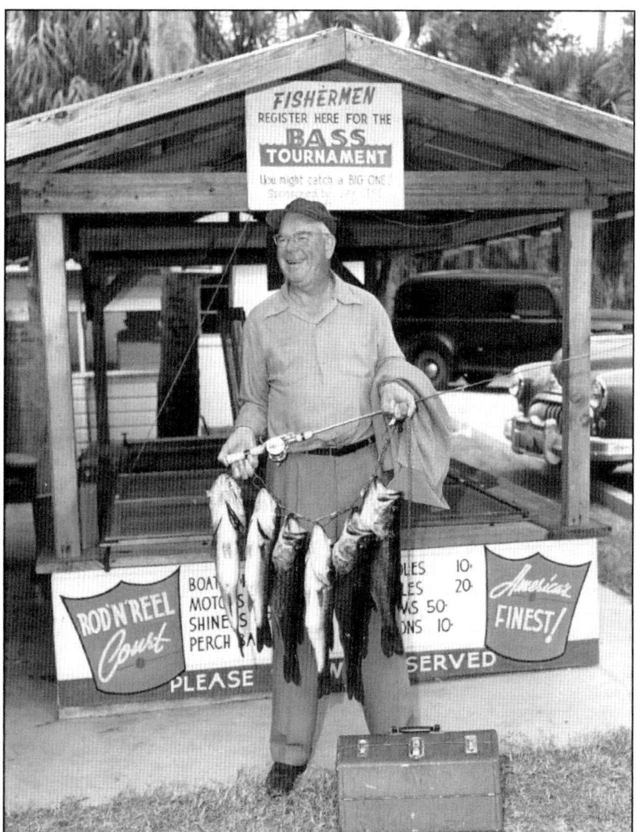

In 1928, Leesburg hosted its first national Fresh Water Bass Tournament. That inaugural competition featured anglers from all over the southeast and Midwest. The most important rule for the two-month-long tournament was that the fish must be taken only from Lake County waters. The largest bass that weighed in that first year was 18.5 pounds, 33 inches long, and 22 inches around its body at the dorsal fin. Above, the winners of that first Fresh Water Bass Tournament have their photograph taken with city and tournament officials. Leesburg mayor Dr. William Alexander MacKenzie is standing in the first row center, in the light suit, and Sen. Truman G. Futch is in the back row, wearing a dark suit at the left edge of the doorway. At left, Wesley "Pinky" Elsten poses with the fish he caught in Lake Harris during a bass tournament in the early 1950s.

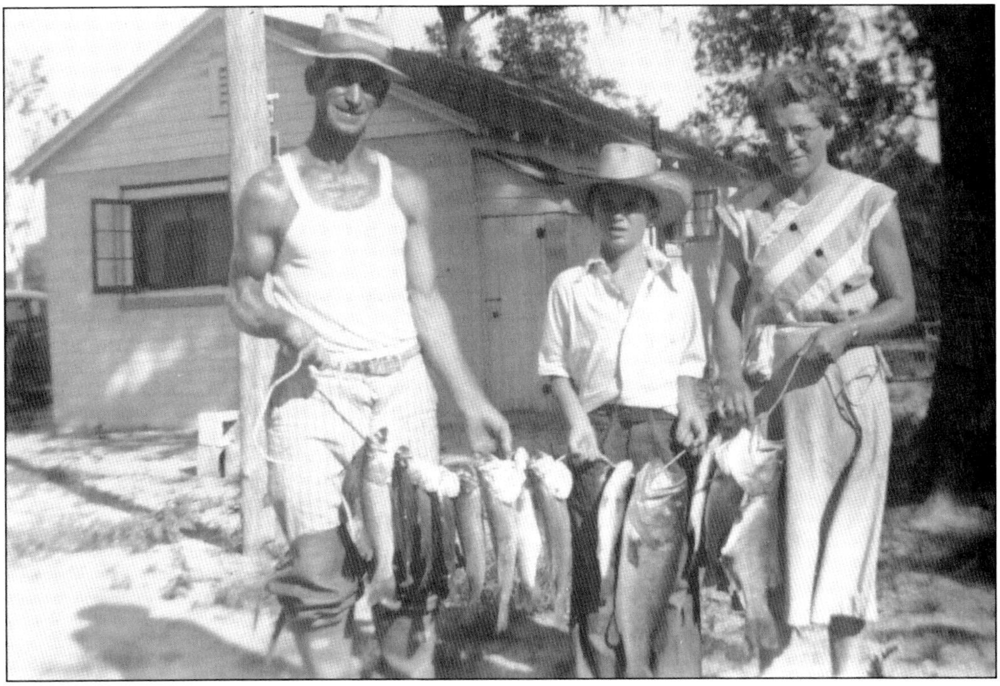

This 1940s photograph was taken at the Frisch Brothers Fish Camp. From left to right are Cloid Victor Frisch, Richard N. "Dick" Pfahler, and Mae D. Witter Pfahler Frisch. The fish camp opened in 1939 and was owned by brothers Cloid and Jack H. Frisch. This great catch was taken from Lake Harris.

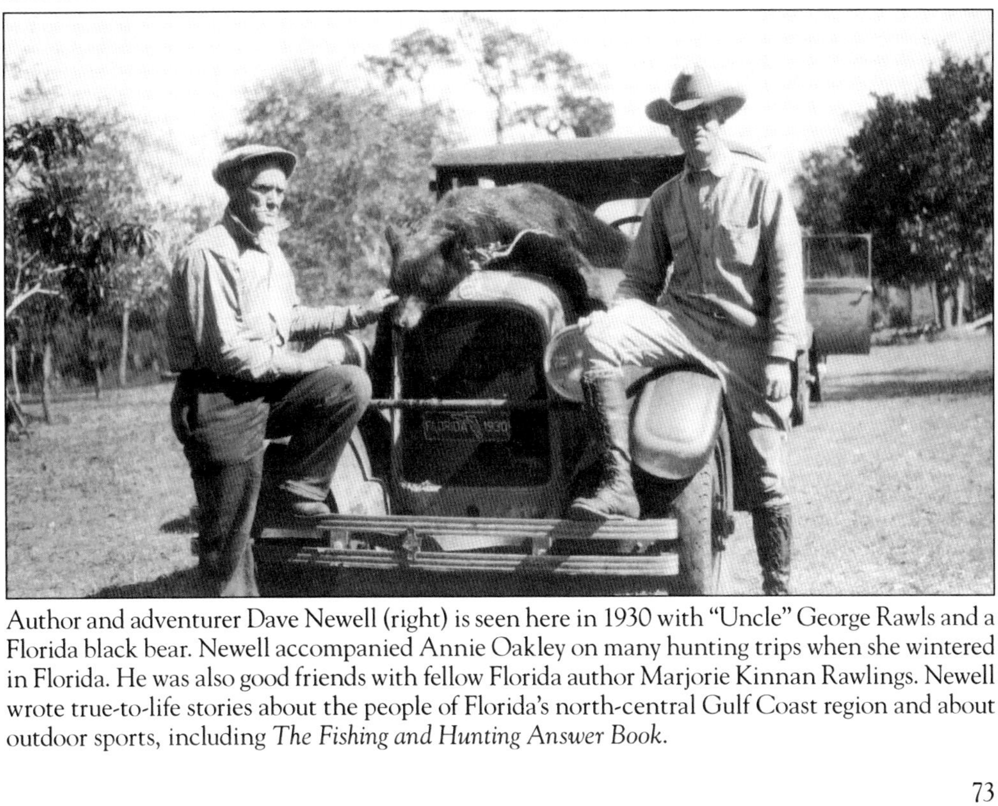

Author and adventurer Dave Newell (right) is seen here in 1930 with "Uncle" George Rawls and a Florida black bear. Newell accompanied Annie Oakley on many hunting trips when she wintered in Florida. He was also good friends with fellow Florida author Marjorie Kinnan Rawlings. Newell wrote true-to-life stories about the people of Florida's north-central Gulf Coast region and about outdoor sports, including *The Fishing and Hunting Answer Book.*

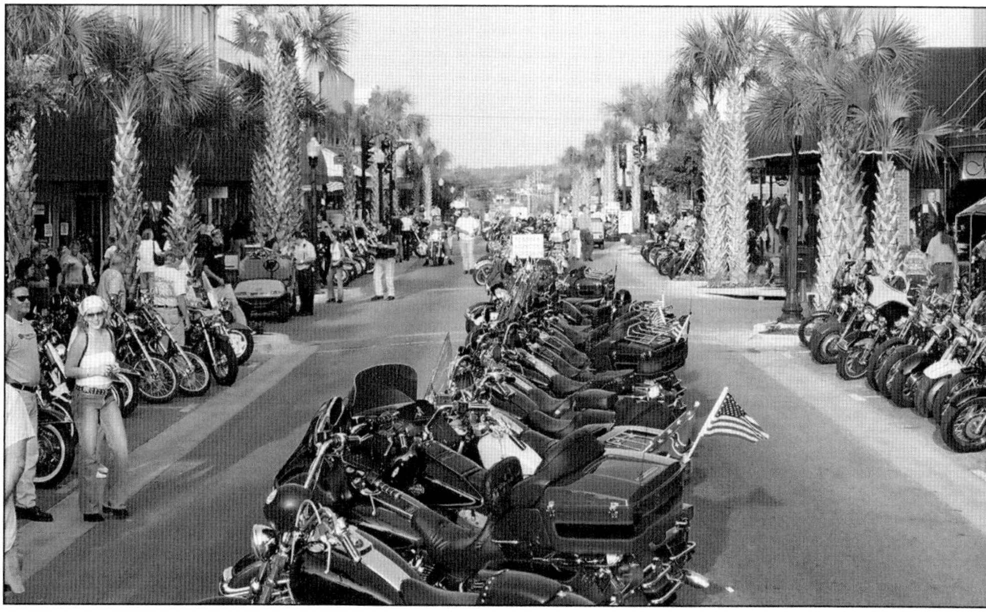

The annual Leesburg BikeFest began in 1997 as a one-day event, but it has grown into a spectacular three-day festival, and attendance has reached 300,000. The Leesburg Partnership is the main event coordinator, with many major sponsors, including Anheuser-Busch and Gator Harley-Davidson. The streets of downtown Leesburg are lined with vendors, and top musical acts have been featured, including Foghat, Leon Russell, and Confederate Railroad. BikeFest 2002 is seen here. (Courtesy of Leesburg Partnership.)

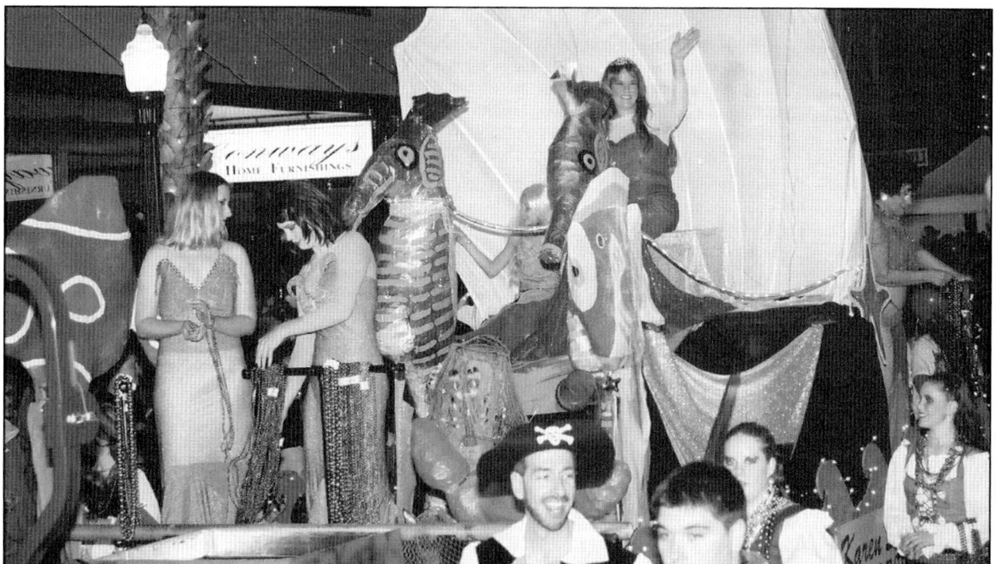

The first Leesburg Mardi Gras Party in the Streets was held in 1998 and has become a popular annual event. The Leesburg Partnership coordinates this street party, which brings New Orleans to downtown Leesburg. The festival includes a children's parade, a carnival, street performers, a spectacular nighttime parade, and lots of beads. A Mardi Gras Ball is held at the historic Leesburg Opera House. The 2004 parade is seen here. (Courtesy of Leesburg Partnership.)

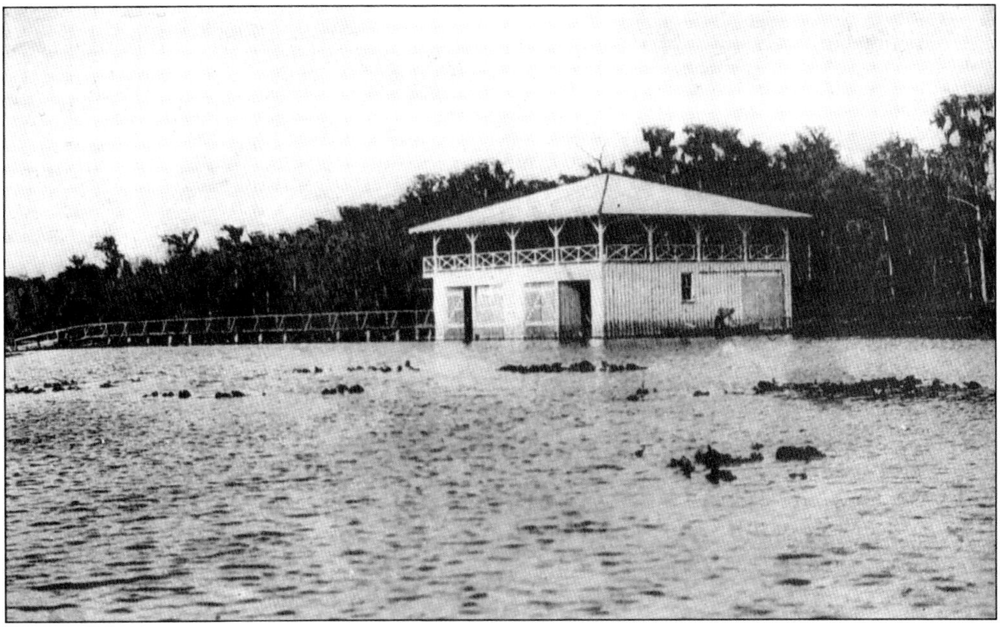

The old pavilion was located on the shore of Lake Harris. A walkway ran along the shoreline from what is now Dixie Avenue at Canal Street. The pavilion was used for dances, parties, graduations, meetings, and many other social events. It burned down in 1925.

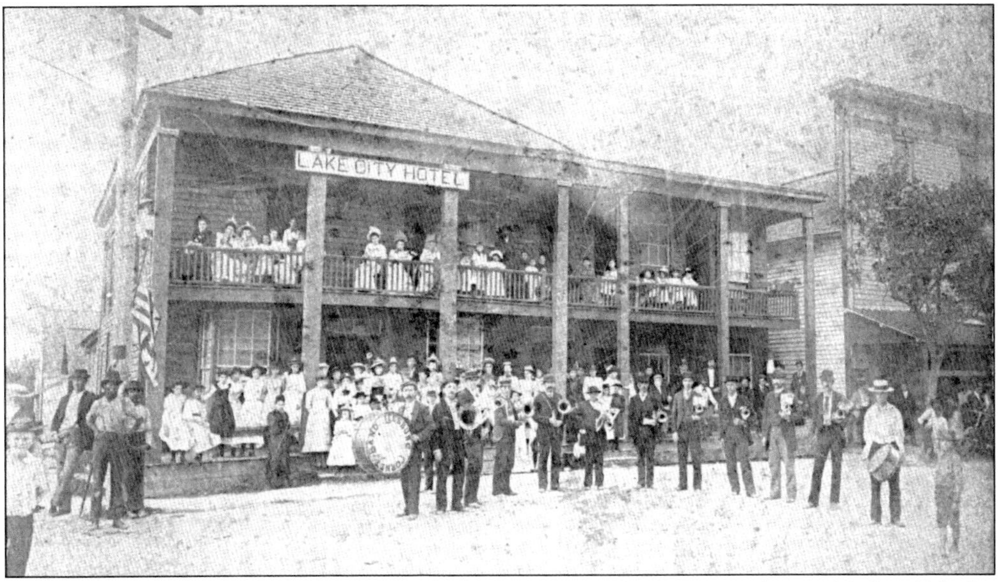

The Leesburg Cornet Band is seen here in front of the Lake City Hotel in 1886. In 1895, the hotel was called the Fuller Hotel. Later, it was known as the Commercial and then the Glyndon. Proprietors of the hotel included the Rainey family and Tom Coyle. The hotel had some fire damage and was moved to a new location in 1912.

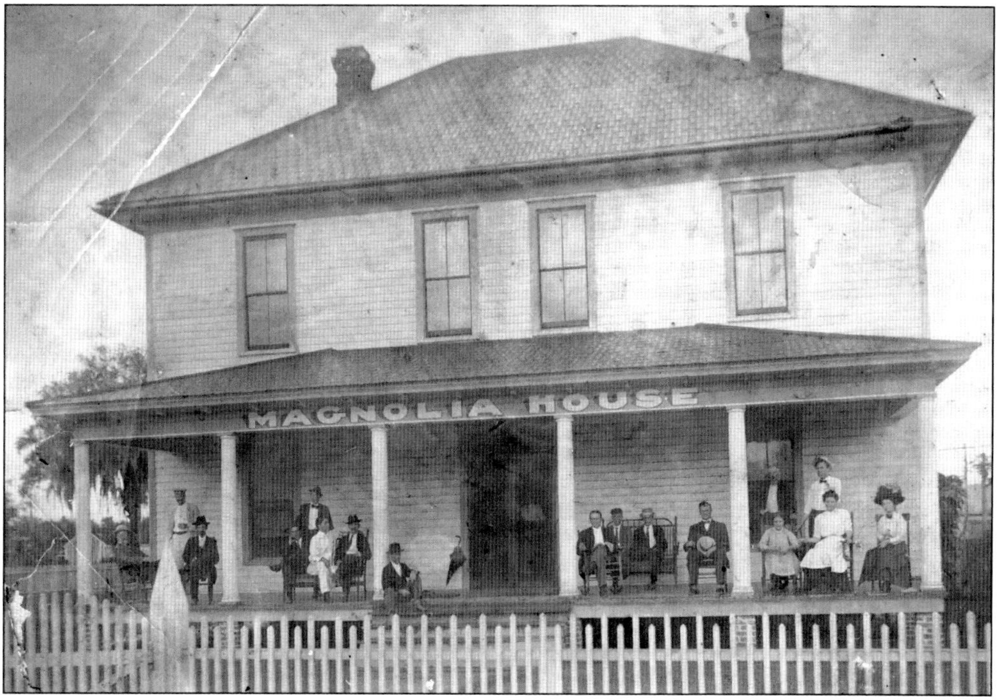

In 1908, Margaret McCormack and her husband, John, returned to Leesburg after being away for 10 years. They expanded a two-room cottage into a six-room, two-story inn on Magnolia Street, which they called Magnolia House. Margaret added more rooms through the years; by 1927, the hotel had 46 rooms and a third floor. The name was also changed to the Magnolia Hotel.

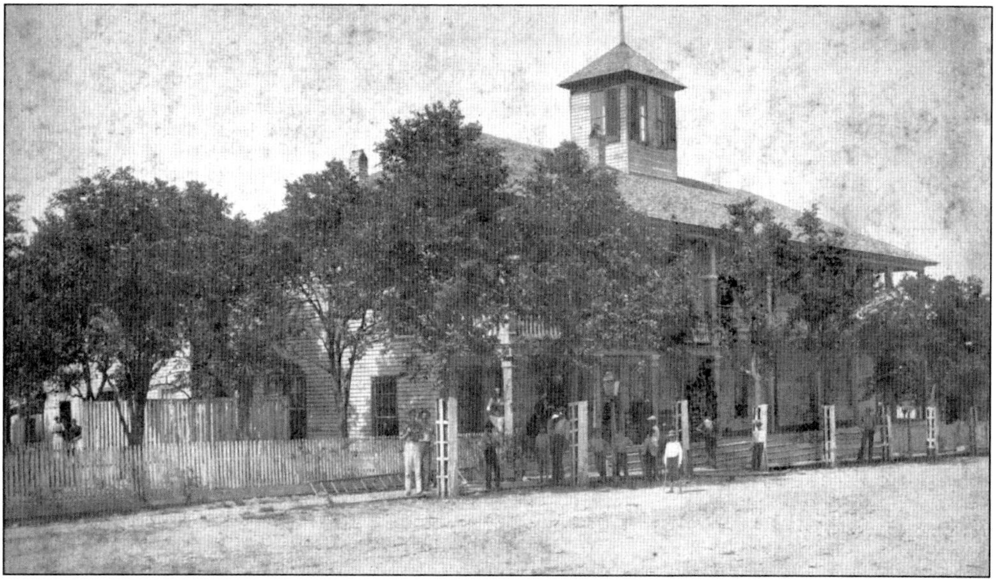

In the 1880s, Margaret "Gillie Ann" Lee Stivender operated a boardinghouse hotel known as Leesburg House and later as the Leesburg Hotel. The 12-room hotel was located on the corner of Main and Palmetto Streets. Around 1885, Edward Mote and Gen. Davis Tilson built the two-story, brick Lake View Hotel. Mote and Tilson moved the Leesburg Hotel down Palmetto Street and connected it to the Lake View.

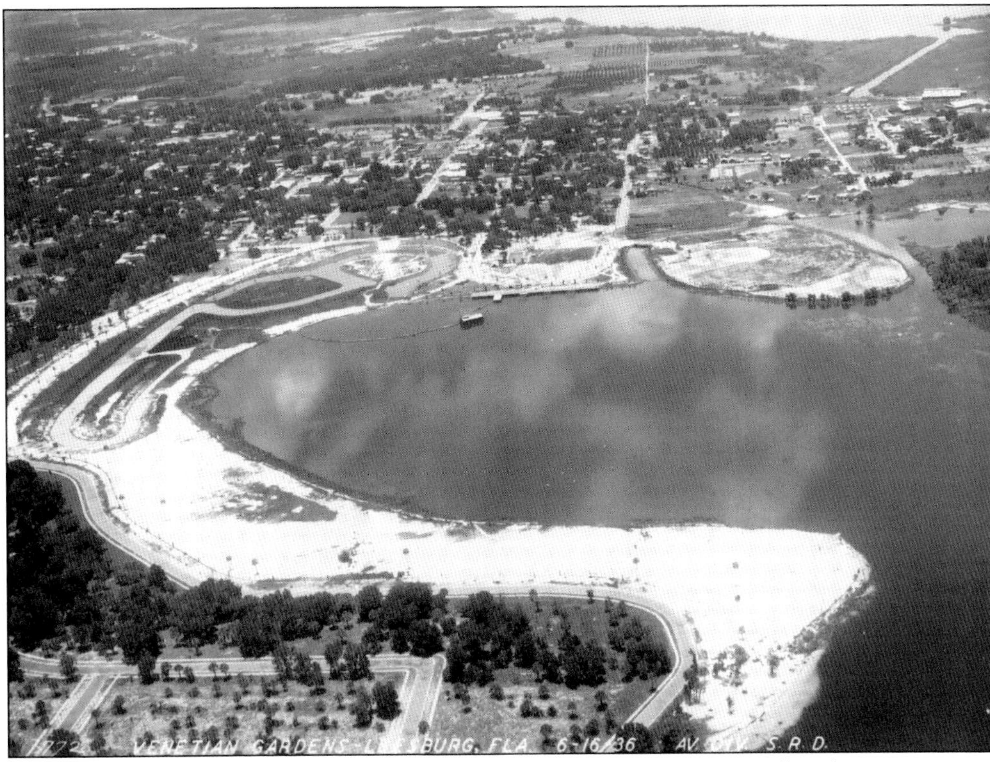

This June 1936 aerial photograph shows the beautiful Venetian Gardens still under construction, which required dredging to create islands and a canal from Lake Griffin to Lake Harris. That canal was never completed. The work turning this saw grass marsh into a unique waterfront park began in 1934 as a WPA project. World-famous landscape architect Richard Forester designed Venetian Gardens.

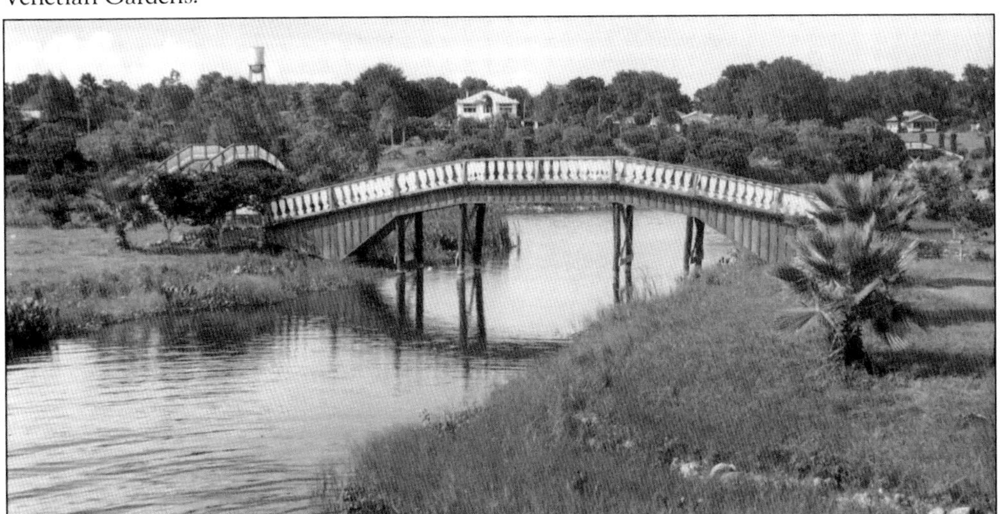

Forester's design plans for Venetian Gardens included large rock gardens, fountains, wading and goldfish ponds, colorful plantings, an open-air dance floor by the lake, a swimming pool, a professional baseball stadium, and ornate bridges connecting the various islands, as seen in this 1950s photograph. This view is from the west side of the gardens looking north.

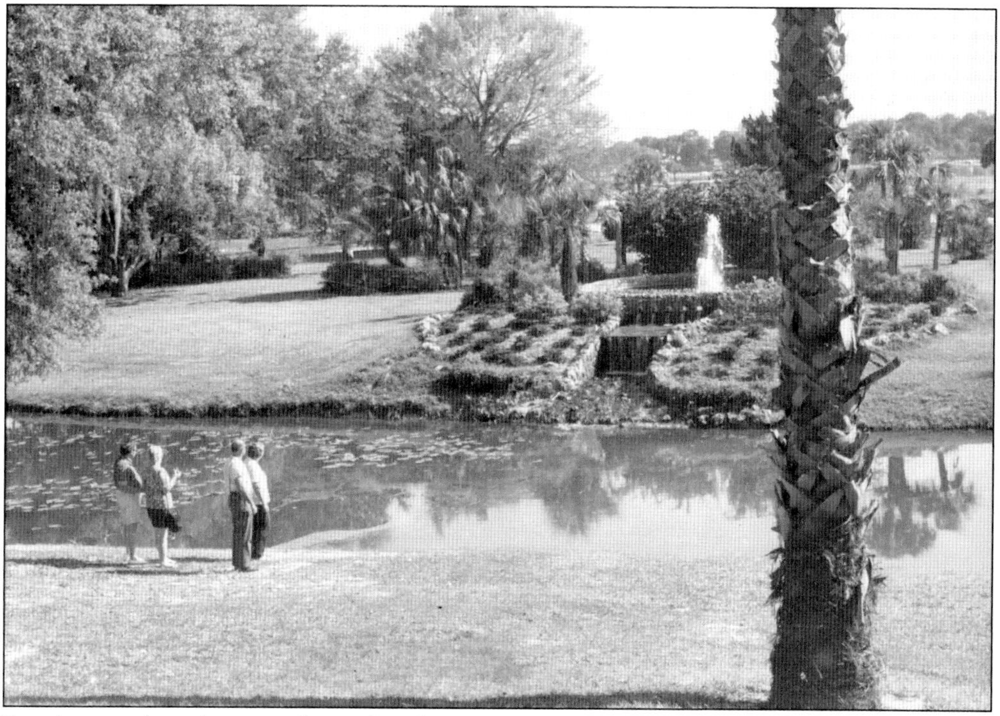

Four large rock gardens were located at the main entrance to Venetian Gardens. Approximately 100 tons of rocks were hauled in from Sumter County to create the extravagant entrance. Goldfish ponds were designed into the rock formations. The water for the goldfish was not pumped in from the lake, but from the city's ice plant in downtown Leesburg. The Venetian Gardens fountain is seen here from Dixie Avenue.

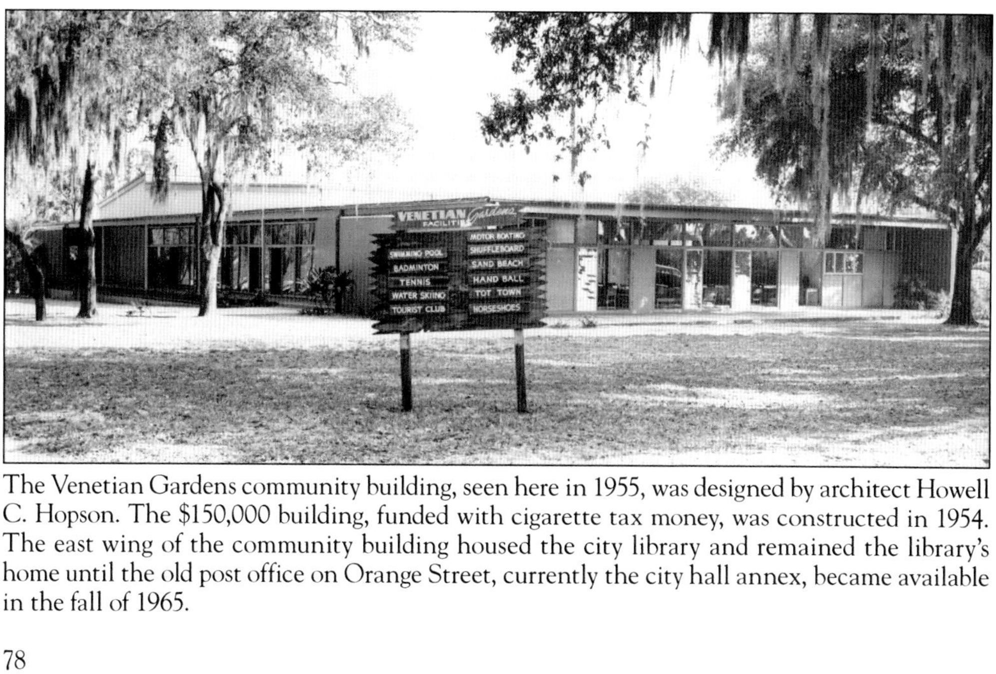

The Venetian Gardens community building, seen here in 1955, was designed by architect Howell C. Hopson. The $150,000 building, funded with cigarette tax money, was constructed in 1954. The east wing of the community building housed the city library and remained the library's home until the old post office on Orange Street, currently the city hall annex, became available in the fall of 1965.

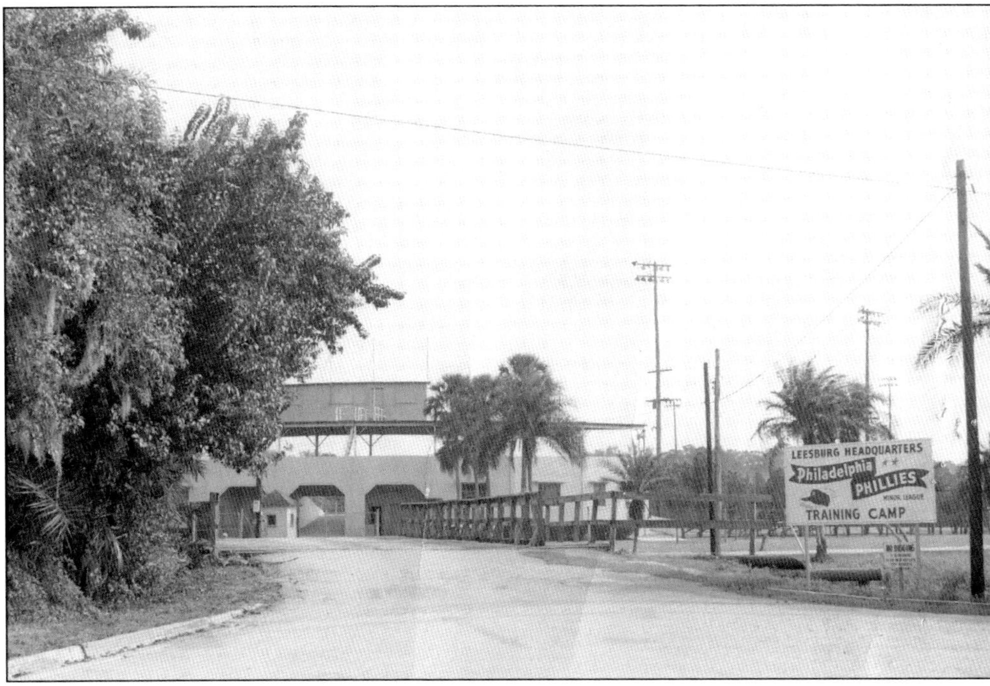

The professional ballpark at Venetian Gardens was built in 1937 as part of the WPA project. The ballpark was built with lights, making it the only place in Lake County for night baseball. One of the ballpark's most unique features was that it was built on an island, keeping with the Venetian Gardens theme. That feature prompted the name of the ballpark: Baseball Island of Venetian Gardens. Completing the park for the start of the 1937 spring training season became a high priority, because a deal had been signed with Oliver French, the president of the Rochester Red Wings, to begin using the ballpark that year. On March 10, 1972, the ballpark was renamed Pat Thomas Memorial Field. In 2003, it was renamed again to Buddy Lowe Field at Pat Thomas Stadium, in honor of Leesburg High School's legendary coach.

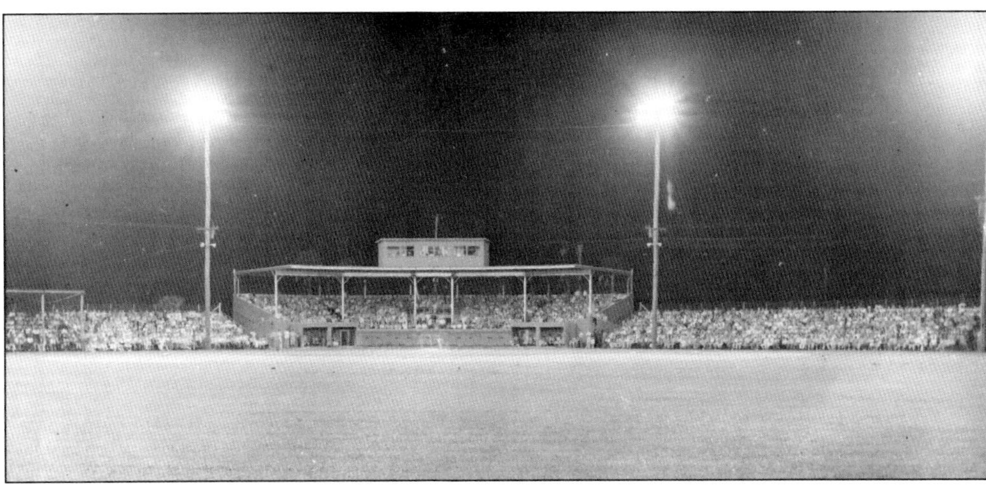

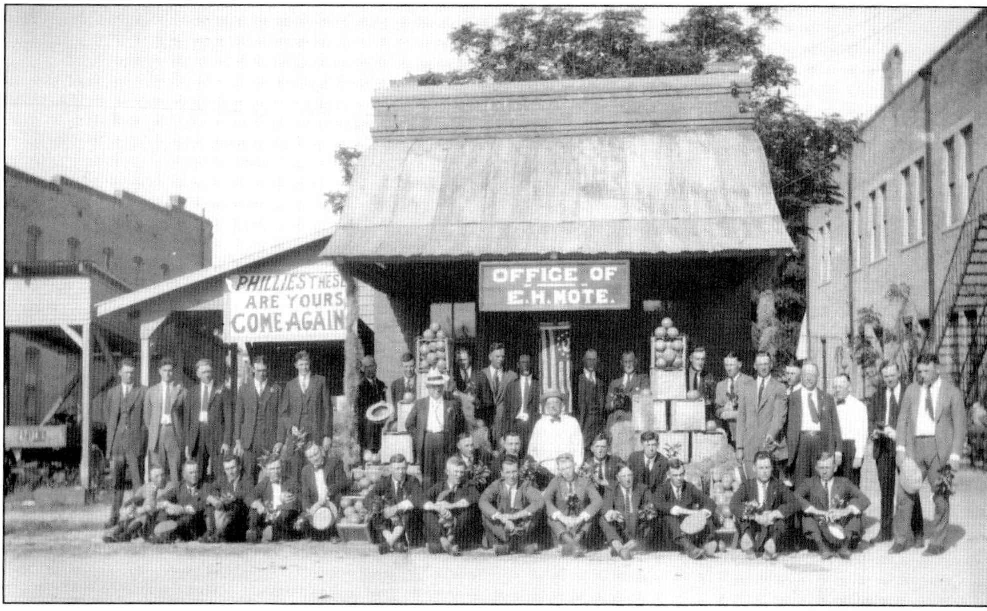

The Philadelphia Phillies first came to Leesburg for spring training in 1922. Though the Phillies' teams of the 1920s featured star sluggers Cy Williams, Cliff Lee, and Curt Walker, the team spent most of the decade at the bottom of the standings. The Phillies are seen here at Edward Mote's office in 1922 before leaving Leesburg for Philadelphia.

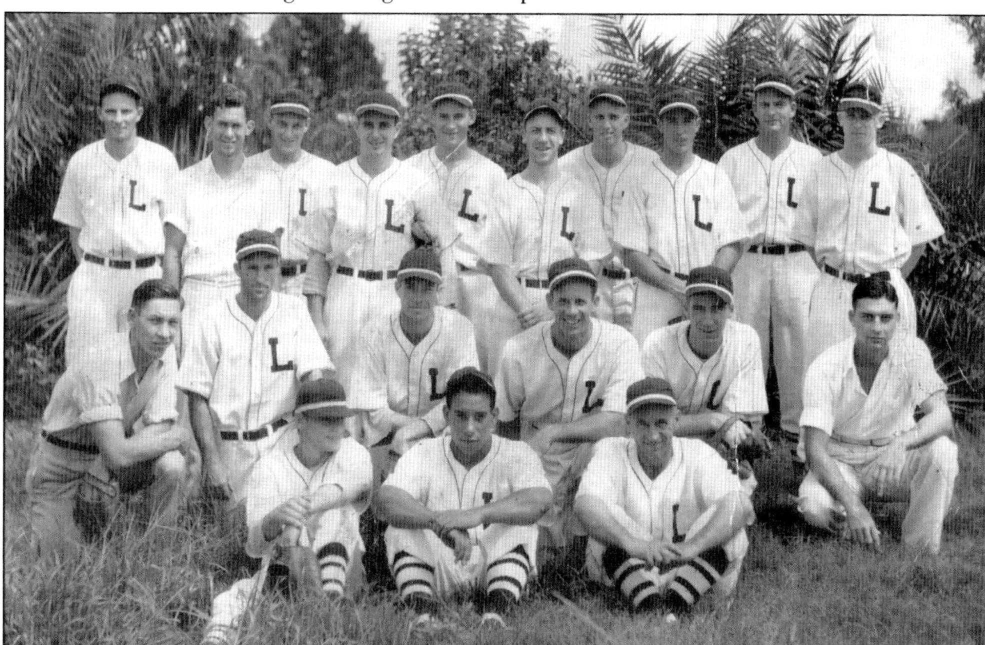

Leesburg and professional baseball have had a relationship since the 1920s. The Leesburg Gondoliers became the city's first professional team in 1937. In 1947, Leesburg acquired its first major league affiliation, with the Pittsburgh Pirates, followed by affiliations with the Milwaukee Braves in 1956 and the Baltimore Orioles in 1960. Seen here are the 1953 Leesburg Lakers, originally called the Leesburg Packers, who played in the Florida State League.

Seven

Leesburg Lines

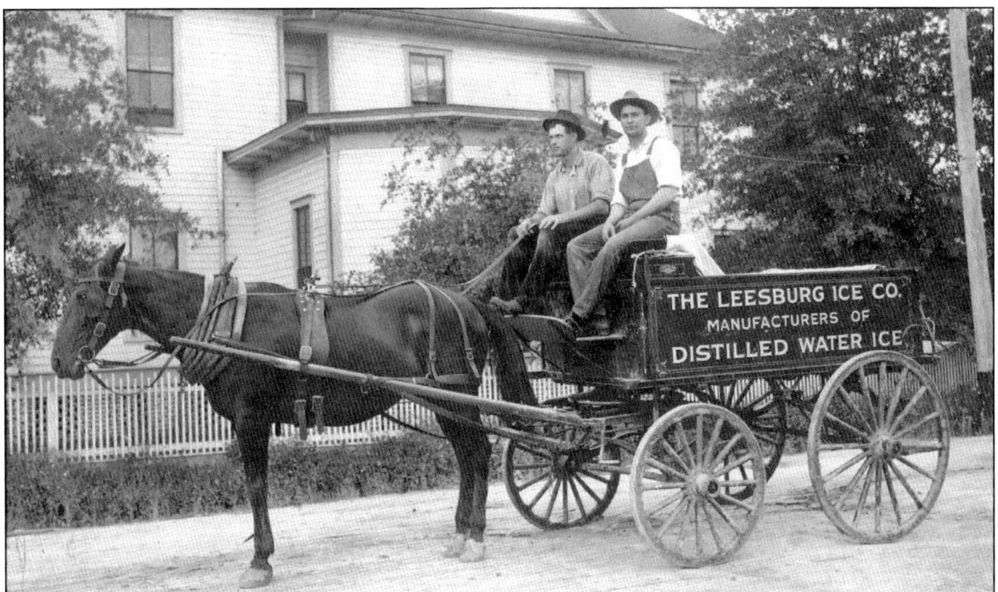

Dating back to ancient times, gusts of wind moved mankind across the water while horses, mules, and oxen moved people and goods across the land. Steadfast horses not only transported families to picnics in the park and to church services, but they also pulled our plows and wagons to deliver goods and wares. Steam lines, rail lines, truck lines, and airlines provided much-needed relief as transportation technology advanced. Jim and Rod Kelley of the Leesburg Ice Company are seen here in 1884.

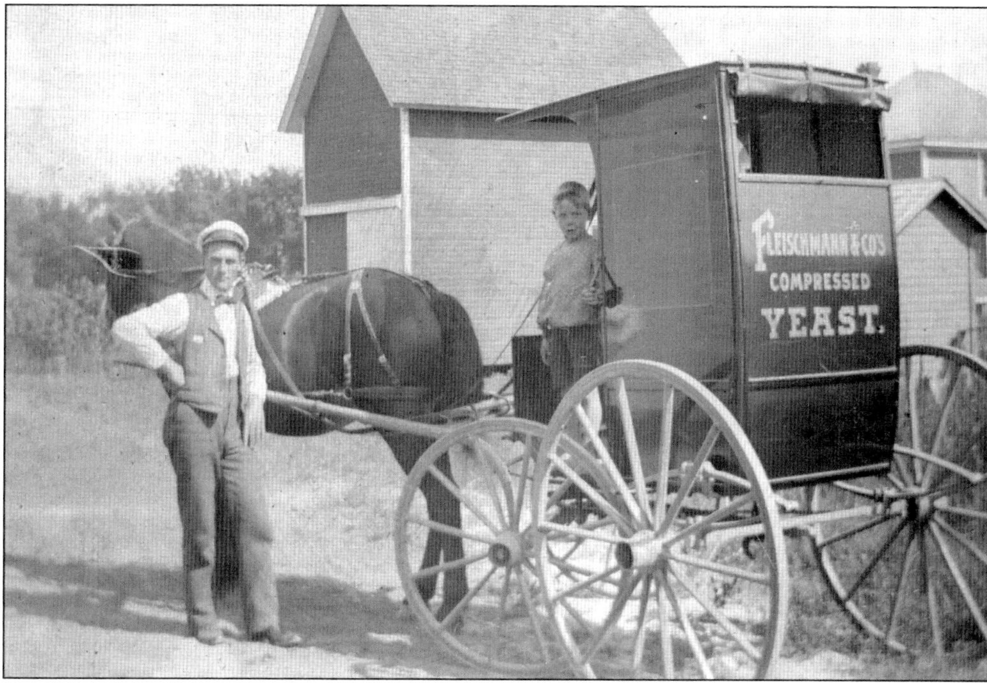

Seen here in the 1890s are L.B. Whitney (left) and his son Melville. Whitney hired out his one-horse delivery wagon, called a fly, to the Fleischmann Company. In 1868, Charles and Maximillian Fleischmann and James Graff, a distiller, founded the Fleischmann Company in Cincinnati. The company manufactured compressed yeast for bread and bakery products, as well as distilled spirits.

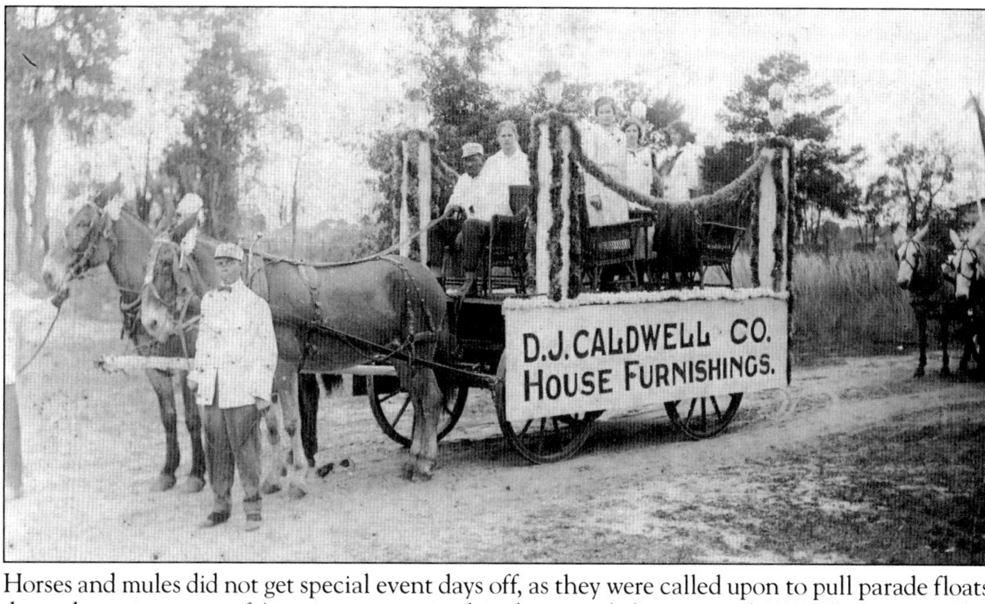

Horses and mules did not get special event days off, as they were called upon to pull parade floats down the main streets of America, as seen in this photograph from around 1910. This team pulled the D.J. Caldwell Company House Furnishings float. In 1908, Caldwell opened a hardware and furniture store in Eustis, Florida, later establishing a branch store in Leesburg under the name Leesburg Hardware and Supply Company.

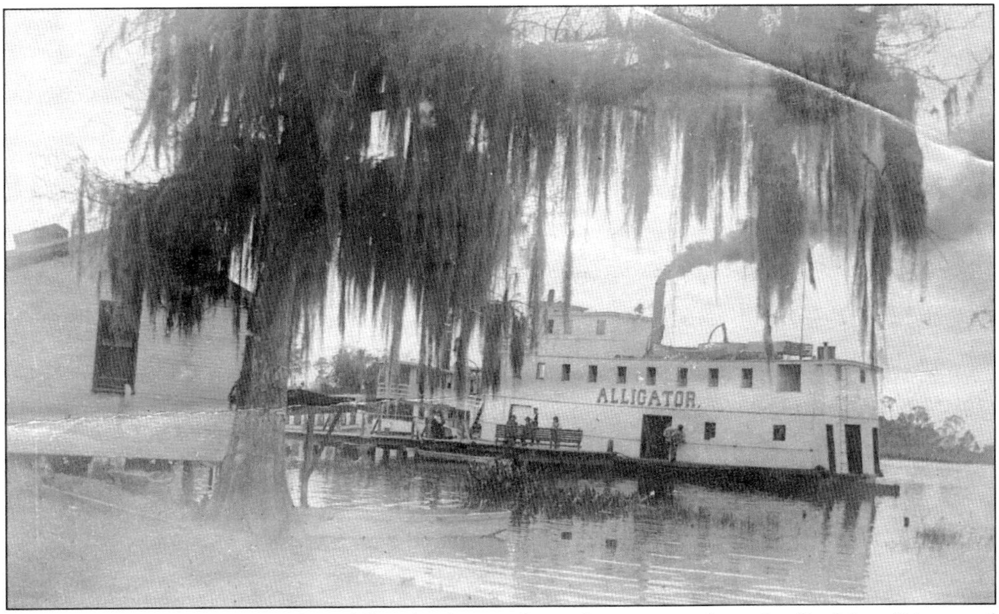

The *Alligator* was an inboard, paddle-wheel steamboat that operated on the St. Johns River and the Ocklawaha. Originally built for Capt. C.W. Howard in 1888, the *Alligator* was owned by Joseph Edward Lucas from 1890 until 1903. This 1905 photograph shows how the *Alligator* looked after it was rebuilt in 1893. "City of Leesburg" appears on the steamer's transom. The *Alligator* burned and sank on November 5, 1909.

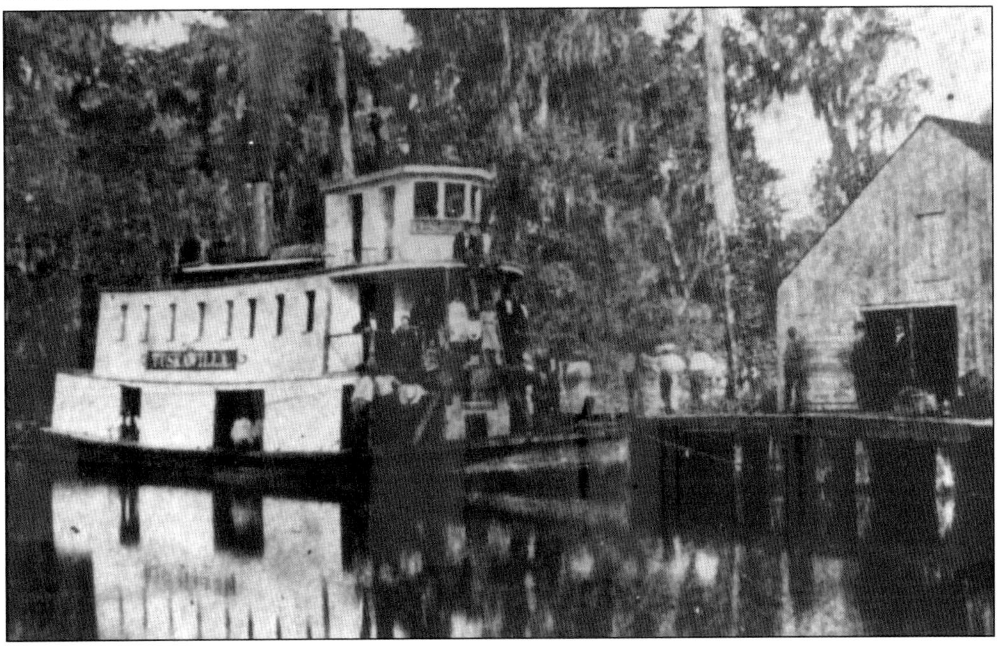

The 76-ton *Tuskawilla* steamer is seen here around 1880 taking on cargo and supplies at the Samuel Agnew turpentine still. The hull of the *Tuskawilla* was built in Leesburg in 1875 and towed to Jacksonville for engine installation. Dr. S.J. Bouknight of Leesburg built and owned the *Tuskawilla*. The steamer carried cargo and passengers during its 15 years of operation, and it disappeared into the history books in the late 1880s.

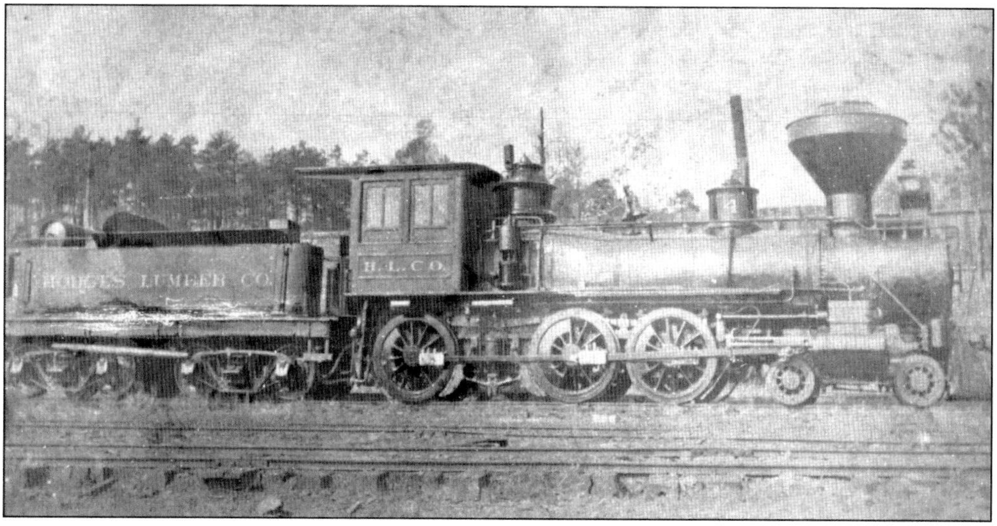

This 1890 photograph shows the Hodges Lumber Company train crossing the Dead River trestle, which opened in the mid-1880s to link Leesburg with Tavares, the Lake Region's leading railroad hub. Lake County and Sumter County were two of Florida's most important timber centers at that time, harvesting virgin pine and cypress.

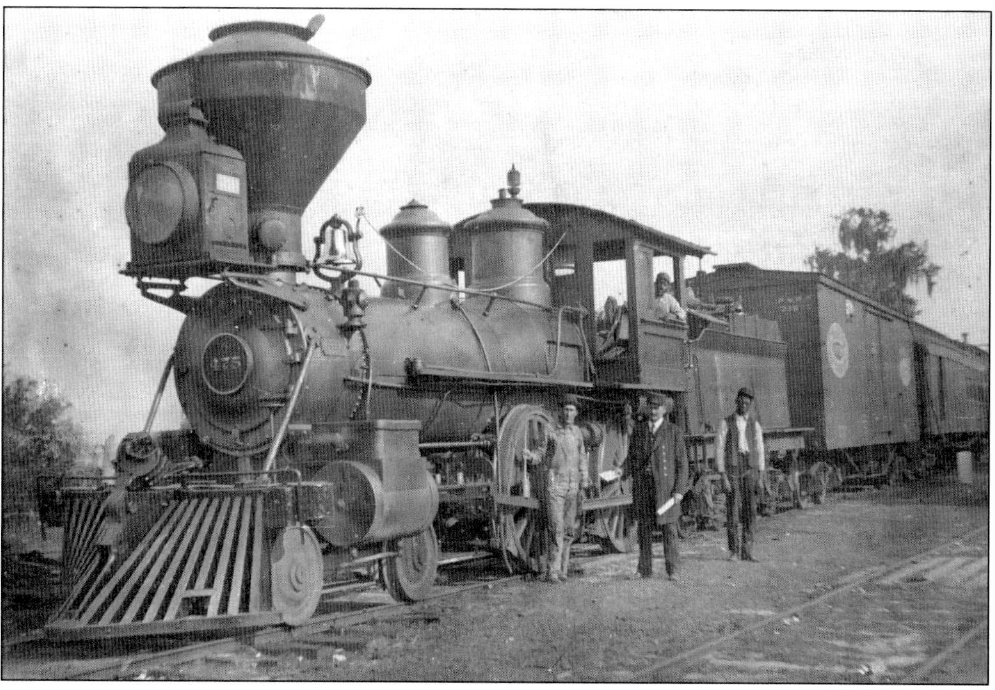

This mixed passenger and freight train is seen at the Leesburg depot in the 1880s. The train ran along the Florida Railway & Navigation Company line, traveling from Wildwood east to Leesburg, and then on to Tavares and Orlando. From left to right are the engineer holding an oilcan, the conductor, and a porter. The man leaning out the cab window is the fireman. Note that the locomotive has a 4-4-0 wheel arrangement.

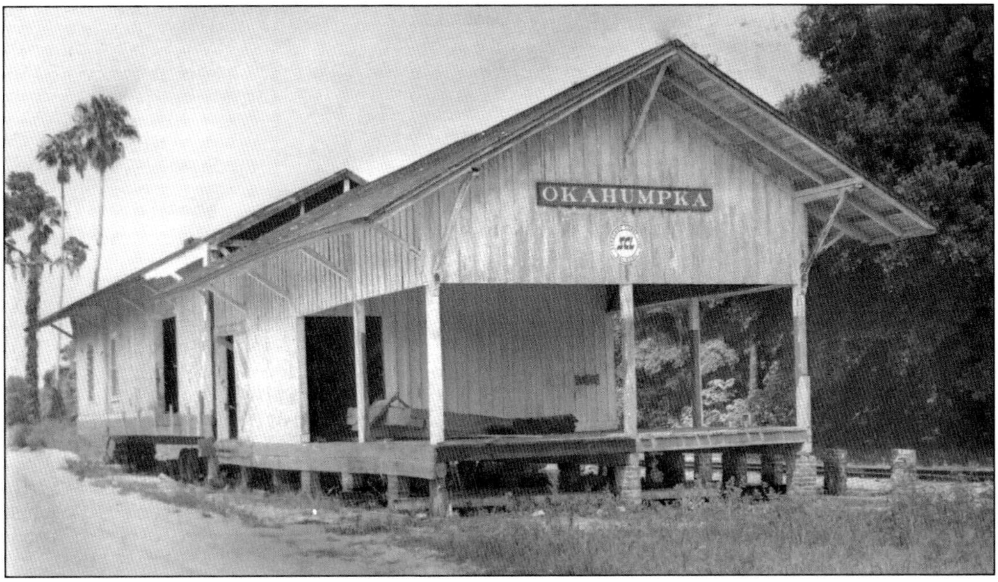

The Okahumpka train depot was built in 1898 as part of the Henry Plant system of railroads and steamboats. This depot was connected to the Plant System section that stretched from Savannah to Tampa. It was a central shipping point for the area's large watermelon crop. In 1978, the Seaboard Coast Line Railroad donated the depot to the Mildred W. and Doyle E. Carlton Jr. Cracker Country Museum in Tampa.

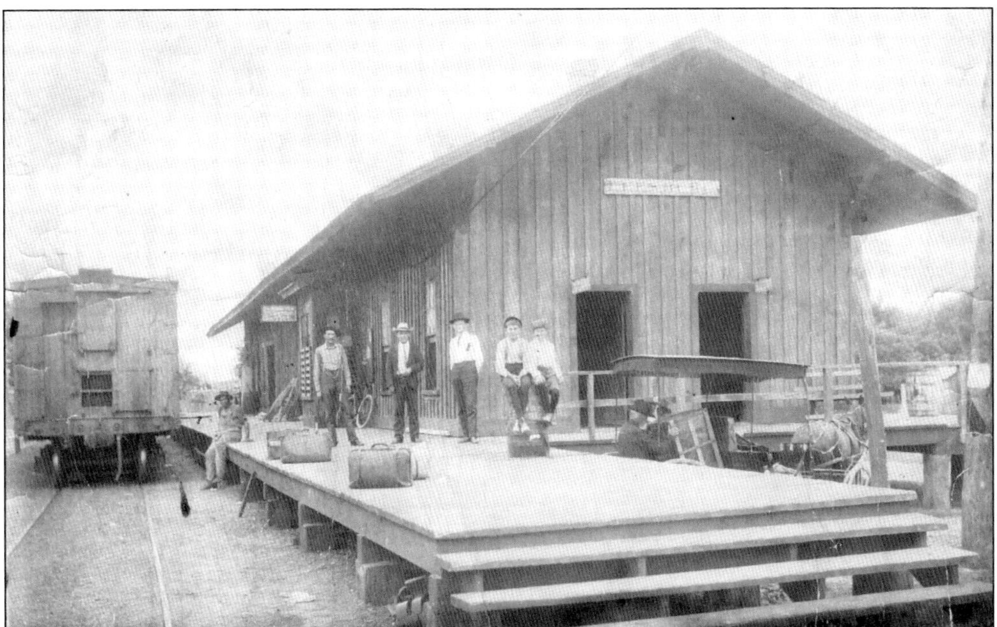

This passenger and freight station was on Sixth Street in Leesburg. This c. 1900 photograph shows a passenger unloading a large chest from a chaise-cart onto the platform and a bicycle leaning against the wall by the telegraph office. This depot was built as part of the Plant System Railroad, which served the southeast region. In 1902, the Plant System was taken over by the Atlantic Coast Line Railroad.

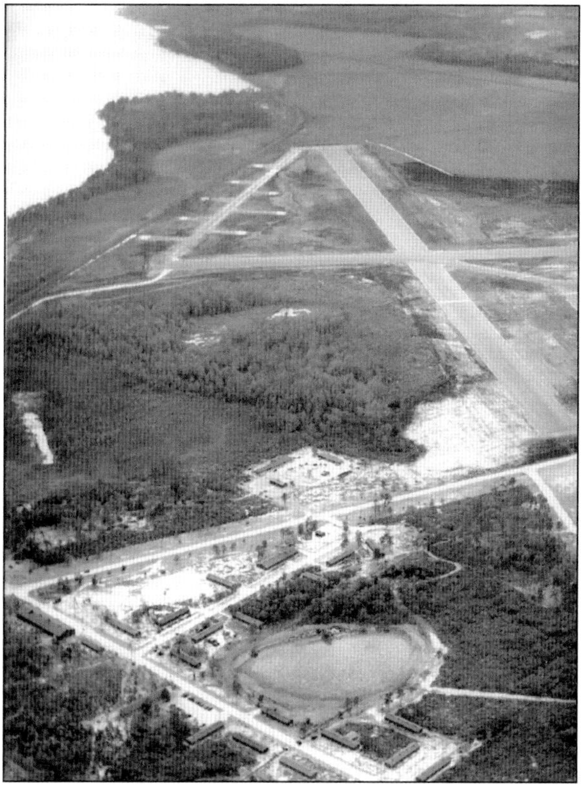

This 1950s aerial photograph of Leesburg Airport looks north toward Lake Harris. Today, the airport is called Leesburg International Airport at Henry Pringle Field. Pringle was instrumental in getting the donation of land from Silver Lake Estates in 1940 to build the airport. A prisoner of war camp, in what was originally the barracks for the pilots, is seen in the lower left of this photograph. Leesburg assumed control of the airport from the War Department in 1948.

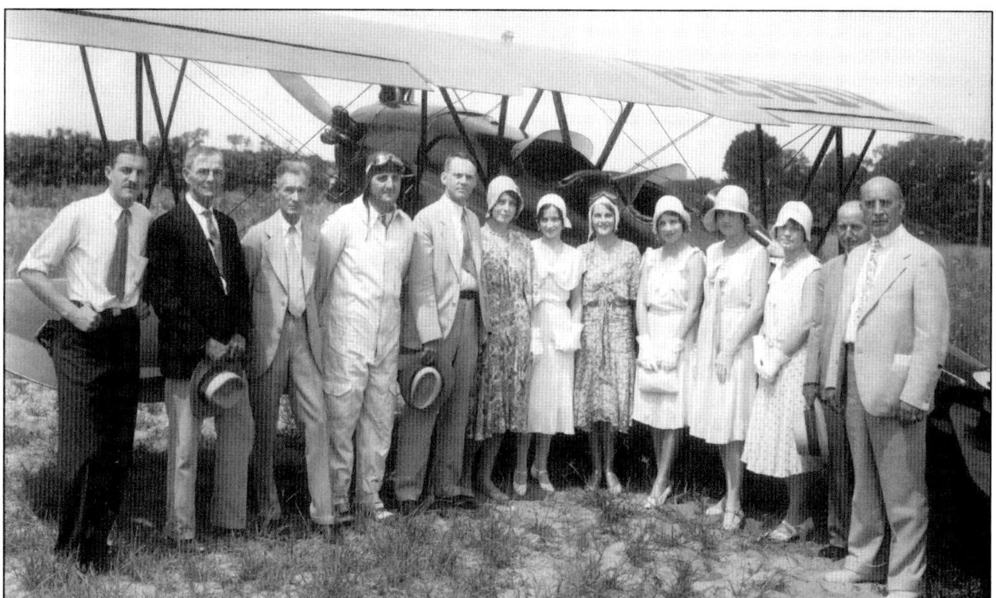

William Herbert Richey (second from left) and friends pose for a photograph at Briles Airfield in 1929. Briles Airfield was also known as Tomato Hill, because it was located on a vegetable farm at the highest point in Leesburg, in the Sunnyside area. Fred Briles received permission to clear a strip of land on Tomato Hill soon after he purchased an airplane in 1928. William Richey served for 20 years as a county commissioner.

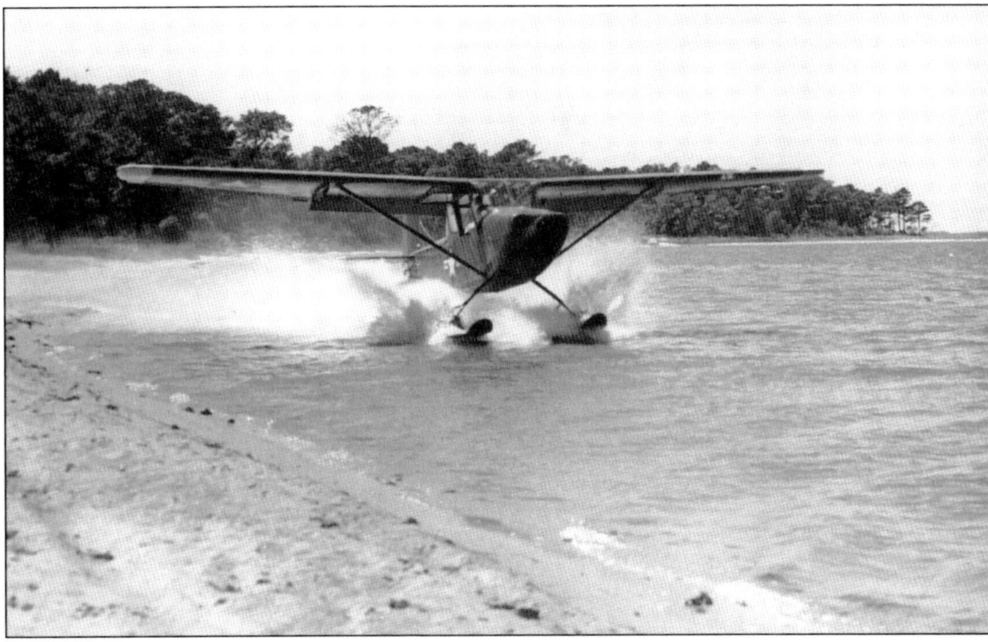

In 1937, nearly 10 years after Fred Briles cleared a landing strip on Tomato Hill, Leesburg began work to build a municipal airfield at what is now known as Beverly Shores, on Lake Griffin. The WPA provided the labor, but the project stopped before it was completed. After World War II, aviator Hal Hoover used the site for his seaplane school. Seen here is a military seaplane on Lake Griffin.

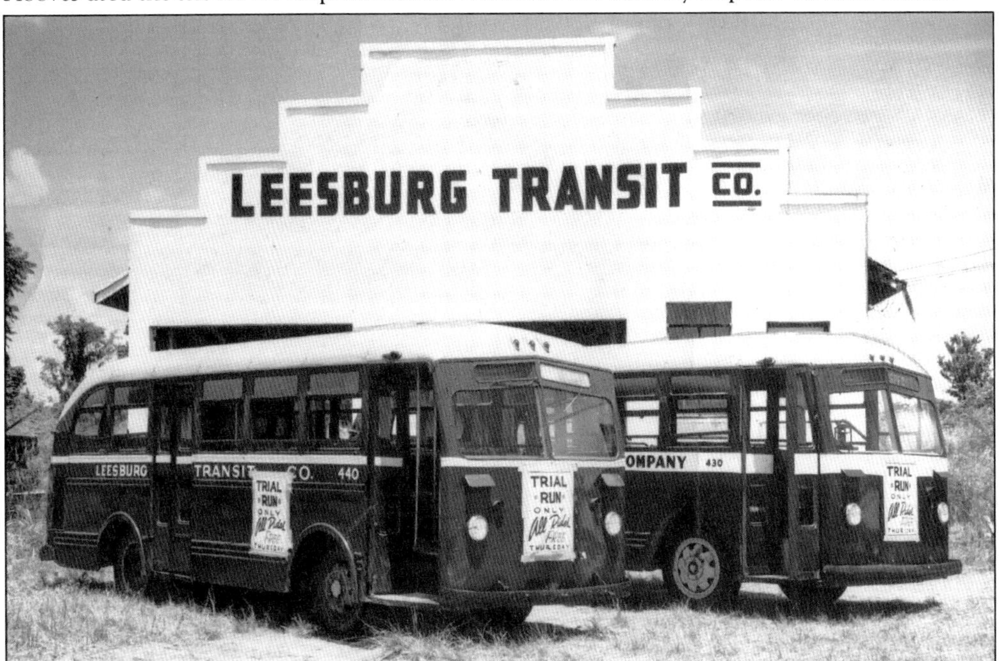

The Leesburg Transit Company, located at 301 South Palmetto Street, made its debut in the 1940s. Buses No. 430 and 440—small, 25-foot "old-look" model transit buses—were first manufactured in 1940 by Yellow Coach/General Motors. Note the signs on the buses, which read, "Trial Run Only, All Rides Free Thursday."

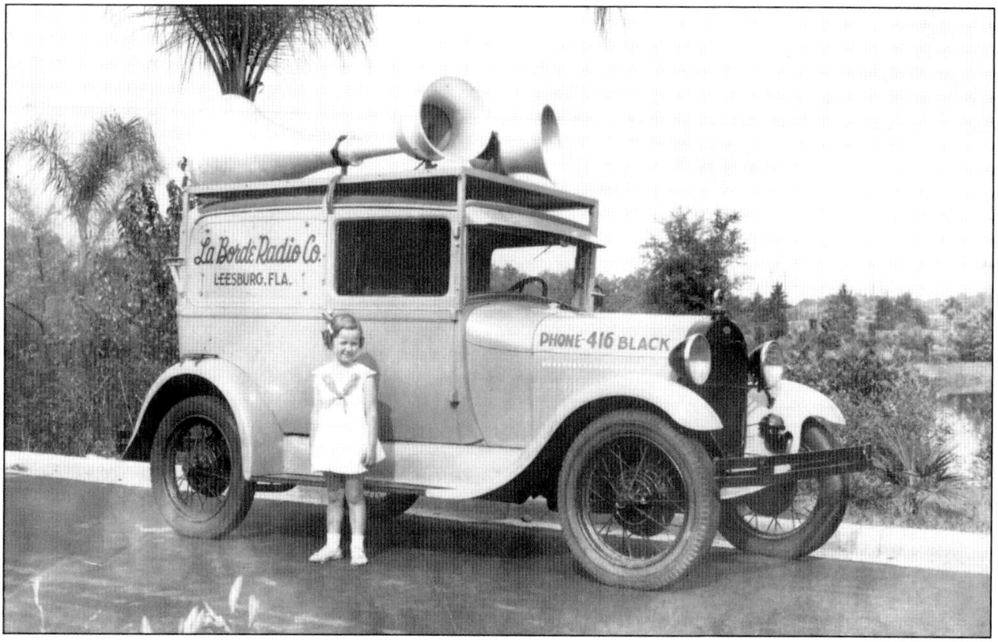

Margaret Ann LaBorde stands next to her parents' sound truck in 1937. The truck, the first of its kind in Leesburg, had two large speakers mounted on top, which were used for broadcasting. It was owned by John and Lucy LaBorde, who owned the LaBorde Radio Company, located at 719 West Main Street. They later expanded their shop to sell household appliances.

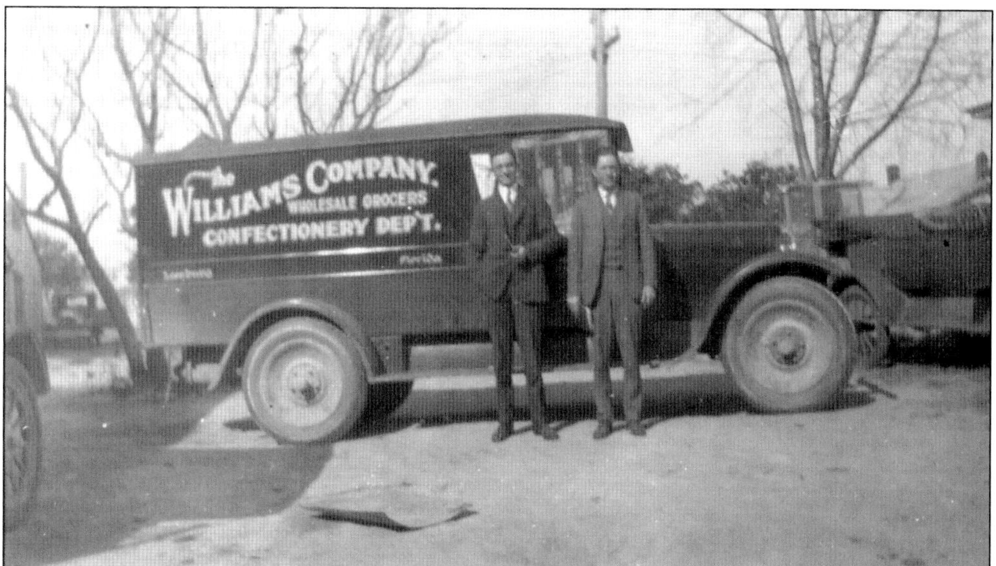

In 1919, James Henry Williams (left) established the Williams Company, a wholesale grocery house. His company built a large trade business in Lake, Sumter, and Marion Counties. The Williams Company was the first in Florida to start delivering goods using its own trucks. James Williams was born in North Carolina on May 7, 1858, and relocated to Leesburg in 1910.

Eight

The All-Leesburg Team

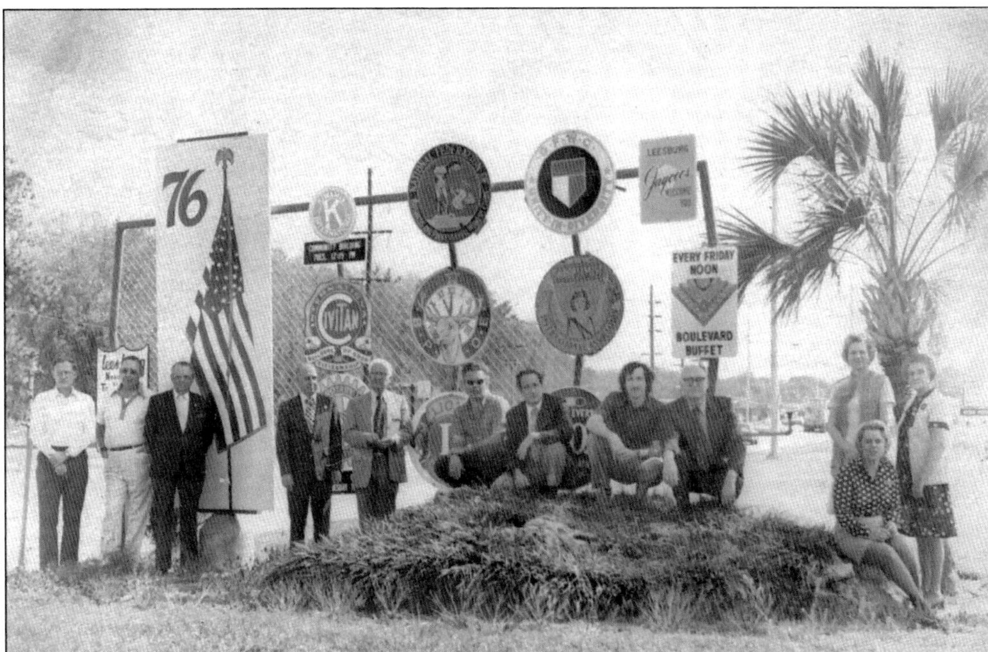

In 1976, several of Leesburg's leaders had their photograph taken at the Gateway to Leesburg sign. Representing Leesburg's many civic organizations are, from left to right, Jack Fredericks, unidentified, Ed Merrell, Don Jones, Clyde White, unidentified, Louis George, Doug Braun, Glyn Faircloth, Ruth Curry, Clair Hollins White, and Beulah Geiger. A past president of the Kiwanis, Clyde White is remembered for his efforts to make Leesburg better.

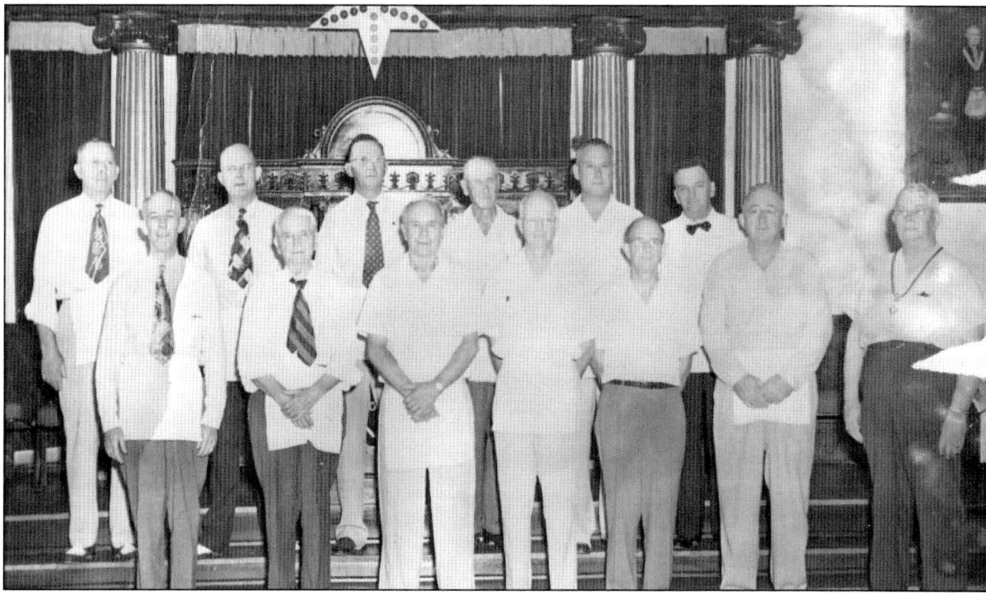

On January 15, 1868, Masonic Lodge No. 58 Free and Accepted Masons was chartered. Melton Haynes was the lodge's first Worshipful Master, and John Robertson was the first Senior Warden. On September 13, 1950, the lodge hosted a past master's night, seen here. From left to right are (first row) Walter A. Ames, Bart Corley, William Dunstan, Henry L. Pringle, C. Earl Schaeffer, R. Perry Butler, and James H. Pegram; (second row) Homer F. Carpenter, John L. Fahs, Boyce A. Williams, Elmer R. Canady, C. Edward Sauls, and George B. Stephenson.

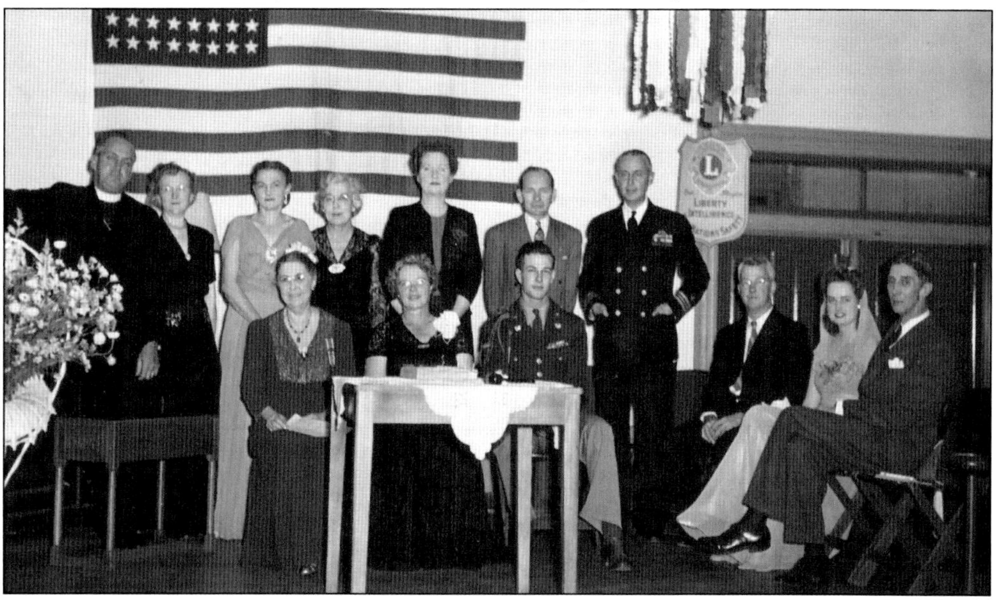

The Bertha Hereford Hall Chapter, Daughters of the American Revolution (DAR), was chartered in 1929. On March 13, 1946, Leesburg dignitaries spoke at a special program hosted by the DAR. From left to right are (first row) Veola Ezell, Lillian Vickers-Smith, Jack Vickers-Smith, Ormond Vickers-Smith, Phyllis Burnett, and Hon. Tim Sellar; (second row) Rev. William Hargis, Clara Freeman Ware, Mrs. William Hargis, Mrs. William Frame, Mary Lowery Lynch, Leesburg mayor Herbert Butler, and Lt. Cmdr. Ed Crandall.

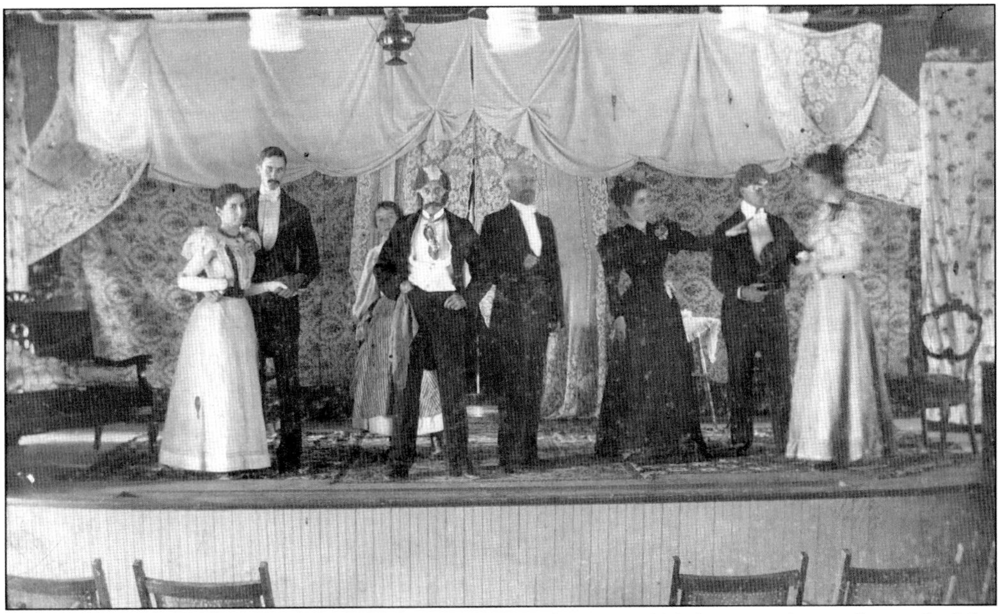

The Leesburg Players, a civic theater group, are seen here in 1898 during a dress rehearsal of the play *Our Boys*, a three-act comedy written by Henry James Byron in 1875. From 1875 to 1879, *Our Boys* was the world's longest-running play, and ranks third in total performances between 1875 and 1919. This photograph was taken by Leesburg photographer R.H. Jocelyn.

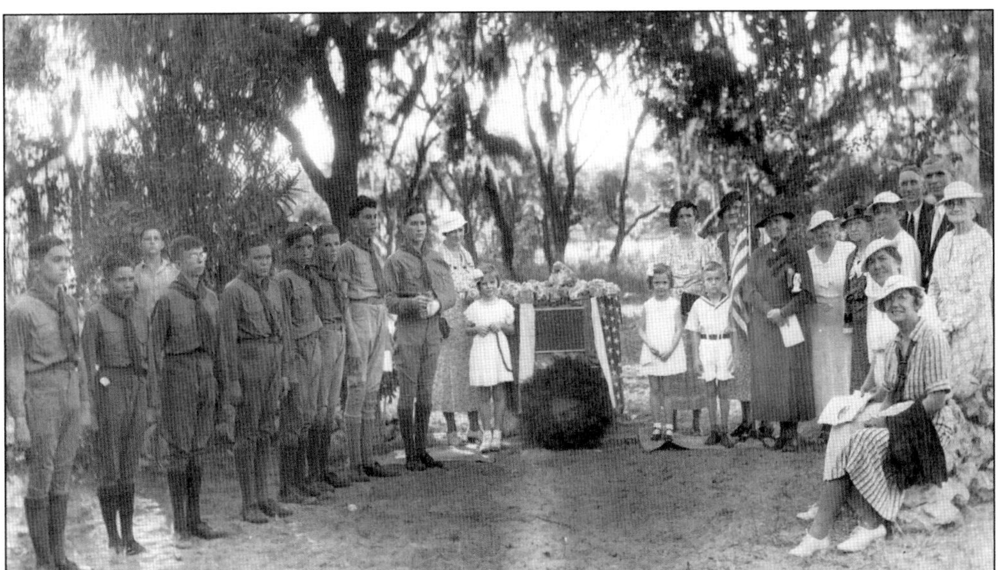

On October 28, 1935, Leesburg Boy Scout Troop 14 and the DAR marked the site of the first Leesburg High School with a bronze tablet. The marker also commemorates the school's first principal, professor J.H. Fulks. It is located in front of the current Melon Patch Theatre on Thirteenth Street.

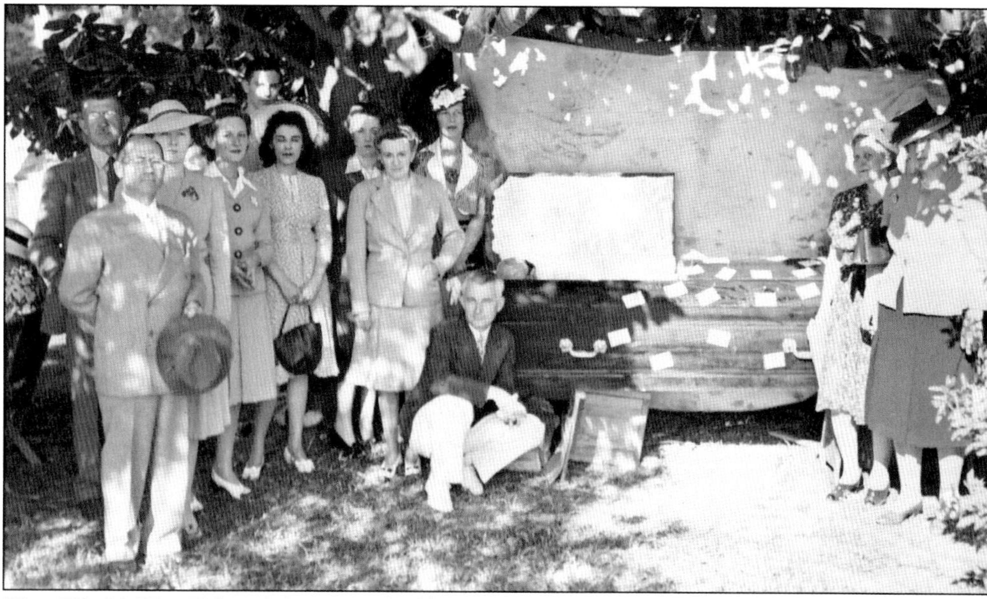

This World War II bond drive was held at the home of William and Minnie Dwight. The Dwight home, known as Pine Eden, was built in 1915 in Fruitland Park. Minnie Dwight hosted this garden party to promote the sale of war bonds. George Rast is kneeling in front of "Hitler's Casket" and Wilma Marsh, the chamber of commerce secretary, is standing next to him. Clara Freeman Ware is on the far right.

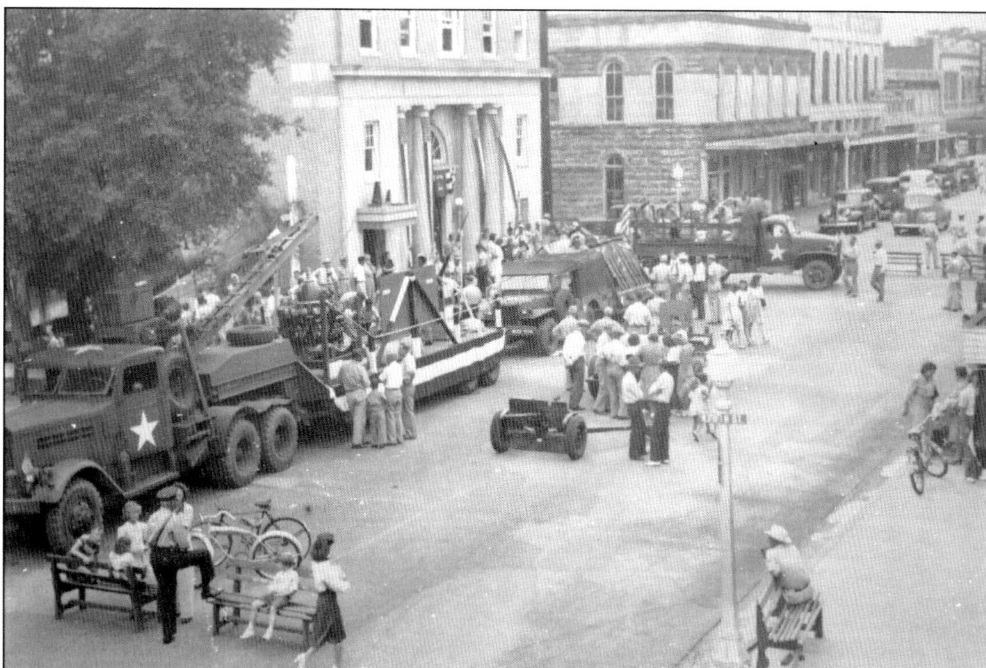

Leesburg held regular war bond rallies soon after the Japanese attack on Pearl Harbor, on December 7, 1941, and until the end of the war. The war bond drive seen here was held in front of the First National Bank on Main Street. More than 85 million Americans purchased over $150 billion in US treasury war bonds.

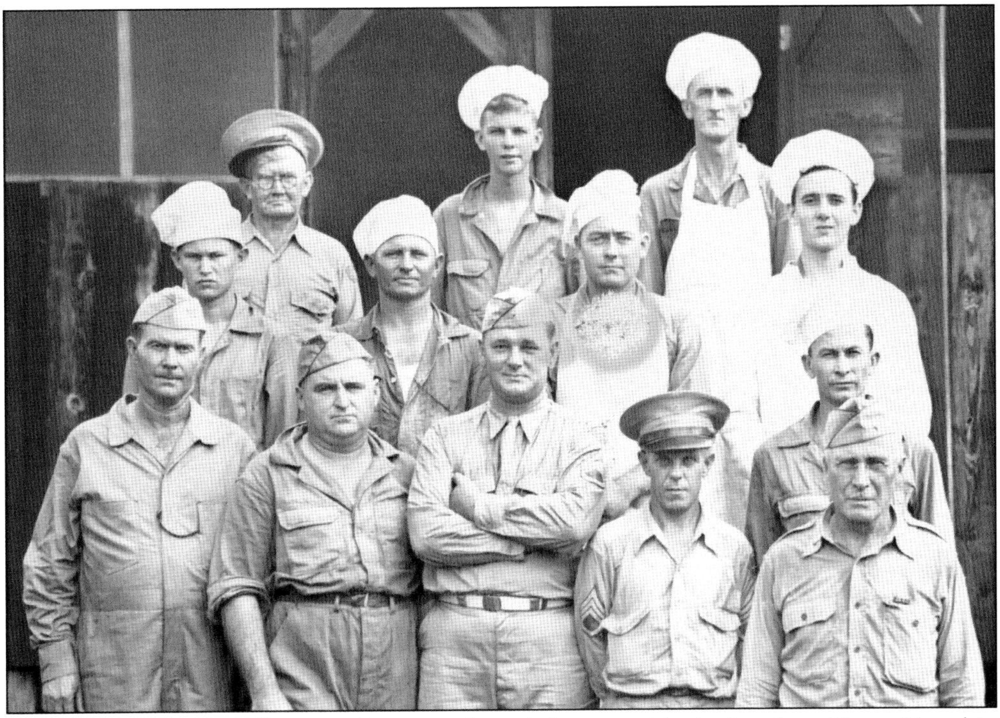

Elmer Robert "Bob" Williamson (first row, far right) poses with the Leesburg Home Guard in 1941. Williamson was born in Barrie, Ontario, Canada, in 1892. He enlisted in the US Army in May 1918 at Wallace, Idaho, and served as a chauffeur in World War I. A casket manufacturer by trade, he married Audrey Sheldon Canaday in Seminole County in 1929. They resided on Line Street in Leesburg.

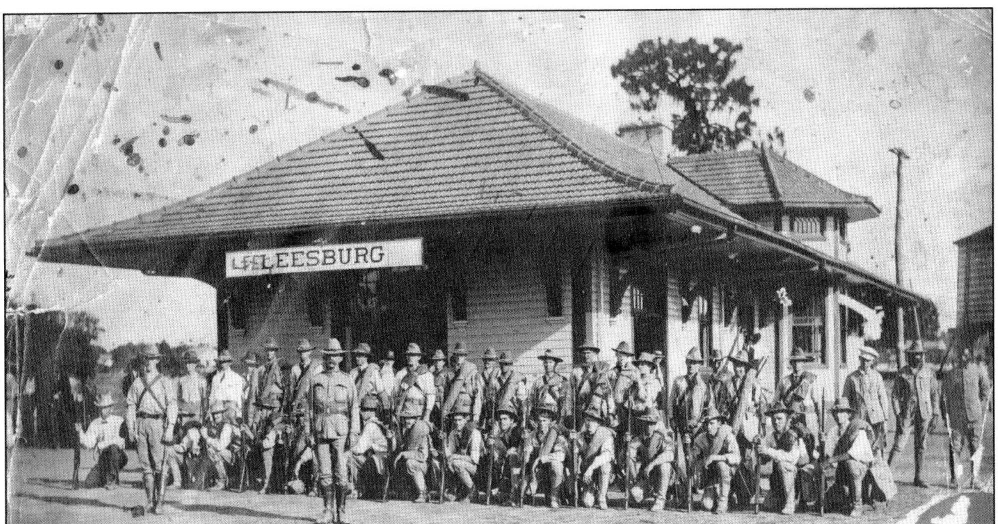

The Leesburg Rifles, Company B, 2nd Infantry, have their photograph taken at the Atlantic Coast Line Railroad depot in 1911. Around this time, many US militia units fought in the Mexican Revolution. The Leesburg Rifles continued a proud tradition of volunteer Home Guard units that began in Colonial America with the Militia and Minutemen of the American Revolution.

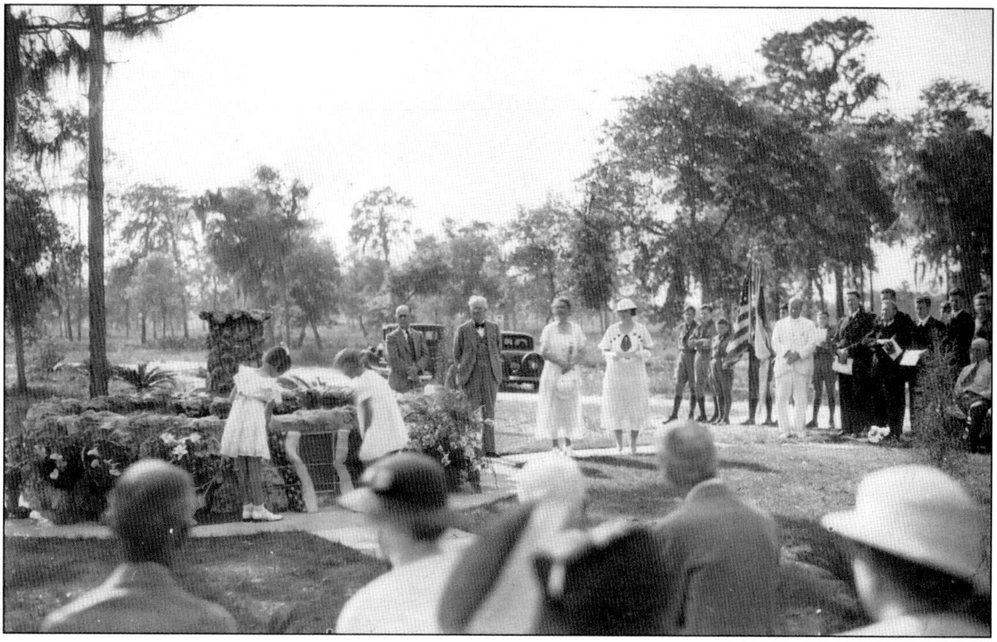

On April 26, 1935, a memorial fountain was dedicated to the soldiers from all wars who are laid to rest in Lone Oak Cemetery. Fannie Ezell, the president of Lone Oak Cemetery Inc., and the secretary of Confederate Gray Chapter 641 United Daughters of the Confederacy (UDC), directed the service. Chapter 641 was founded on December 31, 1902, and is still active today. A total of 12 ladies signed the original UDC charter on that date, including Marian Duncan, Rosalie Peter, Lucy Yancy, Grace McGregor, and Mary Belle Milam. Florida Statute 683.01 (j) commemorates April 26 as Confederate Memorial Day, which is the anniversary of Confederate general Joseph E. Johnston's surrender to Gen. William T. Sherman in Durham, North Carolina, in 1865. Each year on April 26, the chapter holds a memorial service at the fountain in Lone Oak Cemetery.

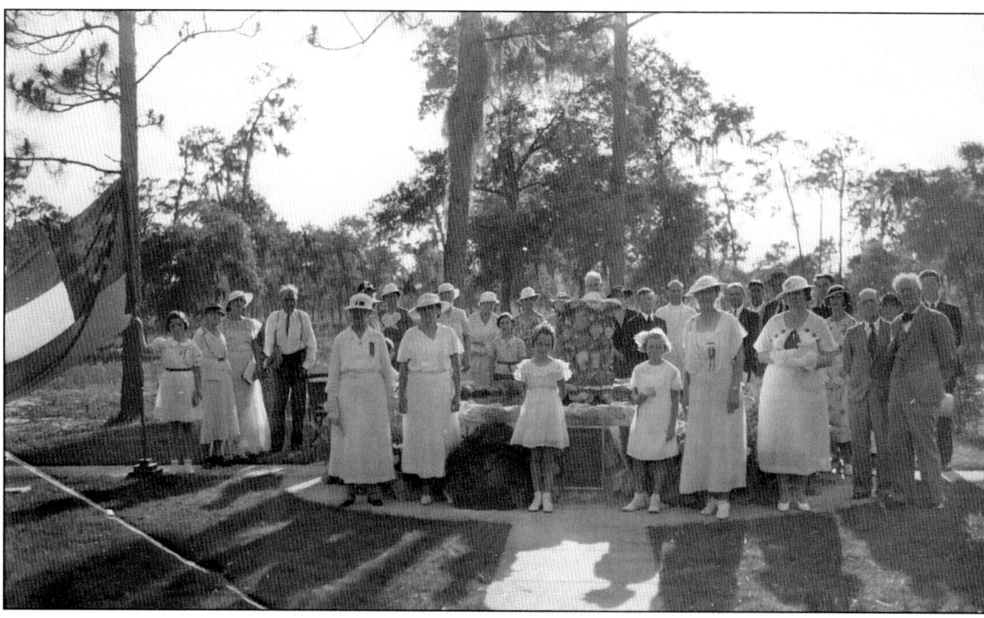

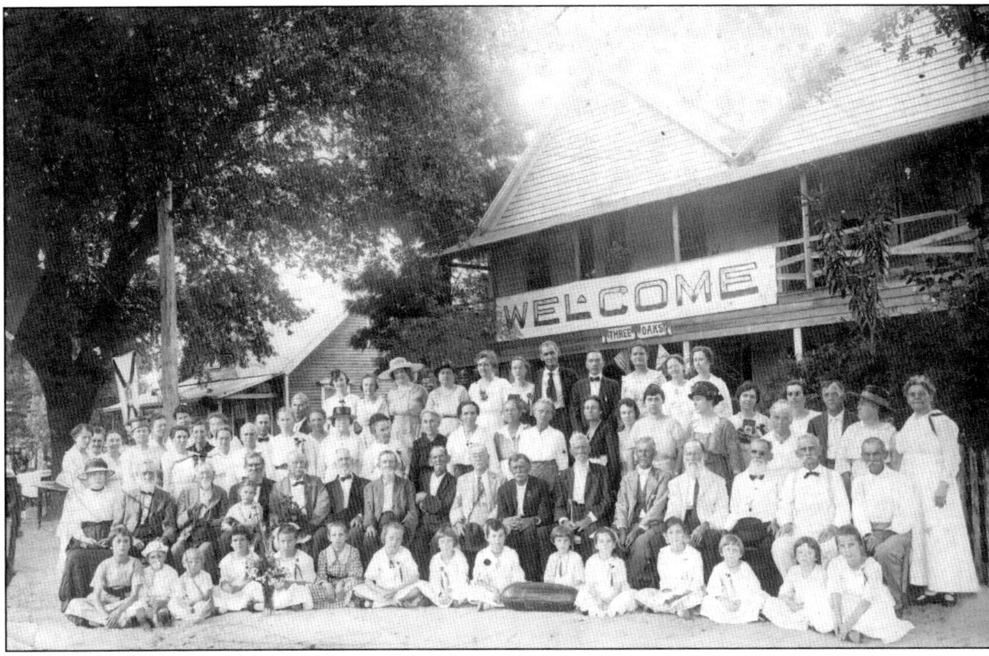

In 1920, the UDC held a Confederate veterans' reunion picnic at the home of Thomas and Fannie Hall. The Hall house, at 1308 High Street in Leesburg, was called Three Oaks. Confederate veteran Thomas Kennedy Hall is seated in the second row, second from the right. The Children of the Confederacy are seated on the ground with Leesburg's trademark watermelon.

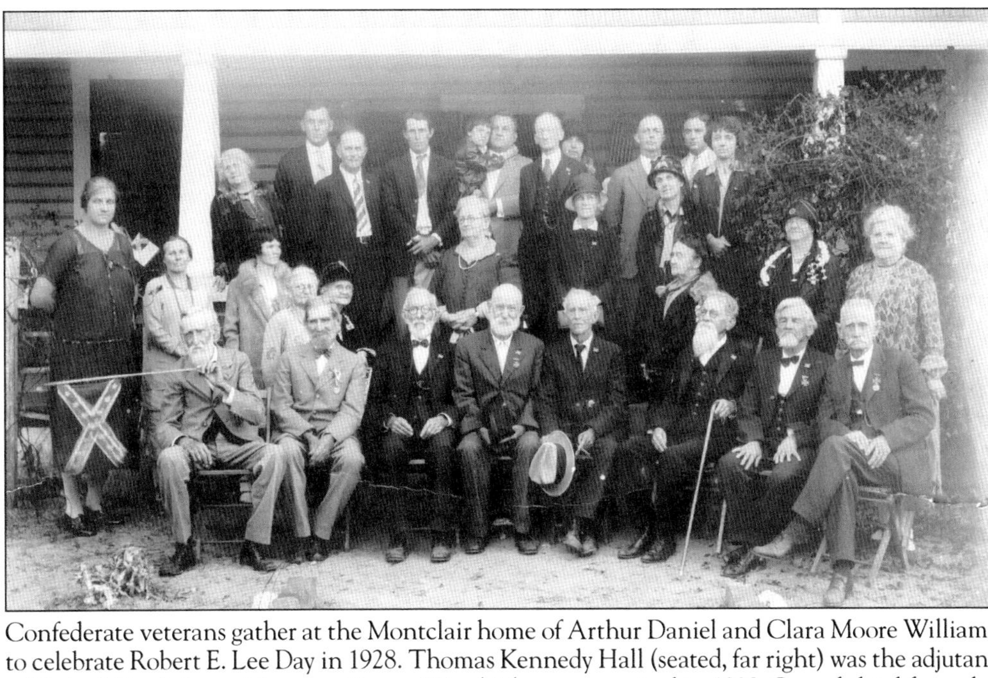

Confederate veterans gather at the Montclair home of Arthur Daniel and Clara Moore Williams to celebrate Robert E. Lee Day in 1928. Thomas Kennedy Hall (seated, far right) was the adjutant of United Confederate Veterans Camp 279, which was organized in 1892. Seated third from the left is Rev. Lacy William Simmons of Lady Lake. January 19, Robert E. Lee's birthday, is a legal holiday in Florida.

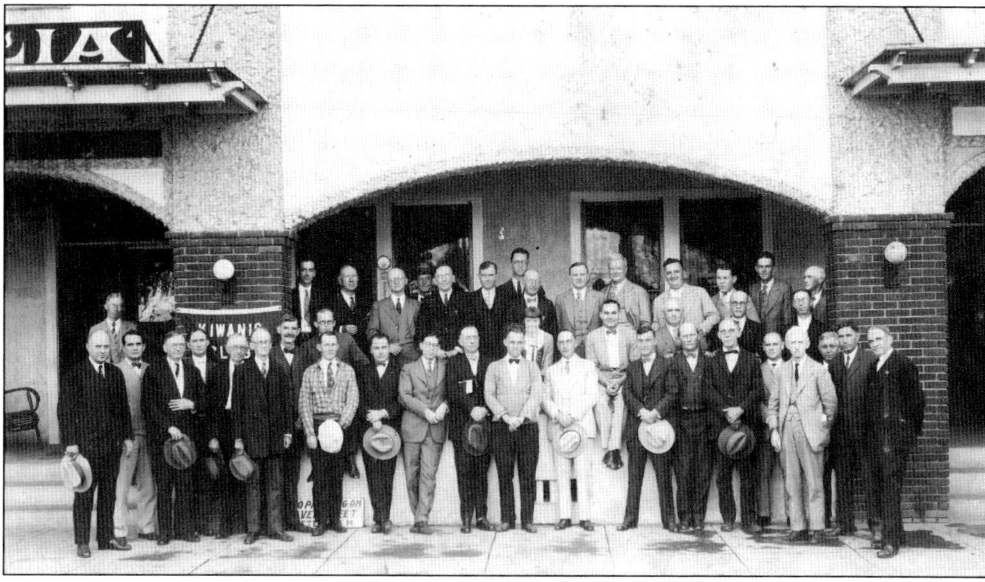

The Leesburg Kiwanis was organized on November 16, 1922. In 1915, the first Kiwanis club was established in Detroit, Michigan; it has become a worldwide service organization dedicated to improving people's lives. Their goal is to make the lives of children healthier, safer, and more meaningful. This photograph of Leesburg Kiwanis members was taken in front of the Magnolia Hotel in the mid-1920s.

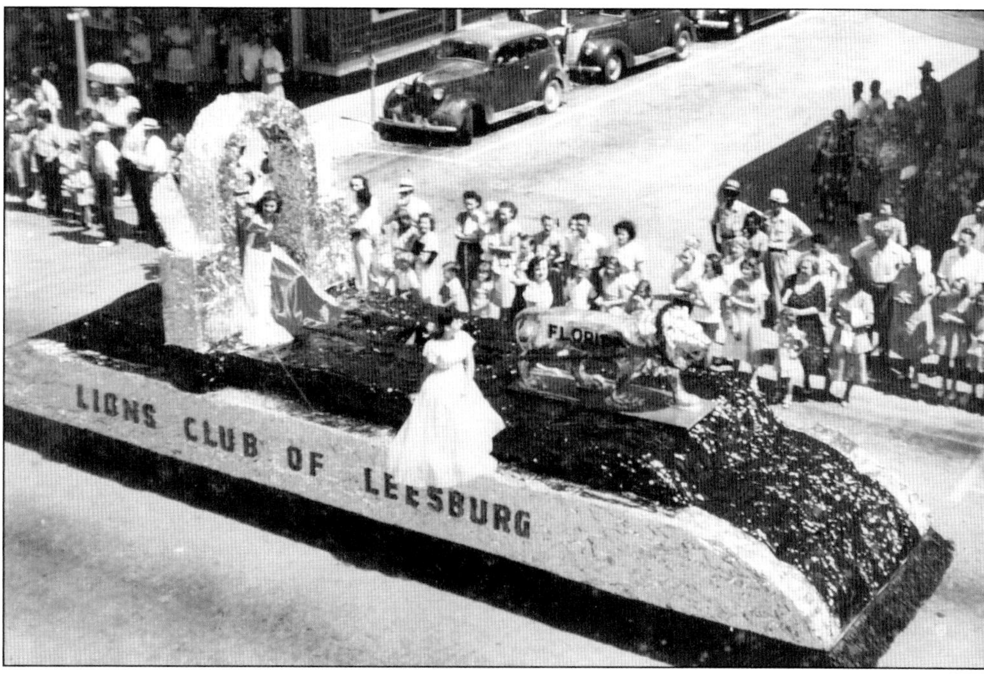

The Lions Club of Leesburg was organized on June 18, 1935. Its first president was Jay J. McIrvin. A Charter Night gala was held at the Silver Lake Country Club at the time, and the first official dinner meeting was held at the Lake View Hotel. The Lions Club of Leesburg disbanded in May 2011. Founded in 1917, Lions Club International's main focus is fighting blindness. The Lions Club float in the 1939 Watermelon Festival parade is seen here.

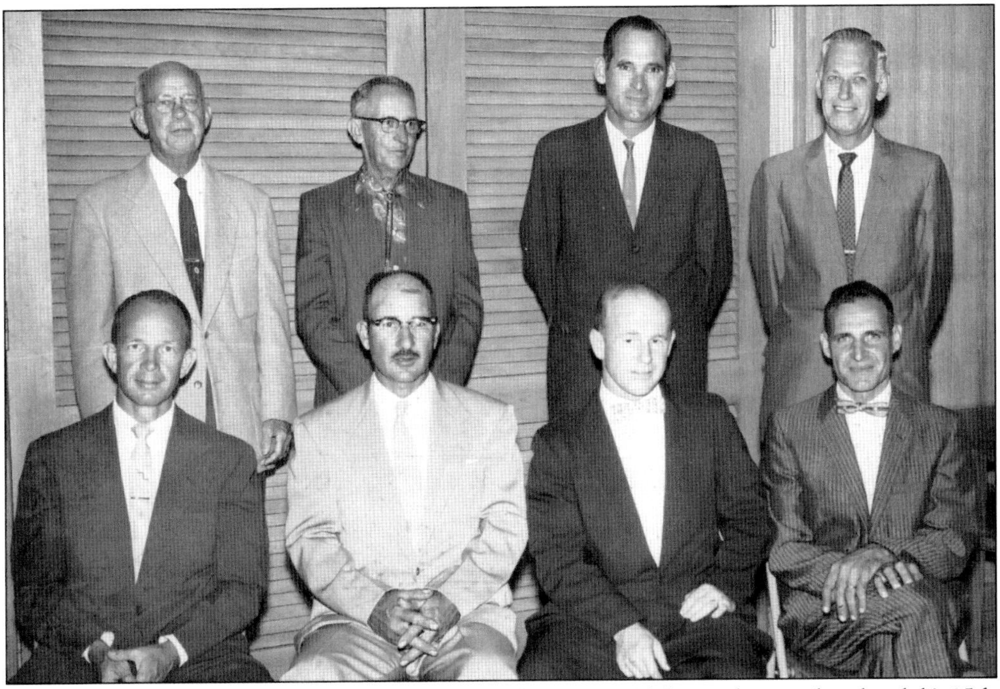

On June 13, 1962, the charter members of the Leesburg Boat Club were honored at the club's 15th annual banquet. The club was organized in October 1946. From left to right are (first row) Robert M. Cottrell, Alfred L. "Brownie" Neil, Dr. John F. Whitt, and Nicholas "Nick" Castelli; (second row) Edward B. Jaques, Morris W. Nelson, Brunson Gibson, and Clarence Aubrey "Slim" Burleson.

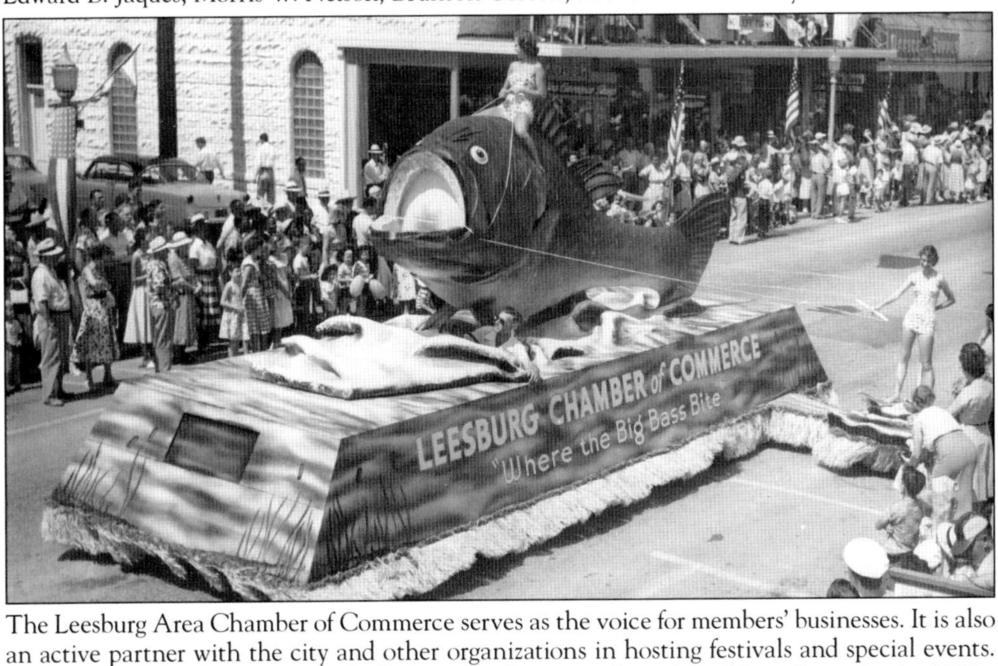

The Leesburg Area Chamber of Commerce serves as the voice for members' businesses. It is also an active partner with the city and other organizations in hosting festivals and special events. The chamber of commerce parade float is seen here traveling along Main Street in the 1950s. The float's theme, "Where the Big Bass Bite," promoted Leesburg's annual Fresh Water Bass Tournament, held from 1928 until the late 1950s.

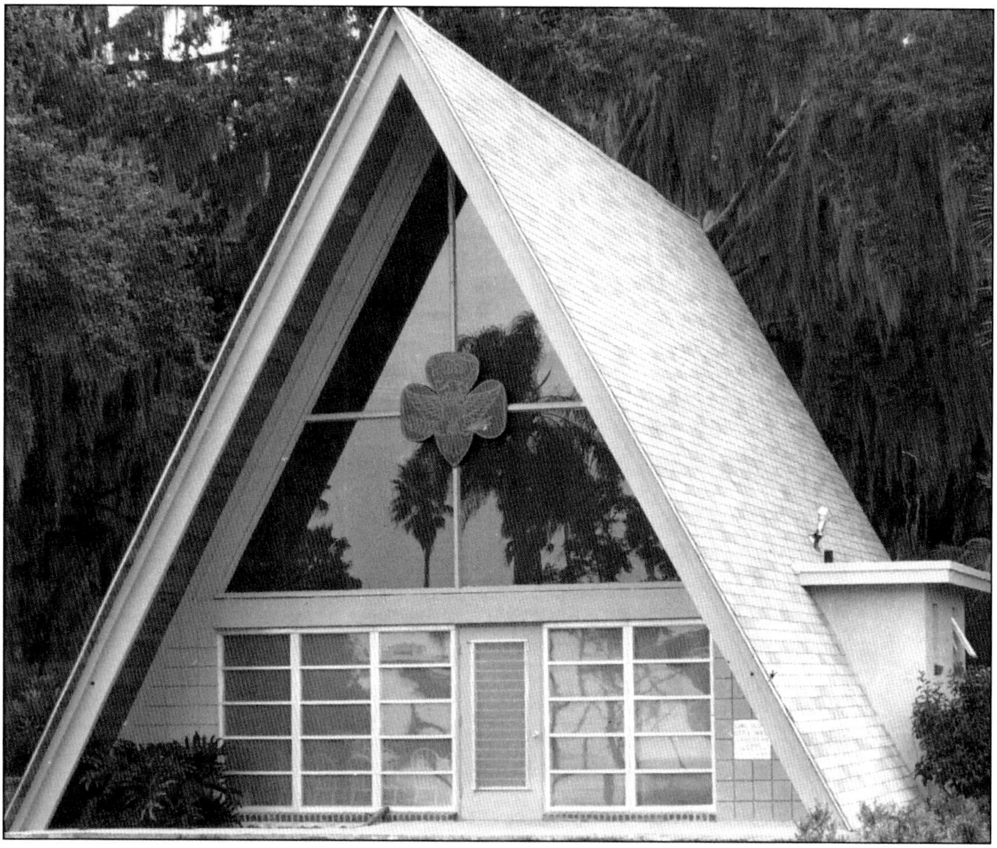

This A-frame building, located in Rogers Park, was the home of the local Girl Scouts of America. It was presented to the Girl Scouts by the Leesburg Triangle Club in 1958. Girl Scouts Marsha Myer, Mary Booth, Patty Evans, Lynna Sannin, Jo Ann Truett, Kay Krueger, and Donna Gail Knight participated in a flag ceremony at the dedication event. The building was razed in 2008.

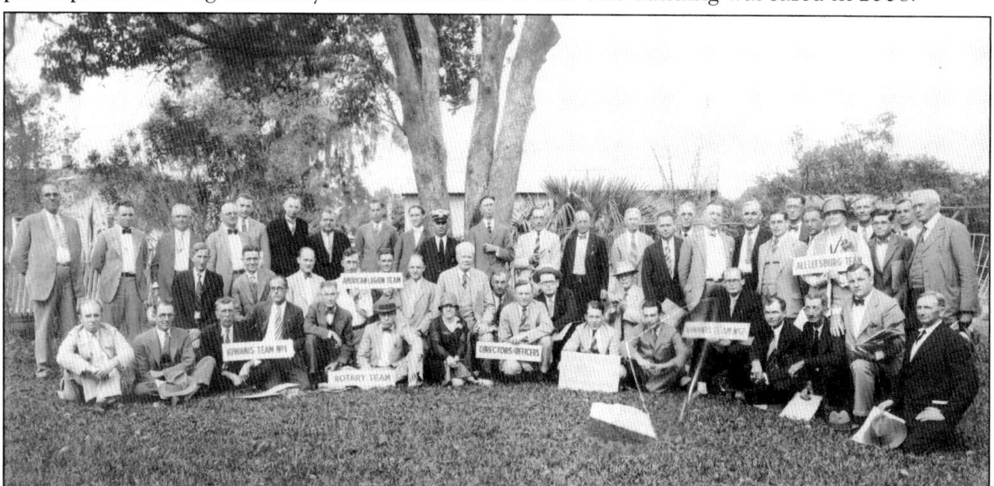

The directors and officers from the Leesburg Chamber of Commerce, the Kiwanis Club, Leesburg Rotary Club, and the American Legion gathered for this late 1920s chamber of commerce "Service to Visitors" promotional photograph. They christened their group the All-Leesburg Team.

Nine

MAKING A LEESBURG LIVING

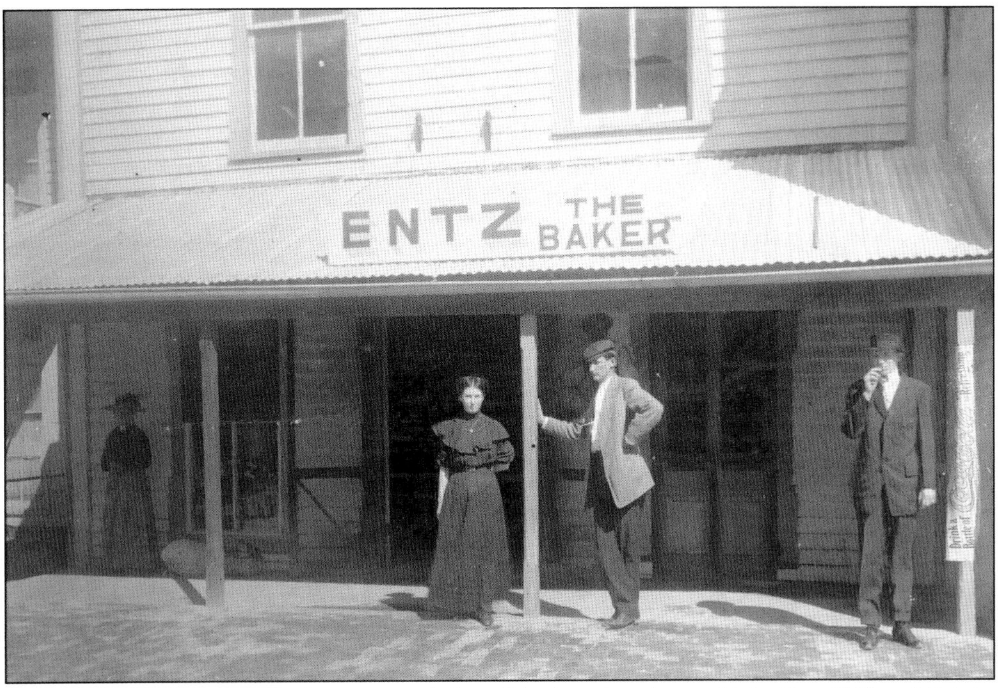

Since Melton Haynes planted orange seeds from "the best fruit he could find" in 1845 and Calvin Lee declared to a New York merchandise supplier, "Ship 'em to Leesburg, Florida," in 1866, Leesburg has been a leading agricultural, industrial, and commercial center in Lake County. In 1905, Michael Entz opened Leesburg's first bakery, seen here. He became famous for his superior cinnamon rolls. Ethel Whatley (center) worked at the bakery.

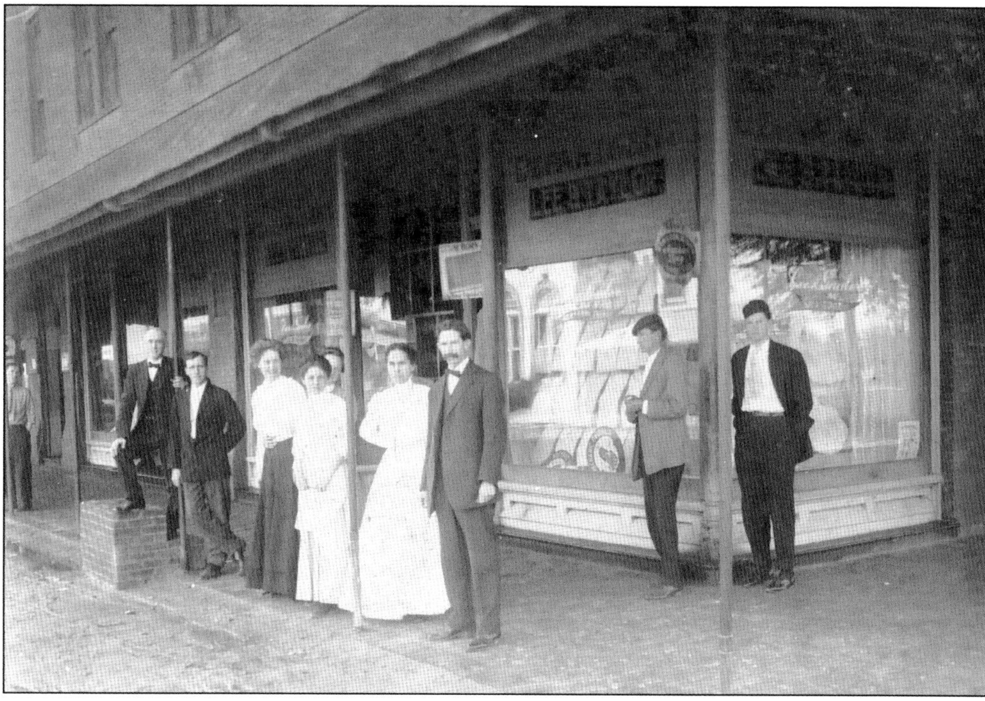

The Lee & Taylor store was located at the corner of Main and Fifth Streets. The clothing store specializing in men's wear was owned by John C. Lee Jr. and Frank and Hillary Amabel Taylor. Frank Taylor, who started out as an associate at the M.E. Weeks dry goods store in Leesburg, died in 1913 from tuberculosis. In 1929, the Lee & Taylor store felt the economic effects of the Great Depression, which prompted Mrs. Taylor to rent spare rooms in her home on Kolb Street. Clerks Winifred Edwards Dunklin and Fletcher Frank Gillespie are seen below.

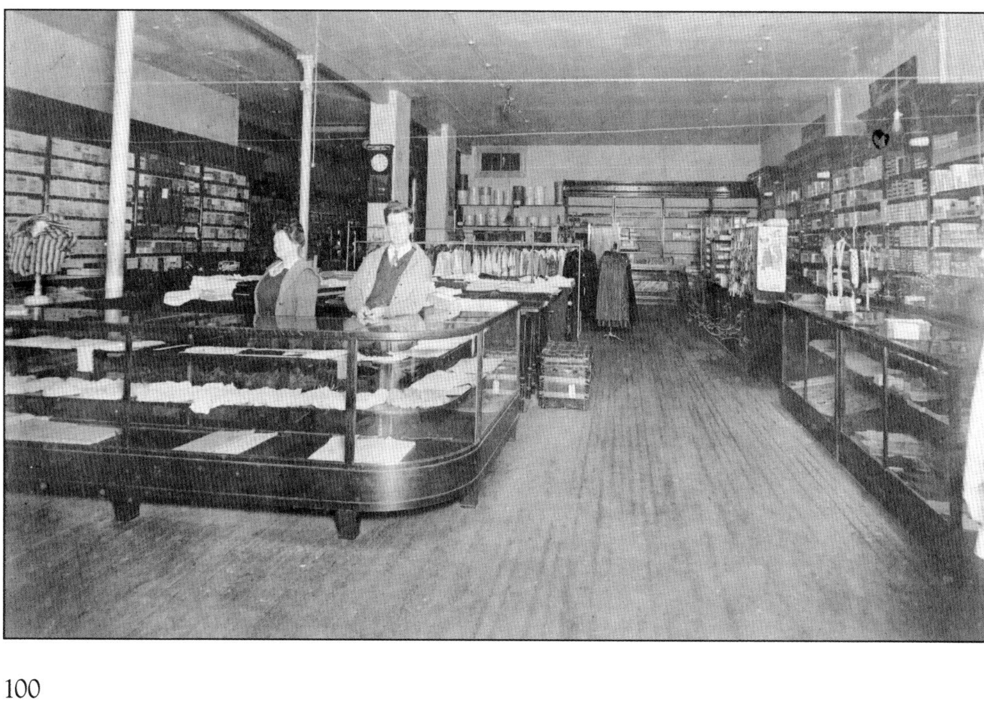

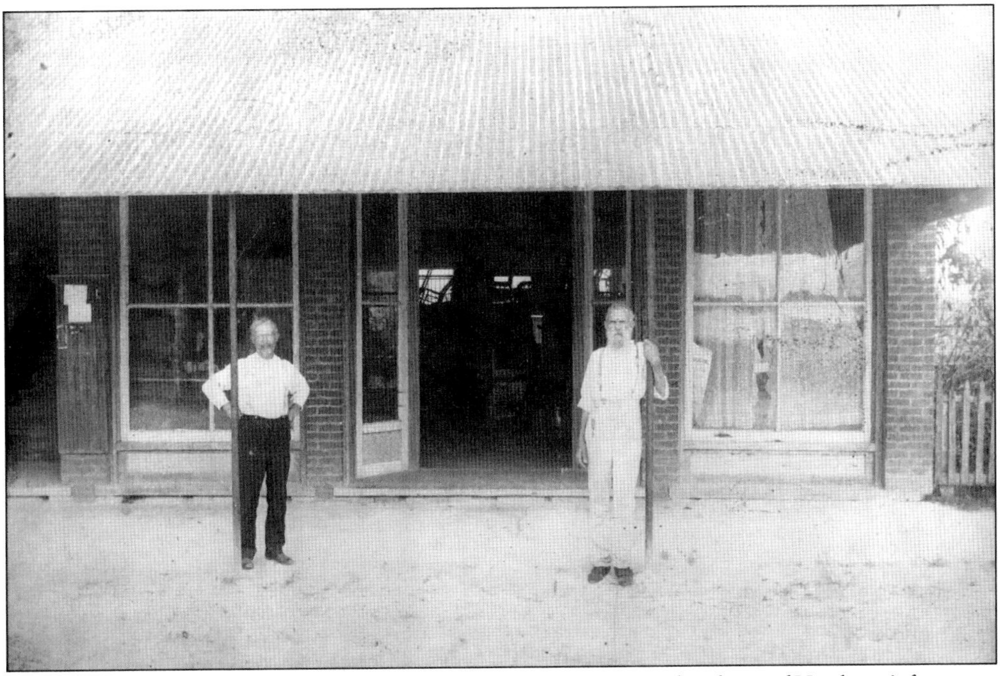

Fred Charles William Kramer (left) and Asa Sleeth Hardman stand in front of Hardman's furniture store on Main Street in 1905. Kramer, who arrived in Lake County in 1892, also made and repaired boots and shoes. Hardman served as the postmaster and justice of the peace.

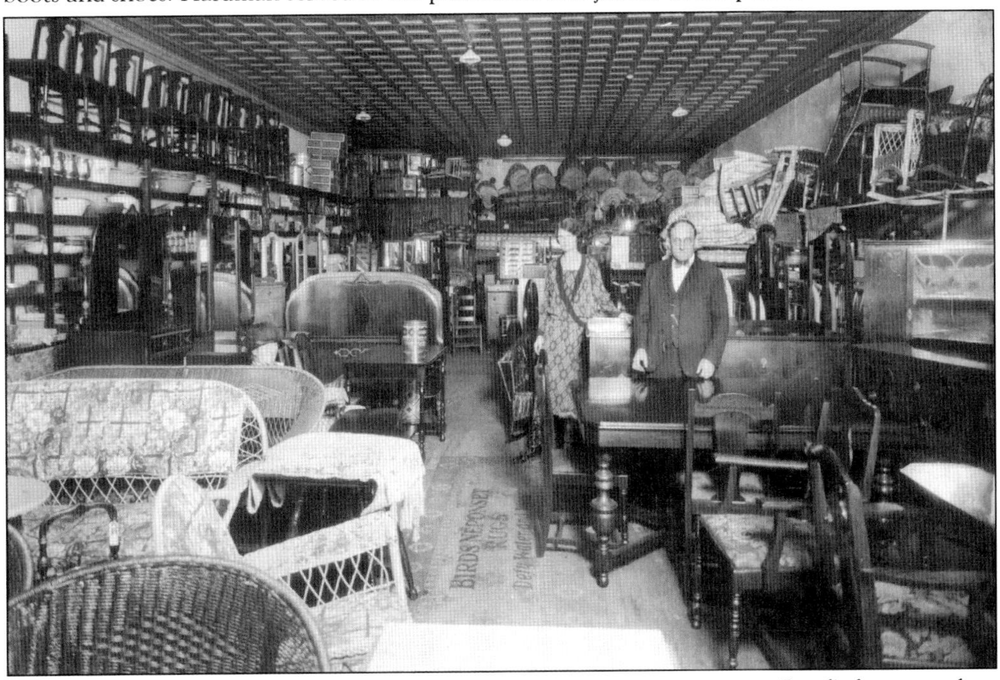

James Arthur and Lilla Harris Boyd are seen here welcoming customers to Boyd's furniture shop in 1927. The Boyds established their store in 1915 on the northeast corner of Main and First Streets. They later moved to this location, on the northwest corner of the same intersection. In 1931, they relocated the store to 208 West Main Street, by the Western Union office.

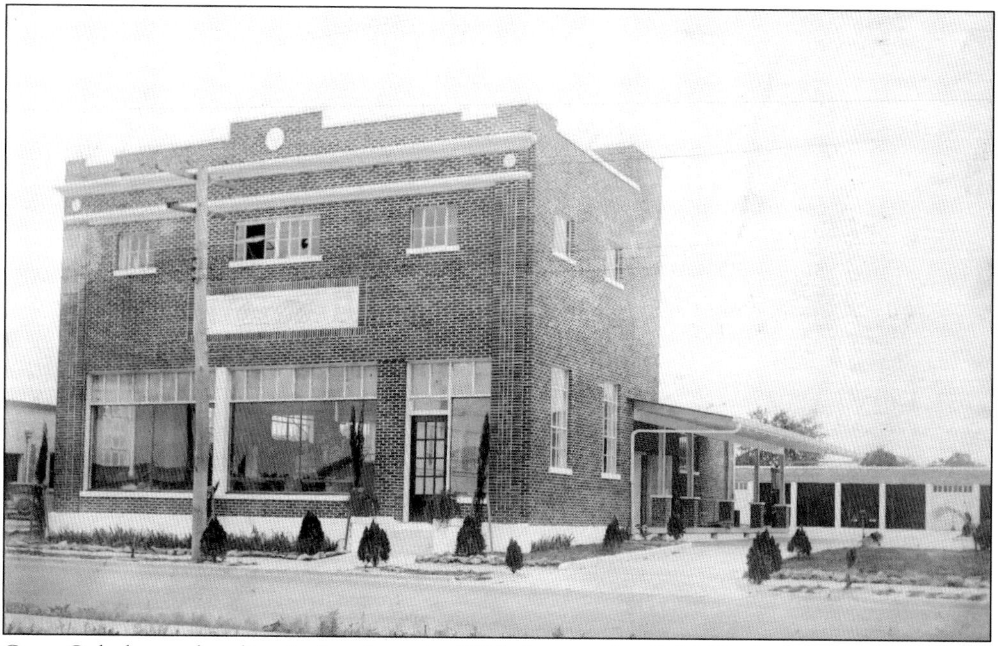

Coca-Cola began bottling in Leesburg in 1908, first in the Gold Block on Main Street. Joe Henderson operated the company. In 1914, he built a new sand brick plant on Sixth Street, across from the city ice plant. In 1930, Coca-Cola moved to East Main Street (seen here) and then to a large new building west of the city in the early 1980s.

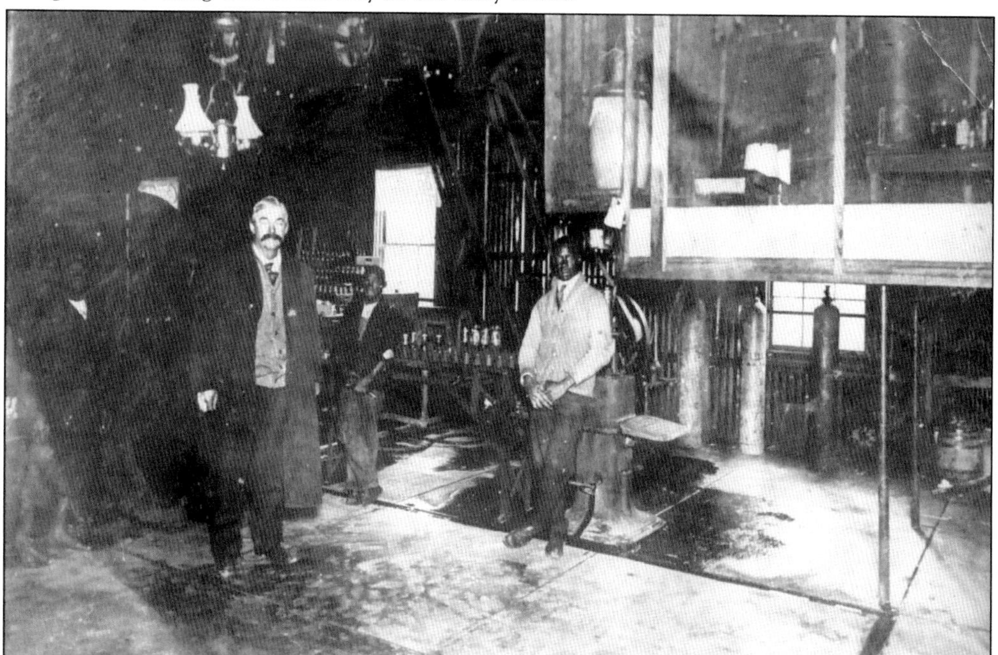

Edward H. Butler (left foreground) moved to Leesburg from Iowa in 1913. He first ventured into the hay, grain, and feed business, and, soon after, purchased the Leesburg Coca-Cola Bottling Company. During those days, the plant produced cases of Coca-Cola in six-ounce bottles. He is seen here inside the plant at 215 South Sixth Street, across from Briles Motor Company.

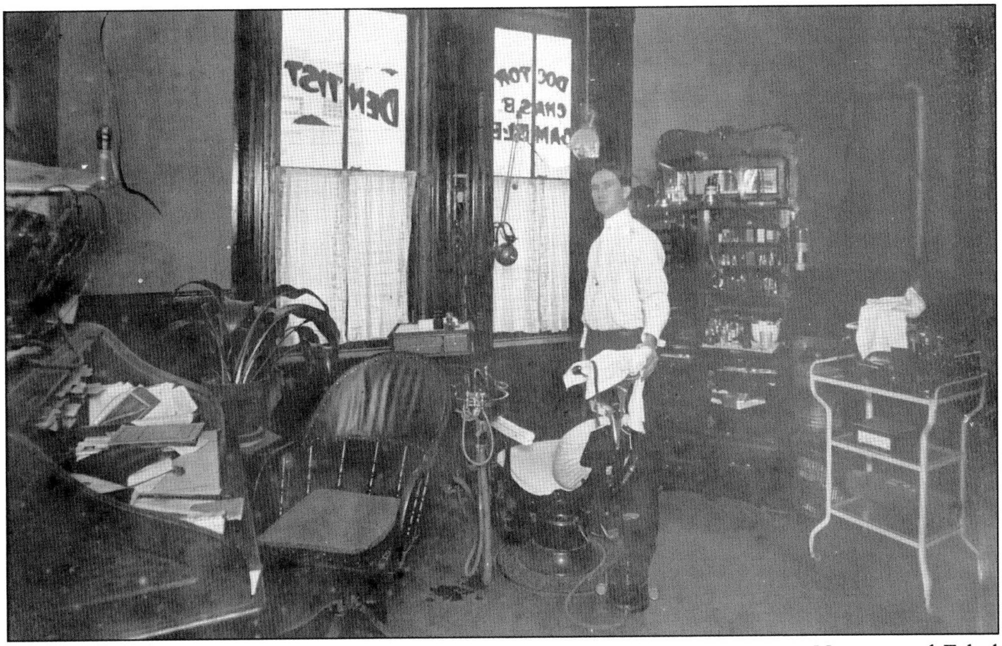

Dr. Charles Byron Gamble began his dental practice in Leesburg in 1908. He married Ethel Schaeffer Meador in 1909, and the couple lived on Ninth Street. Dr. Gamble studied dentistry at Atlanta Dental College. In 1914, Dr. Gamble's office was located in the Mote Block. In 1924, he moved into the Masonic temple building in a partnership with Dr. Wyeth Duncan, who became a dentist in 1921.

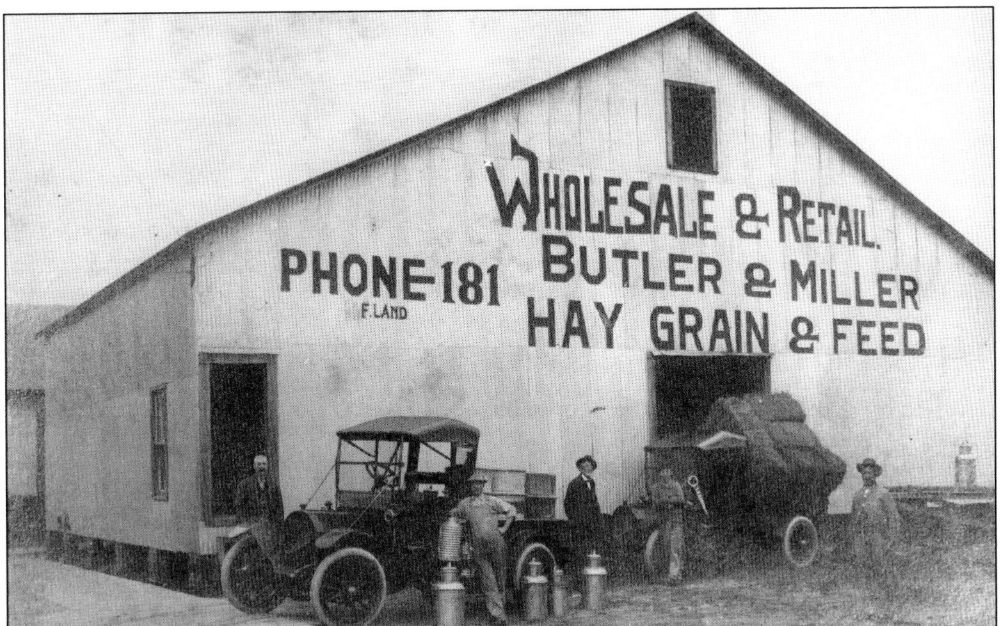

Butler & Miller Hay, Grain & Feed was built on Sixth Street in July 1913 by Edward Butler (far left) and Walter Miller (center, in dark suit). They operated the feed store until 1919. Butler and Miller were friends who both moved to Leesburg from Decatur County, Iowa, in 1913. In 1914, the two acquired the first Gulf Oil dealership in Leesburg.

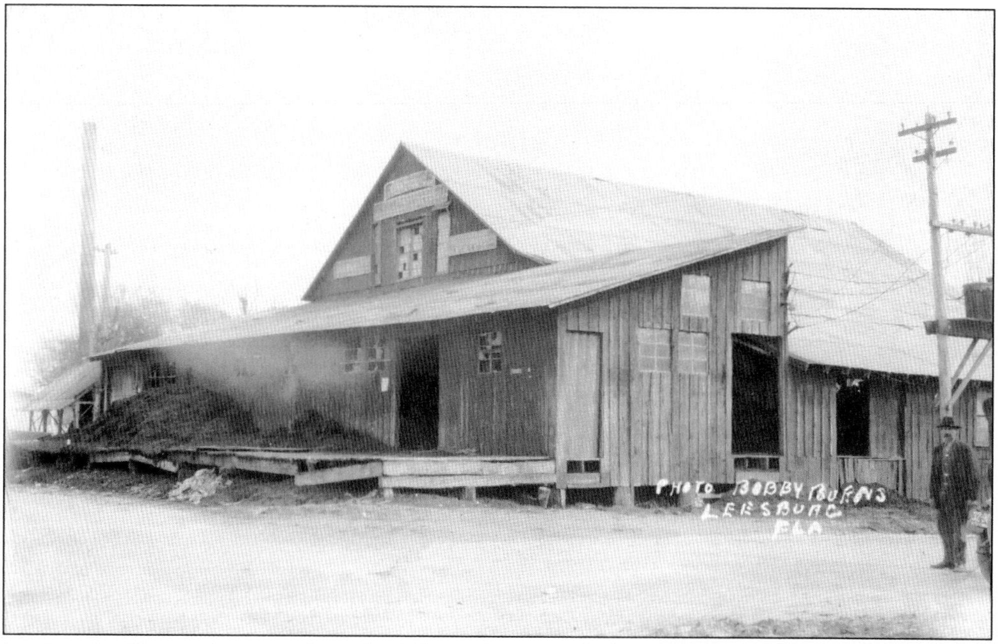

During the Depression, people picked Spanish moss off the trees and sold it for use in sofas, mattresses, and chair cushions. Leesburg had several moss plants in the early 1920s, including the Florida Moss Company, seen here, on Second Street. This building was originally a packinghouse for the Eclipse Orange Grove Company.

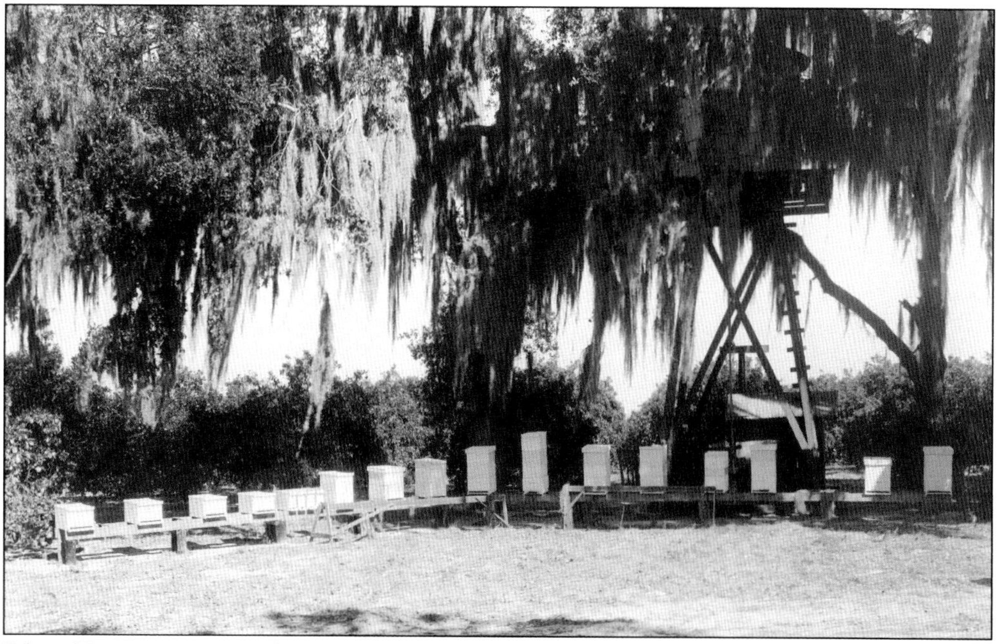

Edward Mote's apiary was located about four miles from Leesburg. He sold honey from it for 75¢ per pound. Oranges and various combinations of citrus are a leading honey source in Florida, as well as the palmetto, which is a good producer of nectar. The honey from orange tree blossoms is usually a light amber color and maintains the orange blossom aroma.

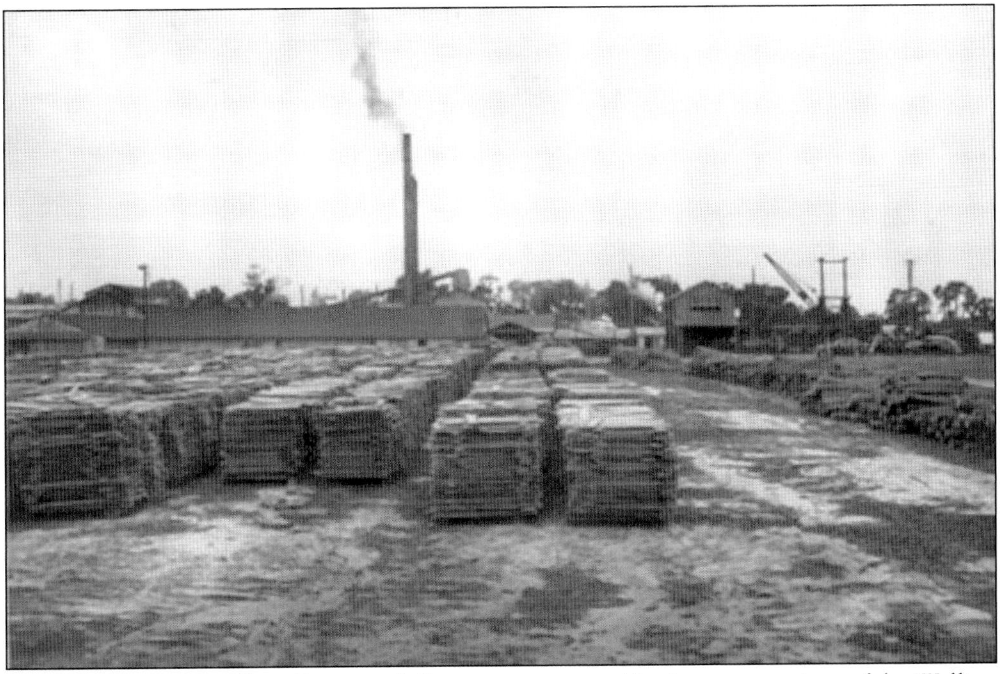

The Walling Crate Mill, on Fourteenth Street, was operated by three generations of the Walling family. In 1916, L.B. Walling moved to Leesburg from South Carolina and bought a sawmill in Weirsdale. In 1917, he purchased 40 acres in Leesburg and relocated the mill there. Later, Walling specialized in making crates for citrus and vegetables. In the mill's heyday, it employed about 150 workers.

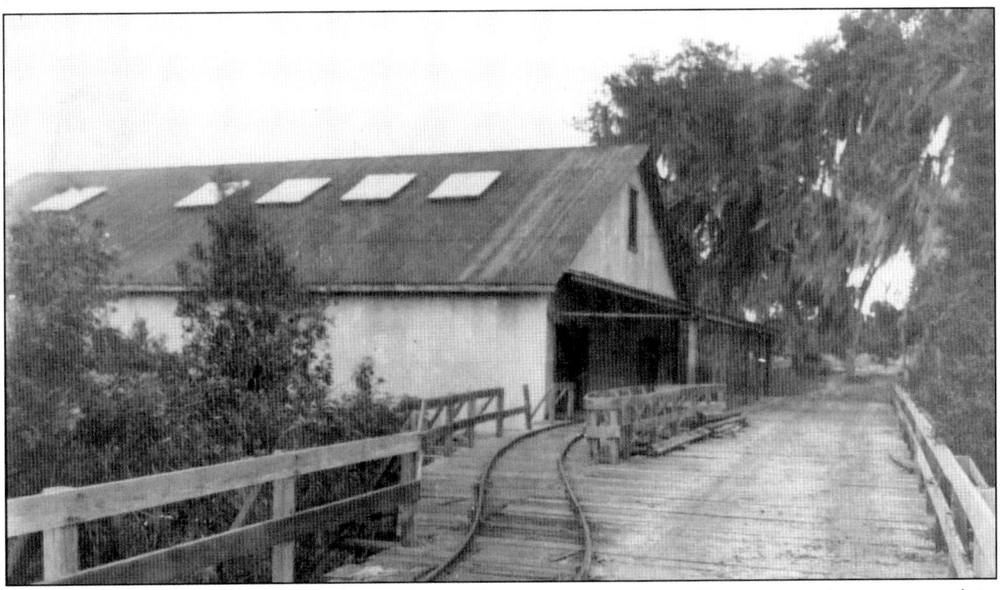

The citrus packinghouse of Robert Perrin Burton is seen here. Burton was instrumental in organizing the Leesburg Citrus Growers Association, serving as one of its directors and largest patrons. He came to Leesburg on November 16, 1885. After first starting out in the drugstore business, Burton bought an orange grove in Emeralda. He married Rosalie Screven in November 1886 in Waycross, Georgia.

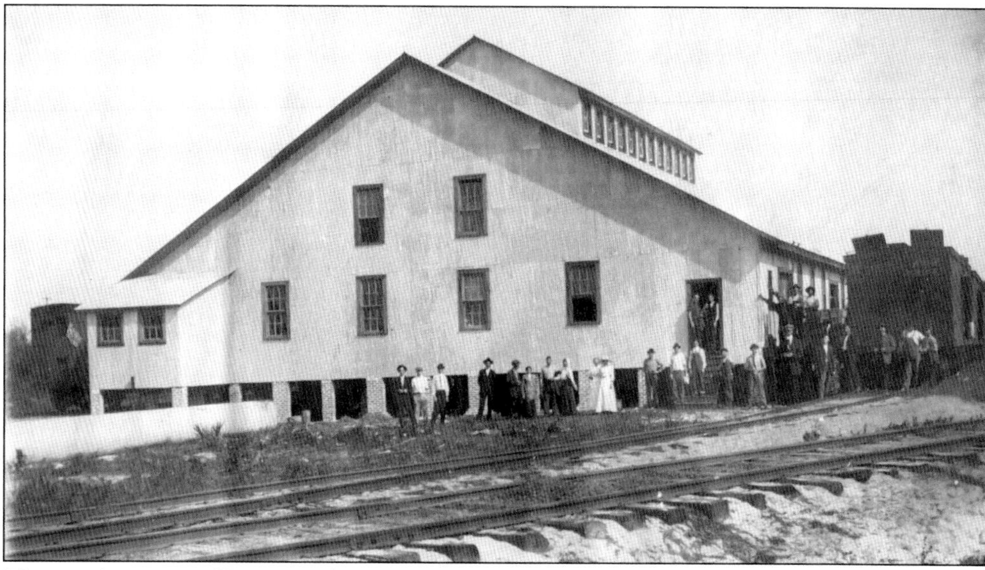

The grand opening of R.F.E. Cooke's packinghouse is seen here in the early 1900s. Born in London, Cooke was part of a group of 150 English colonists to settle in Fruitland Park. He was one of the area's largest orange growers, but was best known as the president of the Leesburg State Bank.

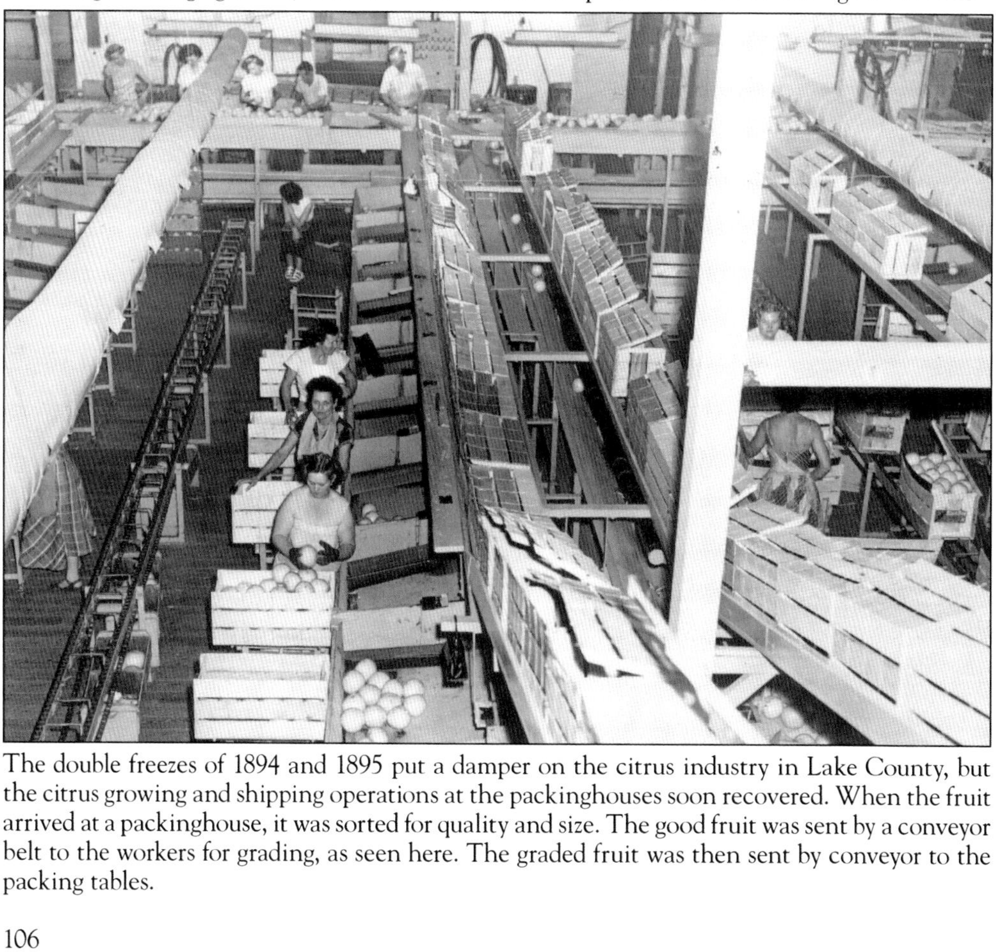

The double freezes of 1894 and 1895 put a damper on the citrus industry in Lake County, but the citrus growing and shipping operations at the packinghouses soon recovered. When the fruit arrived at a packinghouse, it was sorted for quality and size. The good fruit was sent by a conveyor belt to the workers for grading, as seen here. The graded fruit was then sent by conveyor to the packing tables.

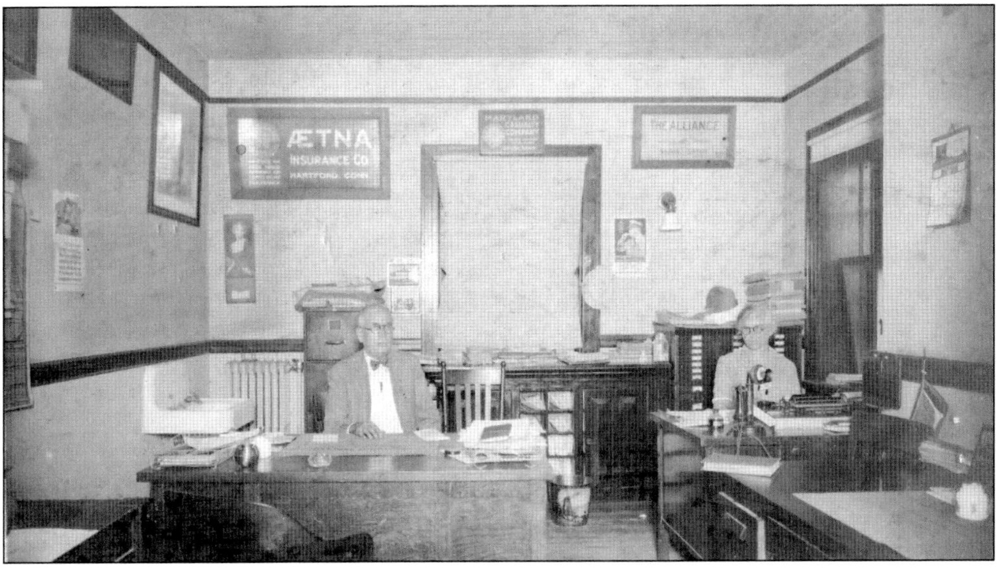

Richard Oscar Bowden and his wife, Willa, are seen above in 1939 at the Consolidated Insurance Agency office, located in the First National Bank Building. Bowden married Willa Bell Gilbert in 1909 in the small town of Lawtey, Florida, in Bradford County. In 1898, he was employed as a railroad agent and telegraph operator for the Seaboard Railroad in Leesburg. In 1930, he became an insurance agent.

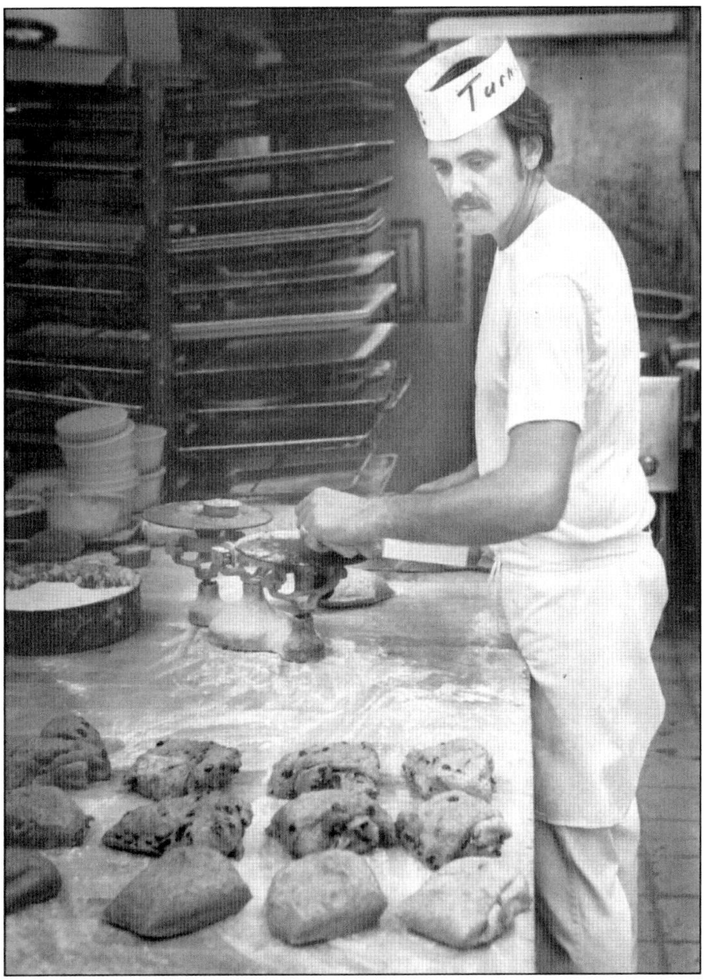

Turner's Bakery, at 116 South Fifth Street, was owned and operated by Herman Woodrow "Buck" Turner and his wife, Laura Evelyn Turner. Born in Council, Georgia, in 1917, Turner lived in St. Petersburg in the 1940s before moving to Leesburg. His son Joe is seen here baking at the family shop around 1960.

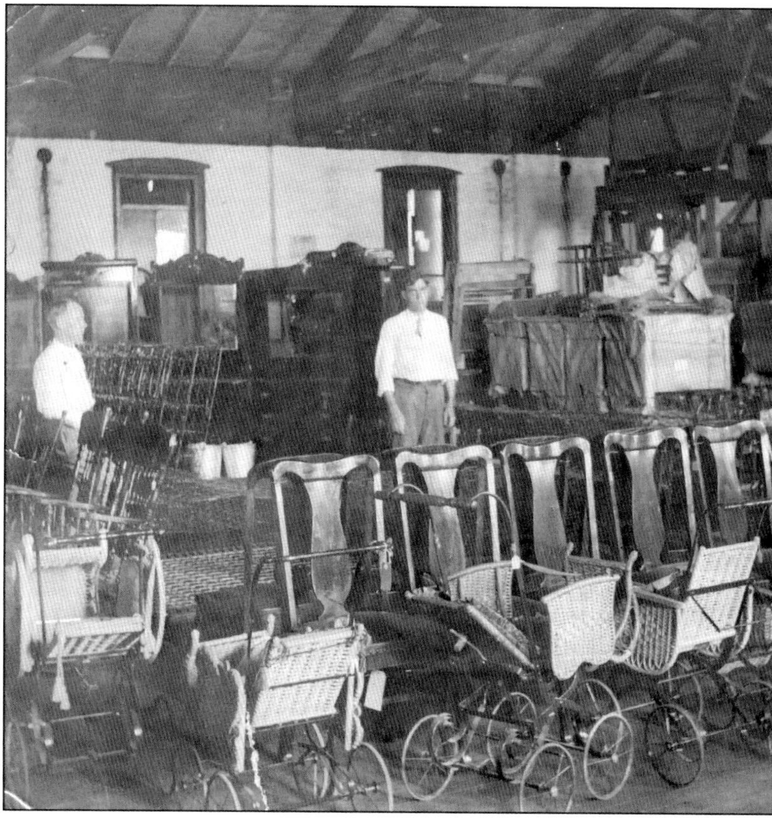

In 1912, Arthur B. Lees (left) owned a furniture and hardware store on West Main Street. William Azariah Abney (right) was a store associate and an in-law, as Lees married Henrietta Abney in 1907. Lees sold the Wonder Ice-Less Refrigerator, which was advertised as the sensation of the day that used no ice, kept things absolutely cool, and saved dollars on your ice bill.

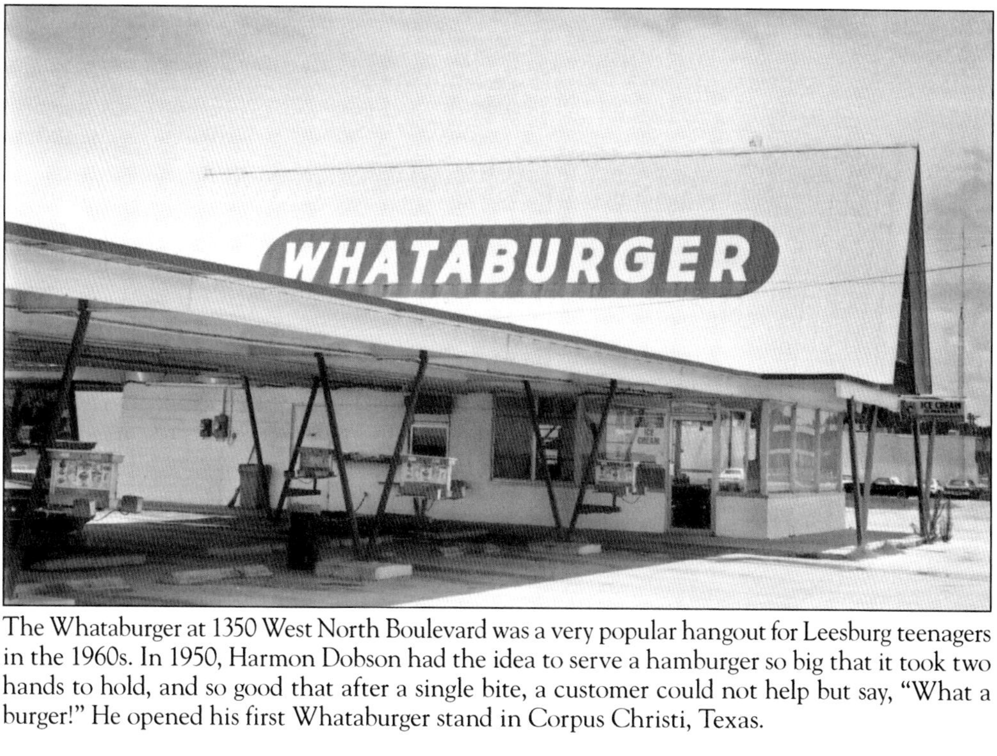

The Whataburger at 1350 West North Boulevard was a very popular hangout for Leesburg teenagers in the 1960s. In 1950, Harmon Dobson had the idea to serve a hamburger so big that it took two hands to hold, and so good that after a single bite, a customer could not help but say, "What a burger!" He opened his first Whataburger stand in Corpus Christi, Texas.

Hewitt's Drug Store was located at 607 East Main Street. The store was owned and operated by John Monroe "Jack" Hewitt Jr. and his wife, Hazel Harris Hewitt. Born in 1908, Jack Hewitt served in the Navy in World War II. Hazel was born in 1912. In this photograph from around 1950, notice the sign on the front door, letting patrons know that Jack and Hazel were out to lunch.

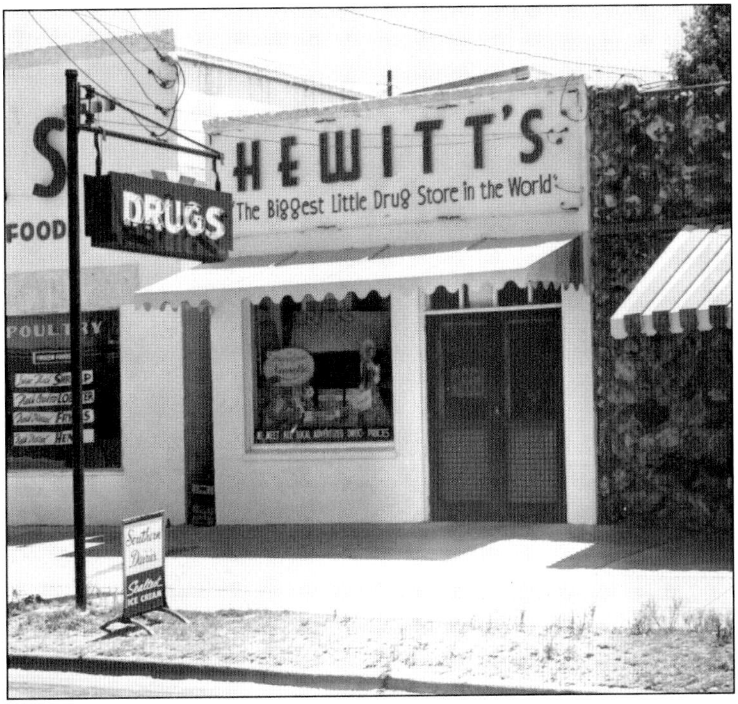

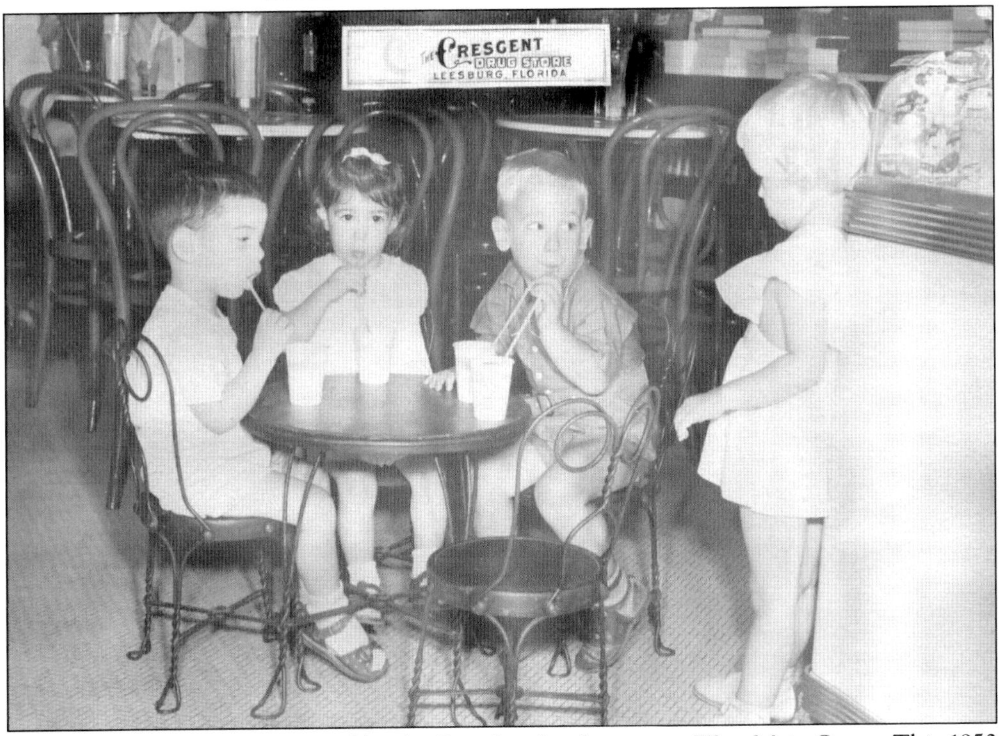

The Crescent Drug Store, owned by the Bragdon family, was on West Main Street. This 1950 photograph shows little Bobby and Butch treating pretty little Marsha Kay and Mary Sue to a soda pop at Crescent's. From left to right are Robert "Bobby" Teese, Marsha Kay Myer Wade Bradshaw, Ted C. "Butch" Prosser, and Mary Sue Faulhaber Stephenson.

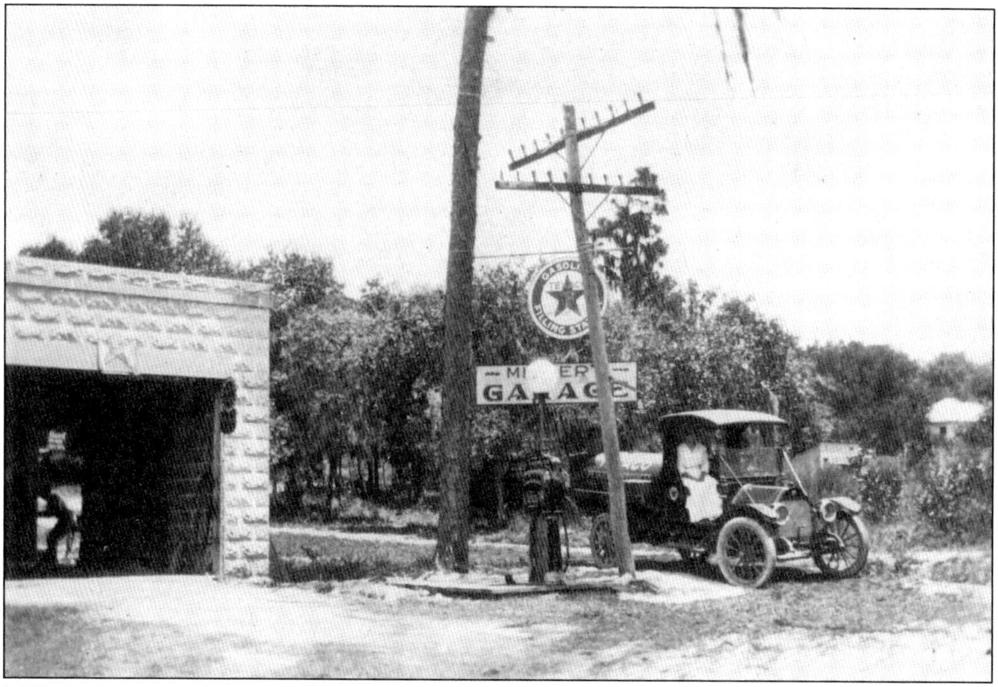

Miller's Garage and the Texaco filling station are seen here in 1916. In the 1920s, the Texaco Company office was located on South Palmetto Street. At that time, Horace T. Morrison, the son of Bishop Henry Clay Morrison, was the local oil company agent. The younger Morrison, who was born in 1874 in Louisville, Kentucky, platted Leesburg's beautiful Palmora Park in 1920.

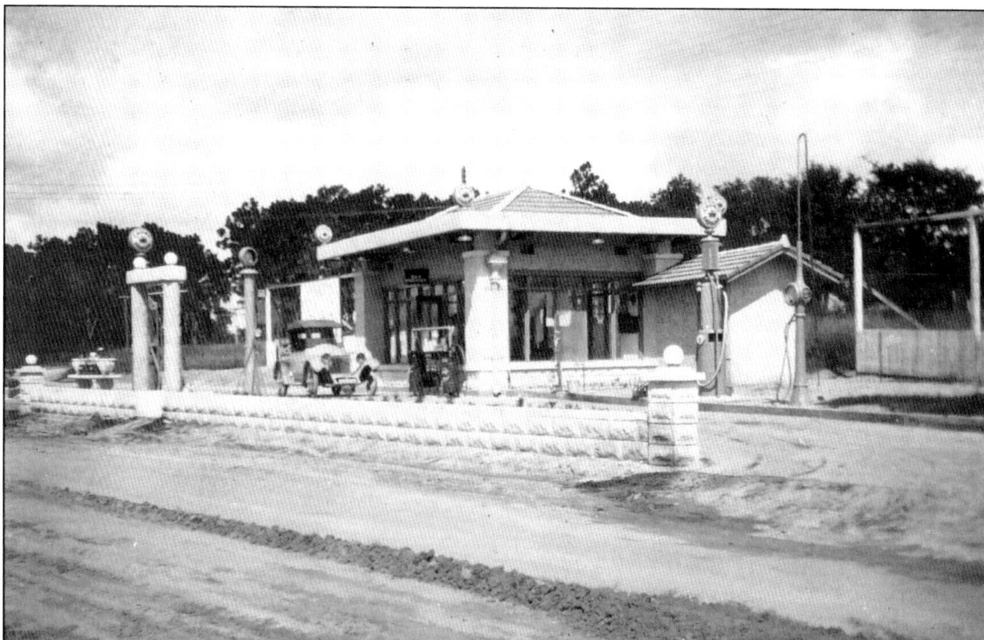
The Landis filling station was located on East Main Street near Sunnyside Drive, east of downtown Leesburg. In 1955, the station was known as the Sunnyside Service Station and run by Norman and Victor Haake, who sold Crown gasoline.

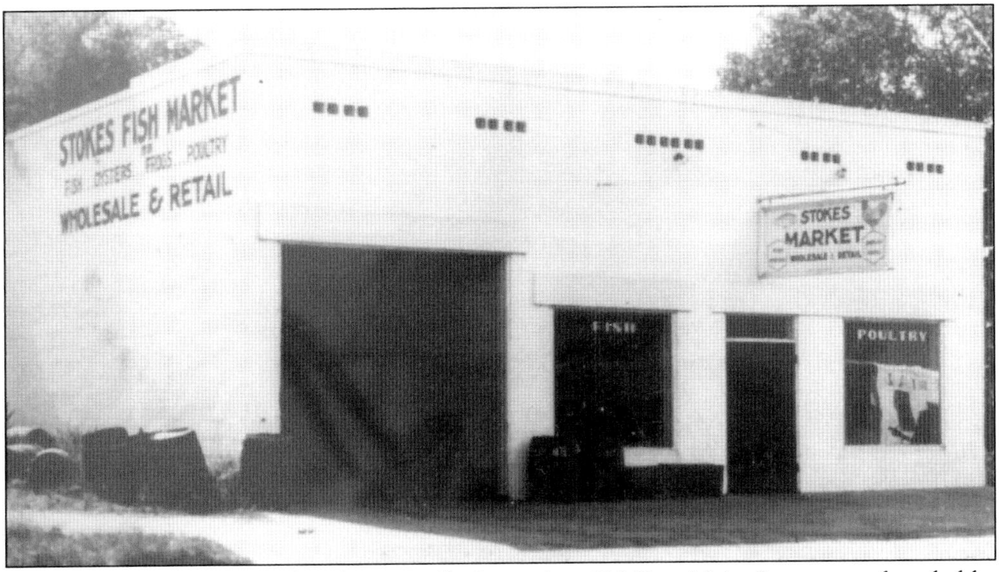

The Stokes Fish Market (above), originally located at 609 East Main Street, was founded by Beryl N. Stokes Sr. (below, third from left) in 1932. When Stokes passed away in January 2003, a tribute in the *Daily Commercial* read, "There were times Beryl Stokes worked from 8 a.m. to 9 p.m. six days a week - dedication that made Stokes Seafood Market successful for the past 71 years. 'He went to that market every day that he could walk,' said Marianne Stokes, his wife. His sons, Beryl Stokes Jr. of Leesburg and William Stokes of Fruitland Park, took over the business about 30 years ago. The business started as a market selling local fish and poultry, but through the years it expanded into a national seafood distributorship."

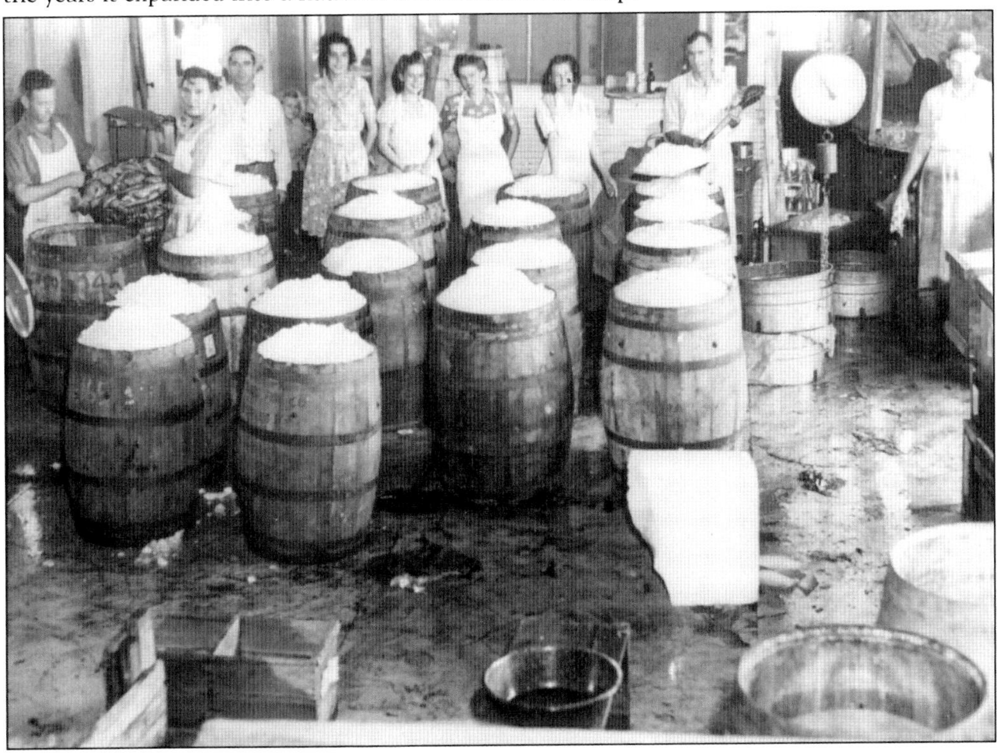

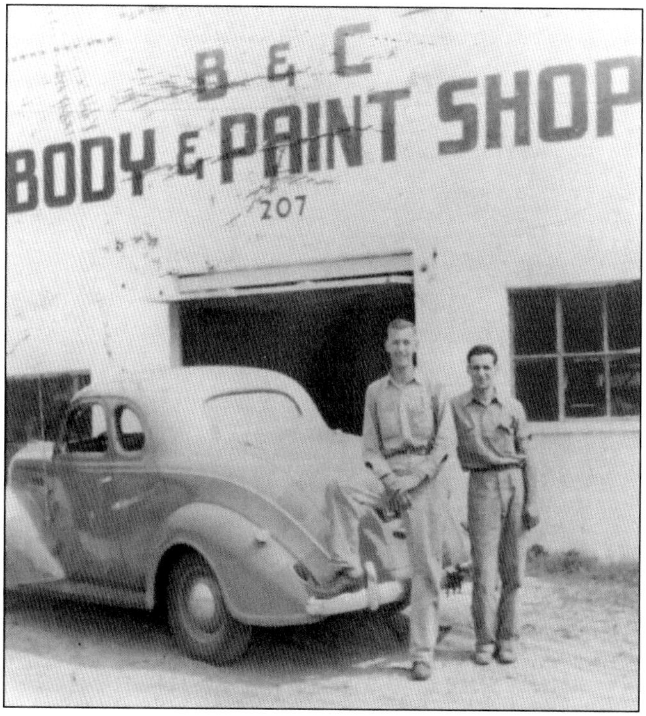

B&C Body & Paint Shop opened in 1946 at 201 East Magnolia Street. It was owned by Clarence Aubrey "Slim" Burleson (left) and Nicholas "Nick" Castelli, who was a staff sergeant with the 91st Air Service Group from 1942 to 1945. He was stationed at Orange Home Tent Camp, near Leesburg, where he repaired military aircraft. Originally from West Virginia, Castelli enjoyed the Leesburg folks so much he married a Leesburg girl named Polly.

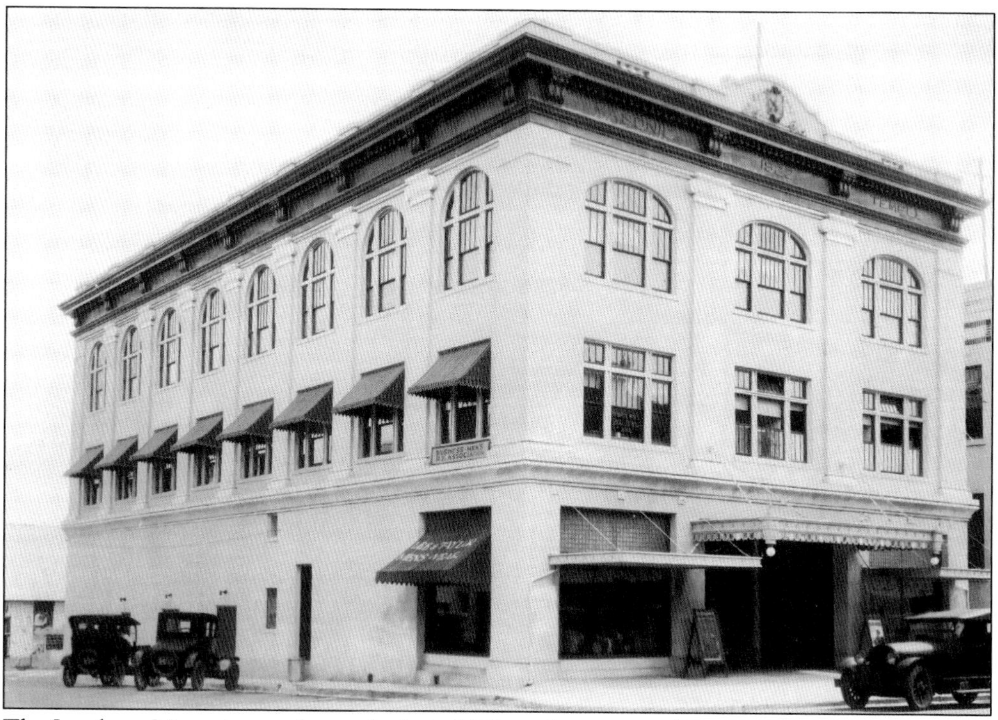

The Leesburg Masonic temple was built in 1922 at the corner of Main and Fifth Streets. Seen here in 1925, the building housed the Palace Theatre and the Lee & Taylor clothing store. The Business Men's Real Estate Association had offices on the second floor, and Leesburg Masonic Lodge No. 58 held its meetings on the third floor.

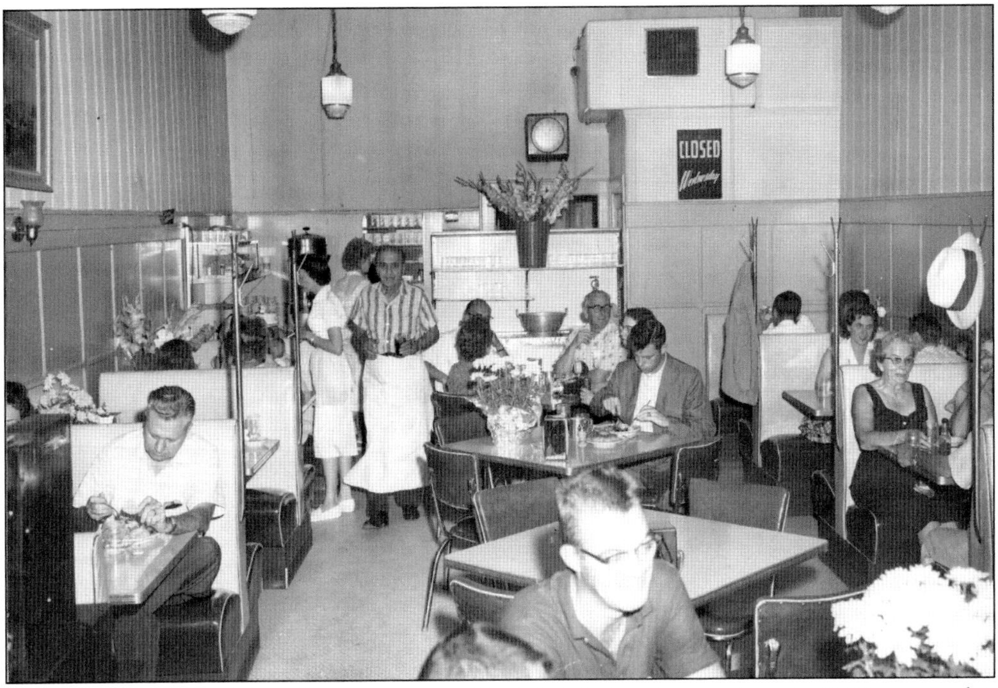

Nick's Café, on West Main Street was owned by Nick Babouris, seen here in 1939 wearing his striped shirt and long apron. Born in Greece in 1894, Babouris worked as a cook in Sanford in 1926. Notice the "Closed Wednesday" sign on the wall—it was traditional in Leesburg for all the stores to close on Wednesdays so the shopkeepers could go fishing.

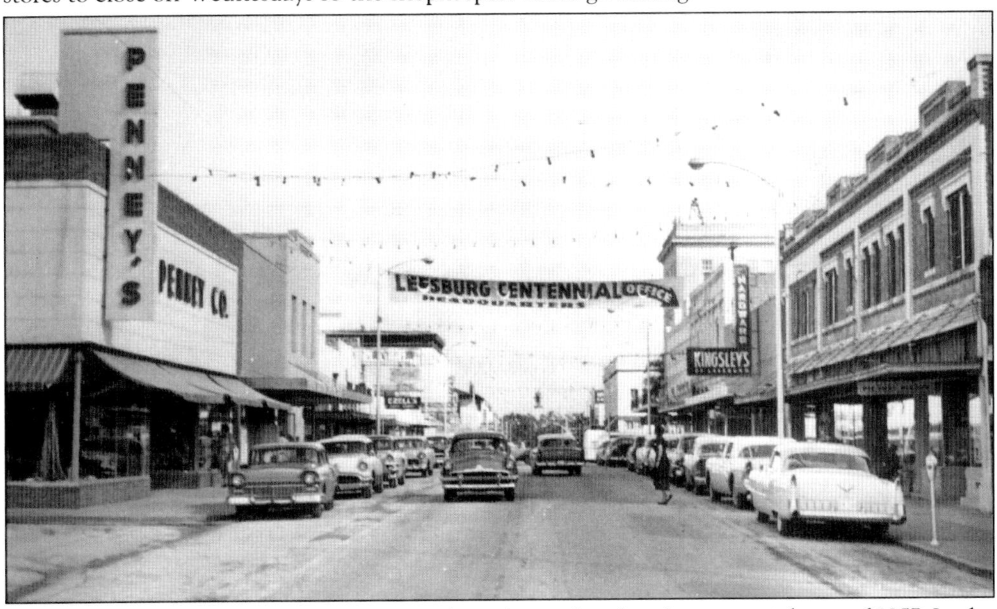

The 700 block of West Main Street is seen here during Leesburg's centennial year of 1957. In the 1950s and 1960s, before shopping malls became popular, chain department stores, such as J.C. Penney's, located their stores in downtowns across America. A Woolworth's opened opposite Penney's on Main Street in Leesburg. Local merchants Kingsley's Hardware and Ezell's Department Store are also prominent in this photograph.

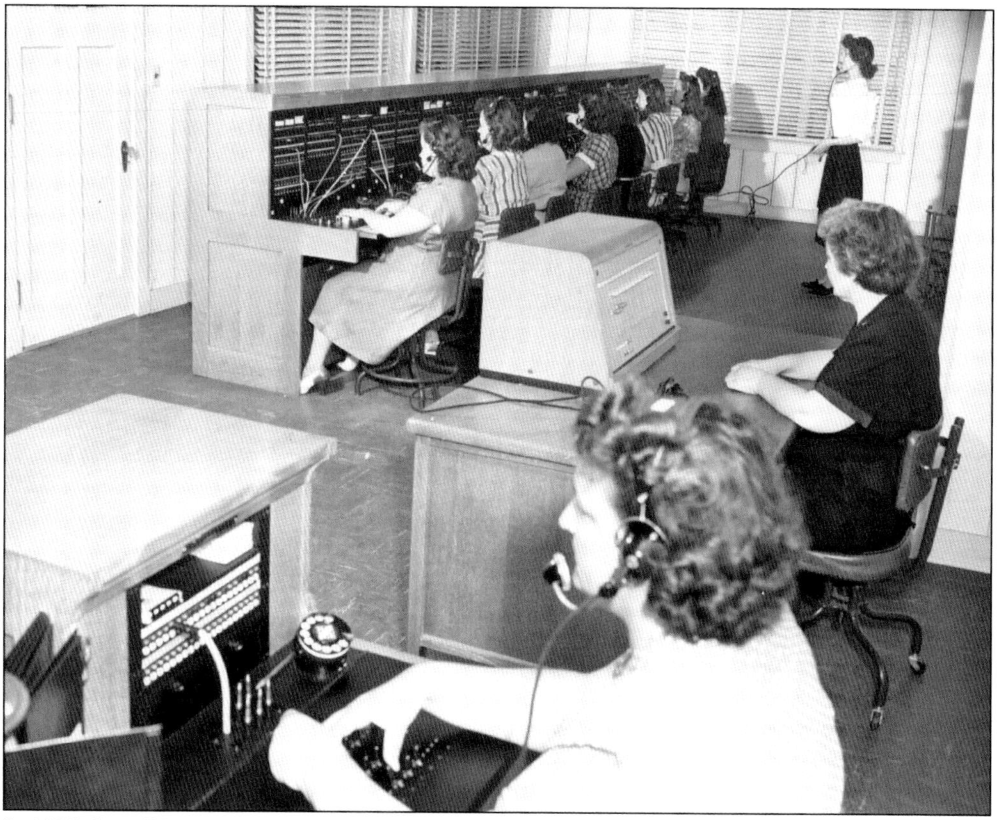

In 1925, Otto Wettstein Jr. created Florida Telephone Corporation (FTC). This 1940s photograph shows FTC's switchboard operators and its chief operator, Christine Mote McClelland (right foreground, in black dress). McClelland lived on North Lee Street and spent her career as a telephone operator. Active in church and community groups, she was also a past president of the UDC and a volunteer for Leesburg Regional Medical Center Auxiliary.

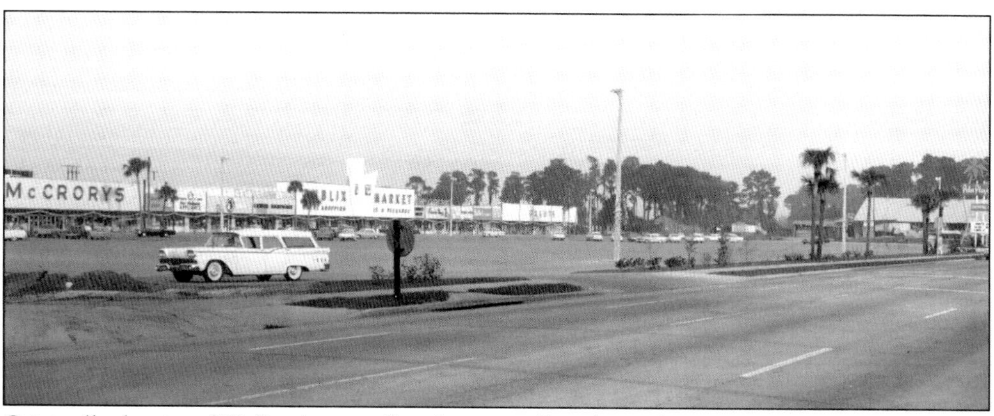

Originally the site of Walling's sawmill and crate mill in the early 1900s, Palm Plaza was built in the late 1950s. To the right of the Grants is Cauthen's packinghouse. Other occupants of Palm Plaza included Liggett Rexall, McCrory's, Home Builder's Supply, Jack's Barbershop/Plaza Beauty Salon, Palm Plaza Camera, Center Hardware, Turner's Bakery, Edwards-Macy, Royal Palm, Butler's Shoes, Toy King, and Publix.

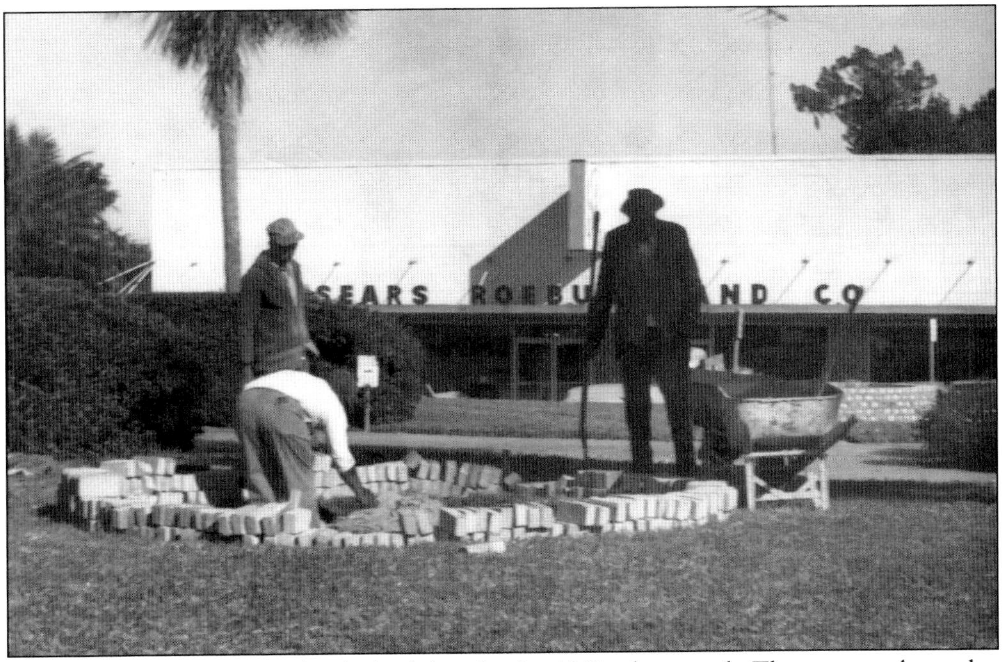

Sears, Roebuck & Co. provides the backdrop for this 1960s photograph. The store was located at 204 North Fifth Street. J.E.D. Inc. constructed the building in 1948, and leased it to Margaret Ann Super Markets. In May 1956, Sears moved in, staying until they moved to Lake Square Mall in 1977. In the foreground, workers construct a chimney for Santa Claus in the city hall courtyard.

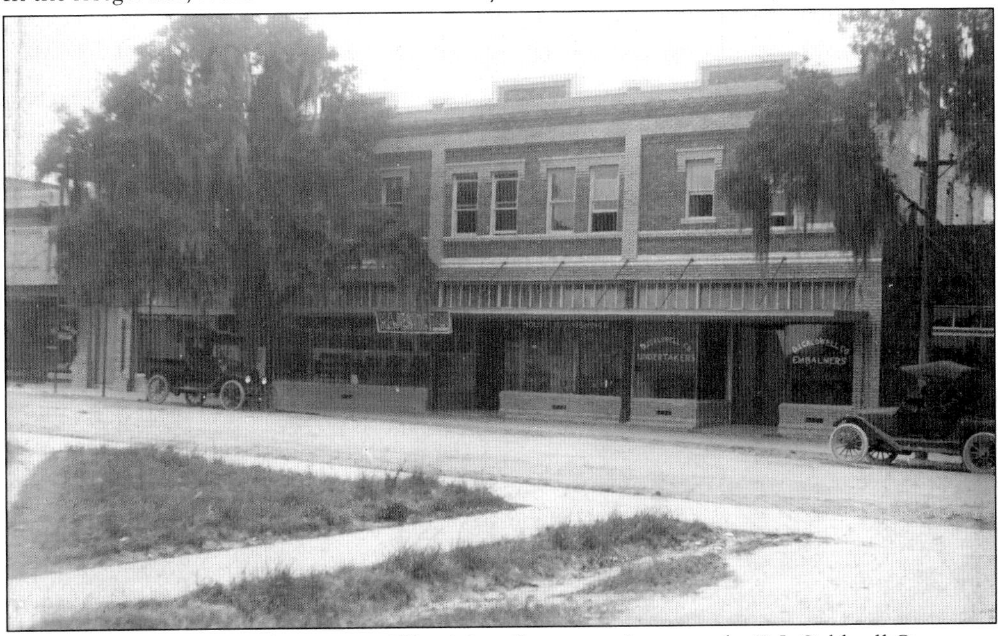

This building, constructed in 1914 on West Main Street, was home to the D.J. Caldwell Company, which sold household furnishings, including the popular Majestic ranges, which were manufactured in St. Louis. D.J. Caldwell also operated an undertaker and embalmer's parlor, a business he bought from J.A. Hanson, who was Leesburg's first undertaker in 1883. Stepp's Hotel was on the second floor of this building.

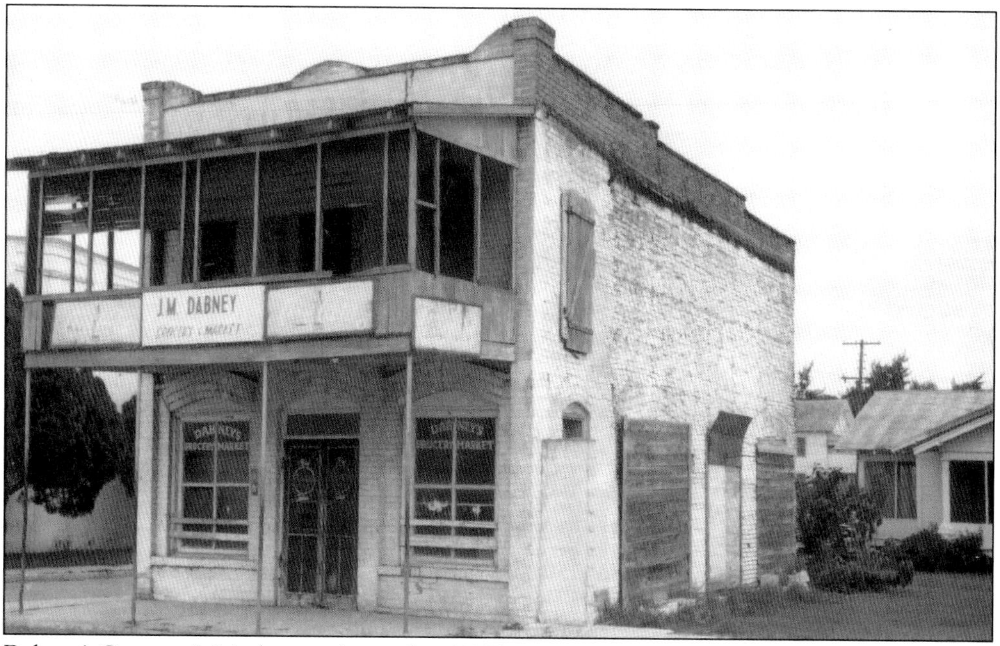

Dabney's Grocery & Market was located at 419 East Main Street. Educator John Morgan Dabney opened the store in the early 1900s. In 1933, he became part owner of the first black funeral home in Leesburg, called Economical Funeral Home. In 1938, he bought out his partners and renamed it Dabney Funeral Home. Dabney's parents, John Butler and Mackey Wright Dabney, were the first black settlers in Leesburg.

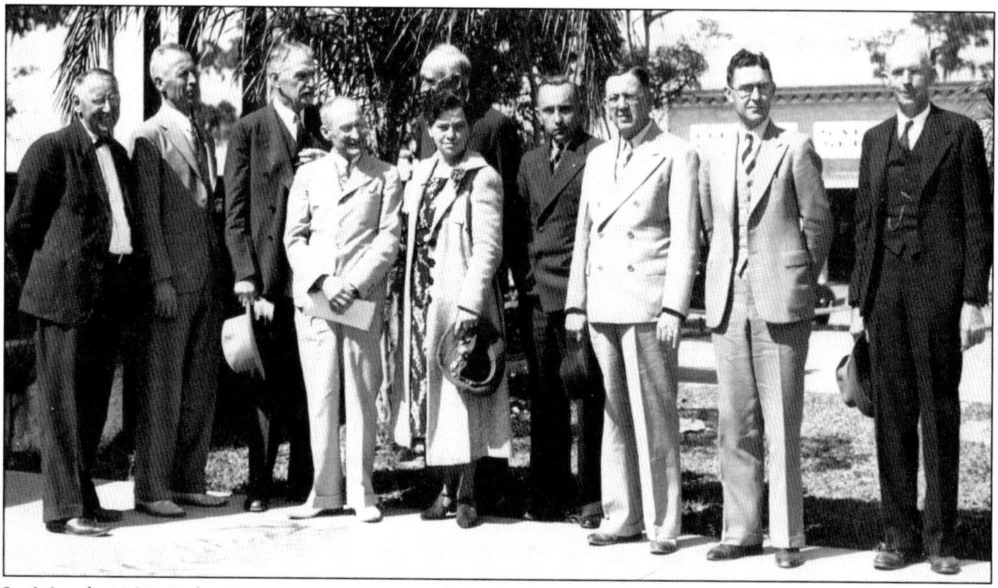

In March 1938, Lake County newspaper editors honored William E. Loomis (fourth from left), the president of the National Editorial Association. The Lake County editors are, from left to right, John Lochner (*Florida Newspaper News*), unidentified, George Keller (*Mount Dora Topic*), William and Anna Loomis, unidentified, Don Lochner (*Clermont Press*), Ralph K. Gore (*Lake County Citizen*), Jess Lantz (*Eustis Lake Region*), and Arthur W. Newett (*Leesburg Ledger* and *Groveland Graphic*).

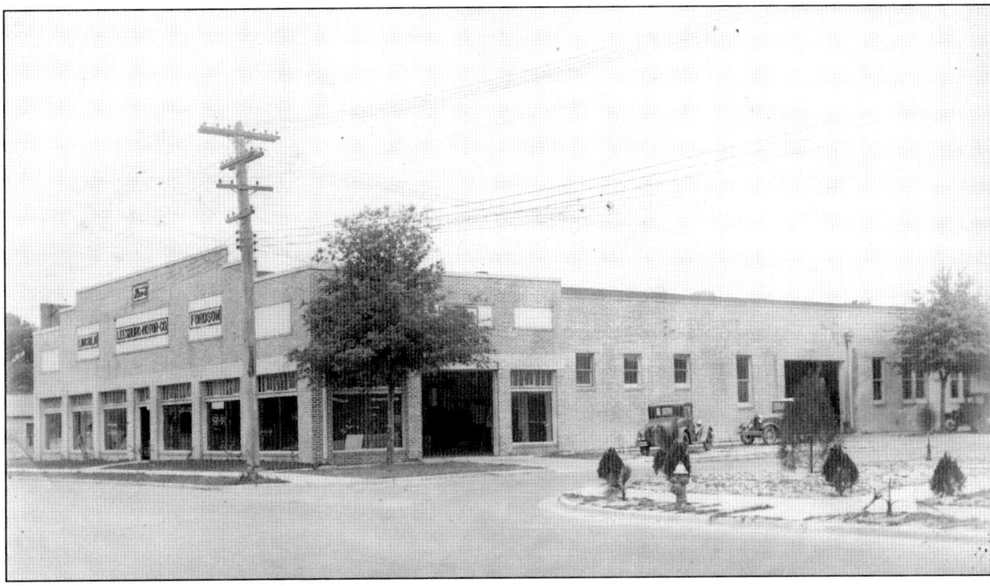

The Kirk Building, located between Seventh Street and Orange Avenue, opened in October 1926. This unique building was constructed so that three more stories could be added if needed. The Leesburg Motor Company was the first tenant to occupy the building. On October 23, 1926, the building's owners, the C.D. Kirk Company, held a grand opening for the public. The new Chrysler 70 was on display for the event.

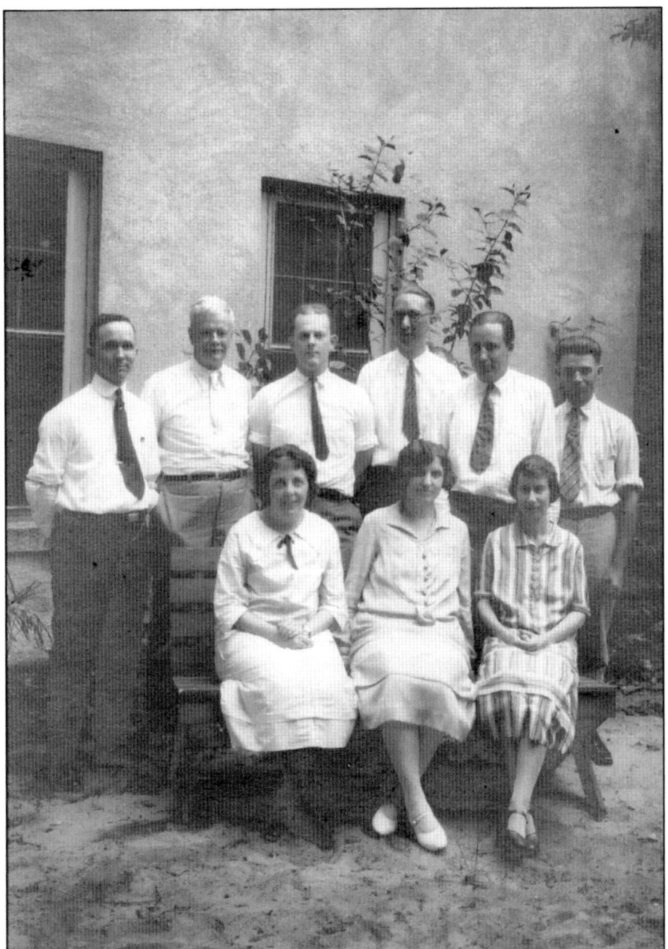

The staff of the Leesburg State Bank is seen here in the early 1920s. From left to right are (first row) Elsie Turner, Kitty Wharton, and Hilda Budd; (second row) cashier George Webster, bank president R.F.E. Cooke, John Fahs, Houston Rogers, L.D. Burdine, and Jack Irwin. John Fahs recalled that everyone but the cashier and the president did a little of everything, from teller's chores to bookkeeping.

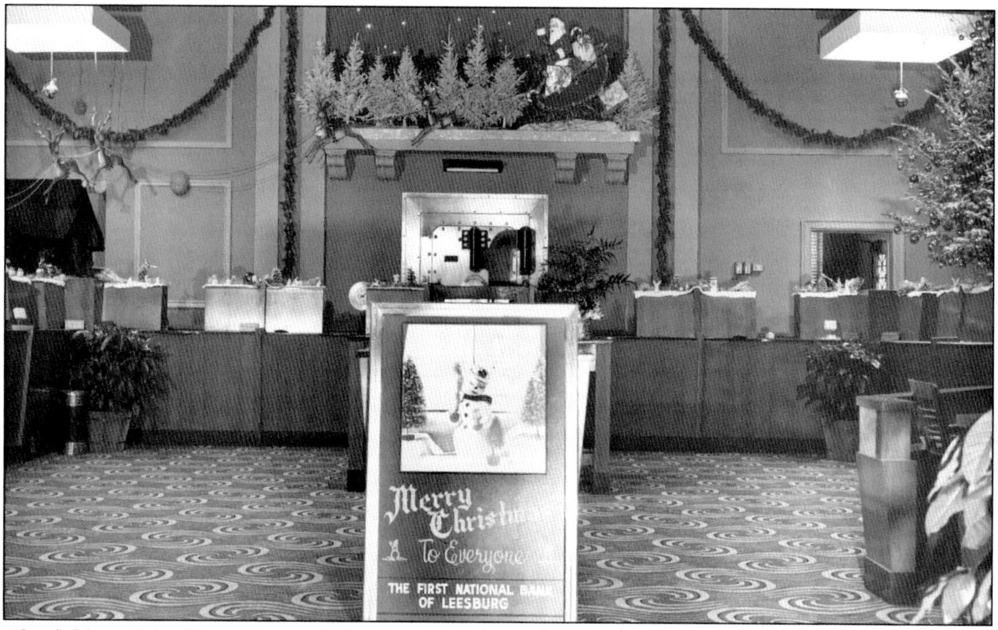

The lobby of the First National Bank is seen here during the Christmas season in 1941. Bank employee George Rast recalled, "For years Ernie Willard, who worked for the Florida National Bank in Orlando, was in charge of decorating our bank lobby. Several other male employees, including myself, always pitched in. We'd spend a whole evening decorating. It became a Christmastime stag party. Afterwards we'd have a good stiff drink of holiday cheer."

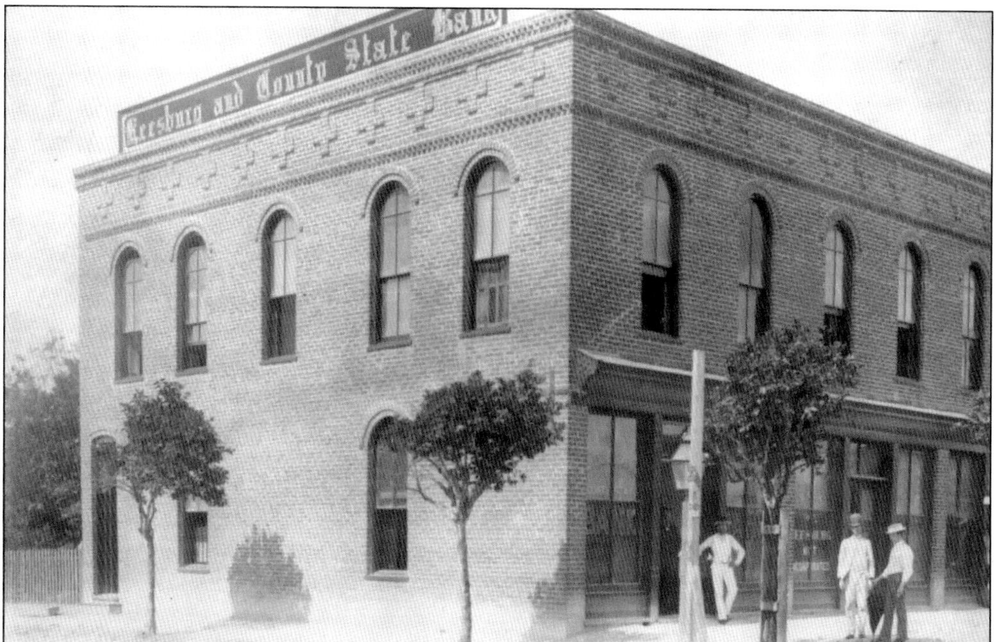

In 1886, R.F.E. Cooke and H.S. Budd opened the Budd and Cooke Bank. In 1907, it became a chartered state bank and was renamed the Leesburg and County State Bank, as seen here. The bank was located on Main Street in the section formally called the Gold Block. After it was chartered as a state bank, R.F.E. Cooke became the bank's president.

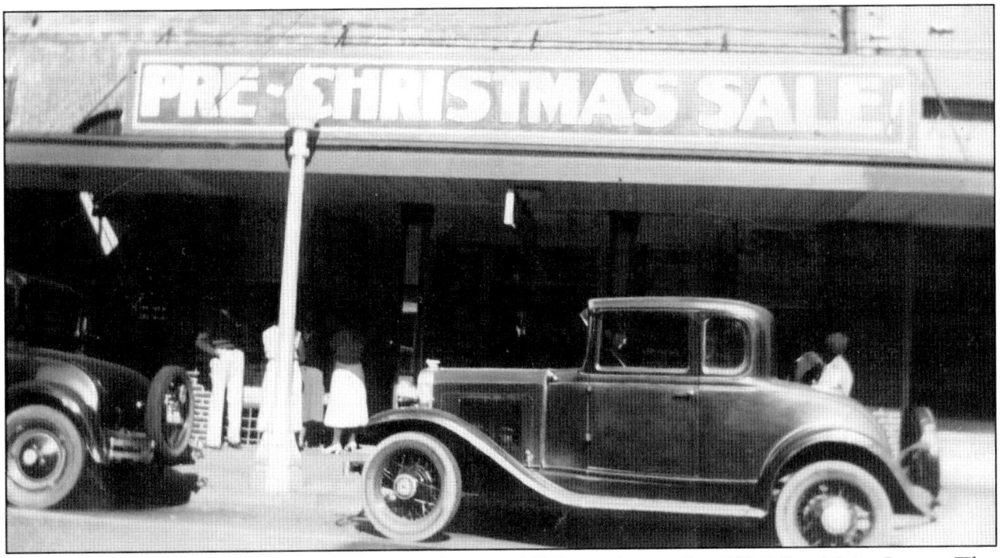

The popular Leesburg Bargain Store, seen here in 1935, was located at 310 West Main Street. The store sold dry goods and shoes. It was owned by Russian immigrants John and Clara Bernstein Lipschitz. The couple came to America in 1897, first settling in Springfield, Massachusetts, and became American citizens in 1906. In the 1920s, they moved to Leesburg with their four children and lived on South Ninth Street.

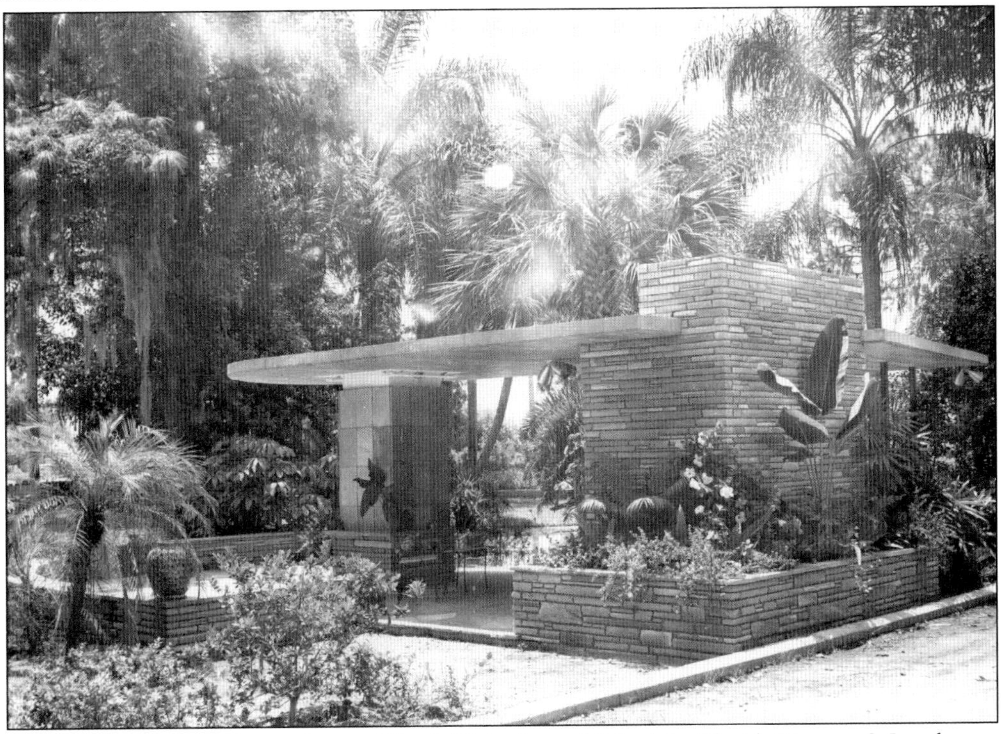

In 1928, landscape architect Gervin Wendal Pringle established the Florida Nursery & Landscape Company, seen here in the 1950s, with his wife, Grace. Gervin Pringle was the company's president and John Y. Clark Jr. was the vice president. The nursery was originally located on Main Street and later moved to 801 North Fourteenth Street.

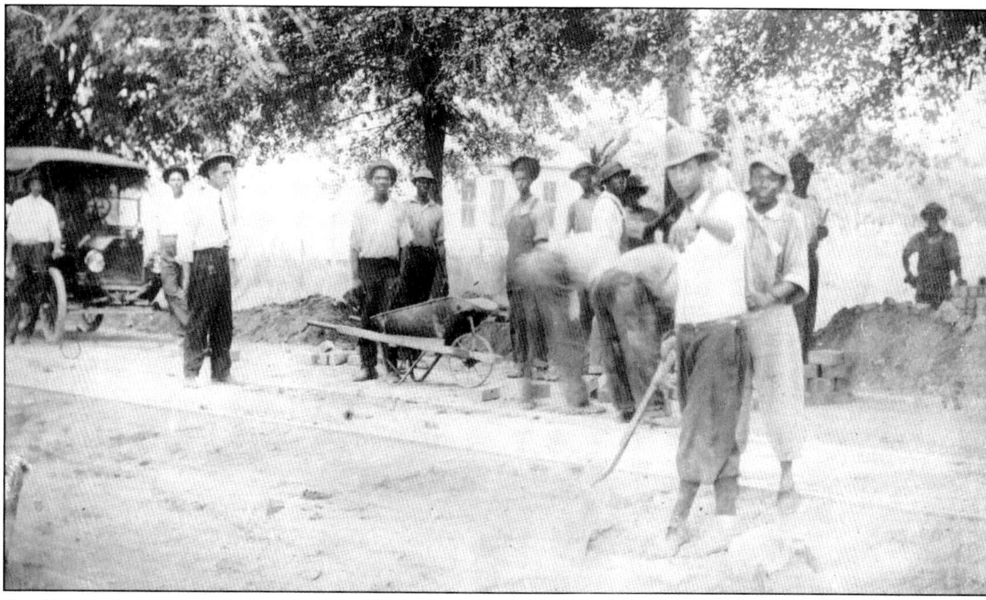

Strolling along Main Street in Leesburg today, one can easily recall memories of days gone by. In the heart of Leesburg, Main Street represents the great American pioneering spirit and the vision of the area's early citizens. Whether by horse and buggy or "horseless carriage," a ride down Main Street reminds one of a time when downtown was the center of social and commercial life. From Lee's general store in 1866 to today's beautiful new Leesburg Public Library, Main Street remains the vibrant hub of the city. Above, in the early 1900s, Tom Lynch (third from left) and his crew pave Main Street with red clay from the Atlantic Coastline Railroad depot to the Lake View Hotel. Main Street was the first road in Florida outside of Jacksonville to be paved with red clay. Below, workers construct a brick building on Main Street around 1900.

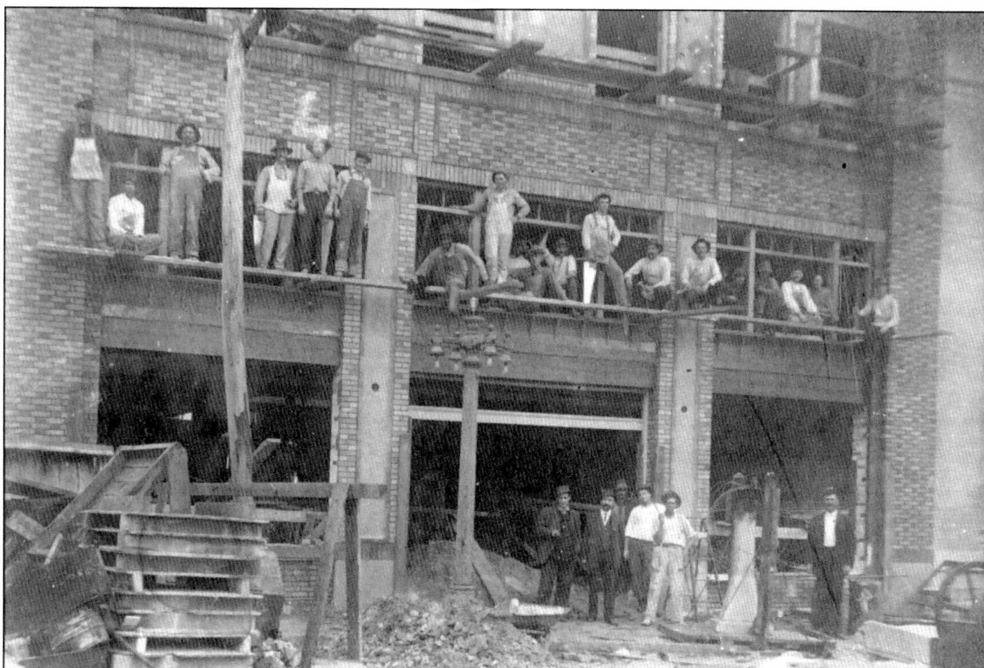

Ten

Leesburg Legacy

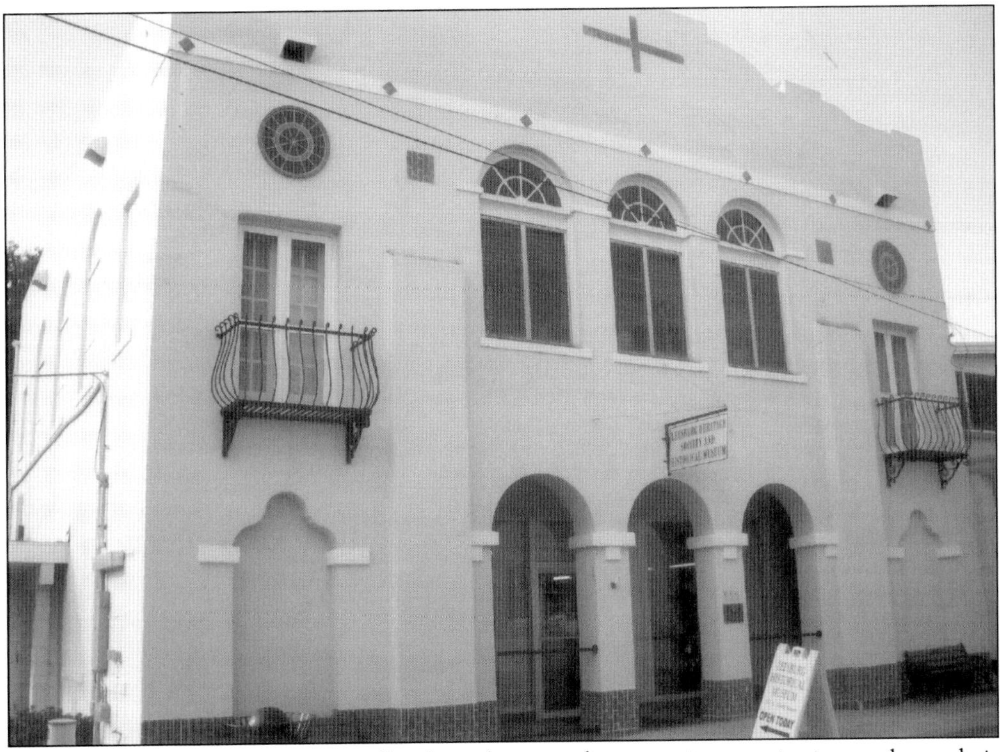

Leesburg's residents, investors, city officials, and civic and community organizations embrace their roles in promoting, protecting, and preserving the city's rich history for future generations. The Leesburg Heritage Society and Historical Museum, seen here, is the home of Leesburg's historical treasures and artifacts. The museum, at 111 South Sixth Street, was constructed in 1922 and was the original home of the Leesburg Women's Club. (Courtesy of the Bob Grenier collection.)

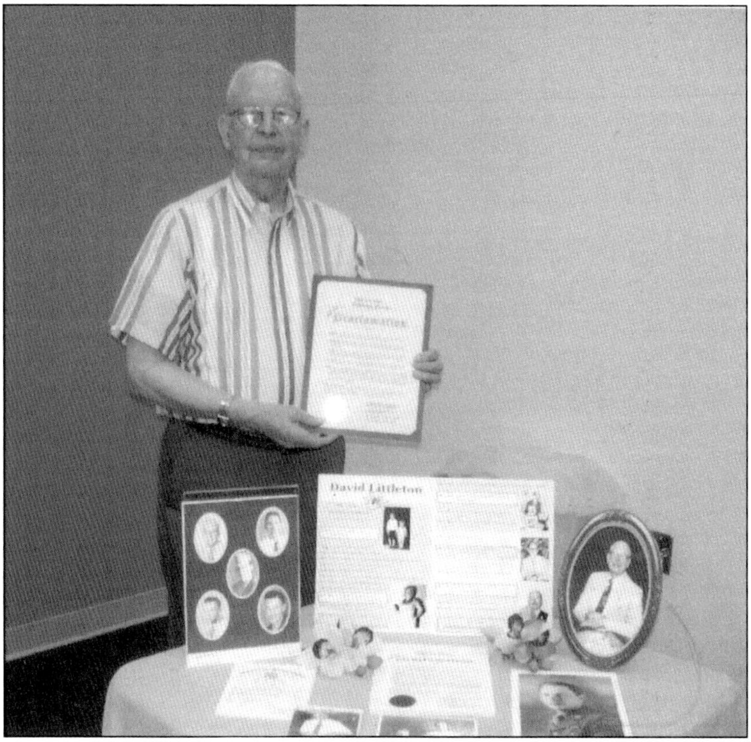

David Harold Littleton, born on May 7, 1922, was a native of Leesburg and a 1940 graduate of Leesburg High School. One of his proudest moments was being named Florida's Outstanding 4-H Club Boy in 1940. A World War II Air Force veteran, Littleton retired in 1984 after 43 years in the banking industry. He was the cofounder and past president of both the Leesburg Heritage Society and the Mid-Lakes Orchid Society. He passed away in 2009.

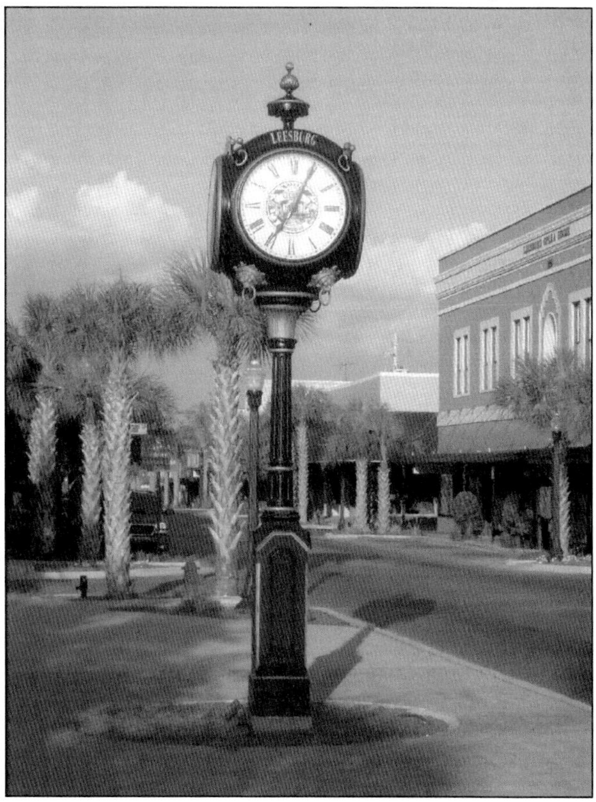

In 1998, the Greater Leesburg Community Redevelopment Agency purchased two Main Street properties to build a town square in front of city hall. On March 3, 2000, the Leesburg Towne Square was completed and dedicated to the residents of Leesburg. On January 1, 2000, the Towne Square Clock was dedicated to the memory of Marvin and Marie Bowden by the Kiser Hardaway family.

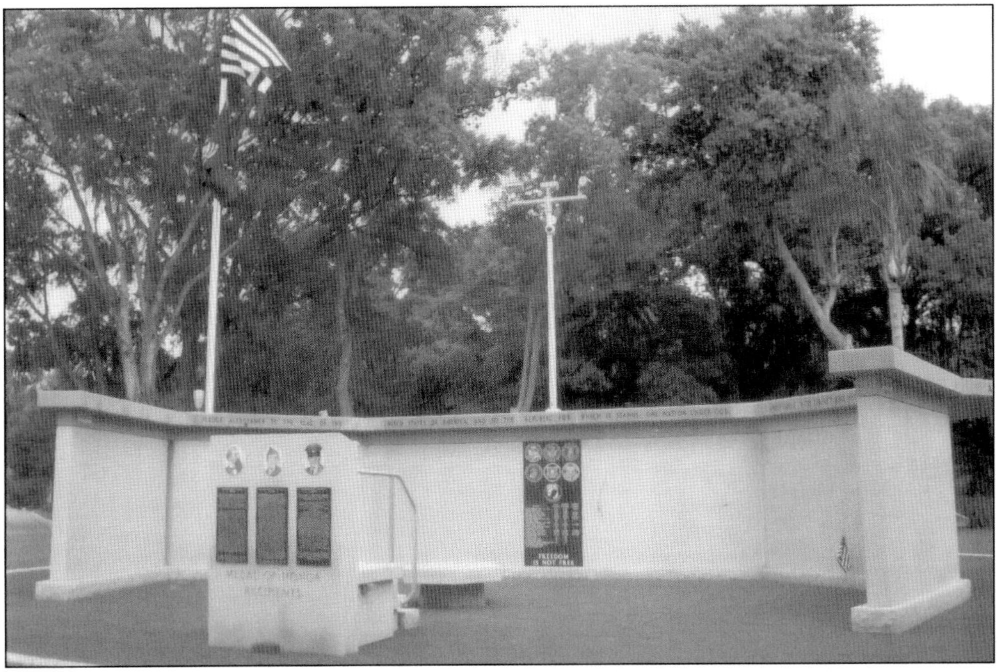

The 2,800-square-foot Veterans Memorial at Fountain Lake Park (above) honors veterans from Lake, Sumter, and Marion Counties. It is one of the largest memorials in the southeast. On May 19, 2012, executive director Donald Van Beck hosted a dedication ceremony. The event included an appearance by the Rolling Thunder, a national veterans' motorcycle group. Speakers included Sen. Carey Baker, Brig. Gen. Tim Sullivan, and Maj. Gen. Polly Peyer. (Courtesy of the Bob Grenier collection.)

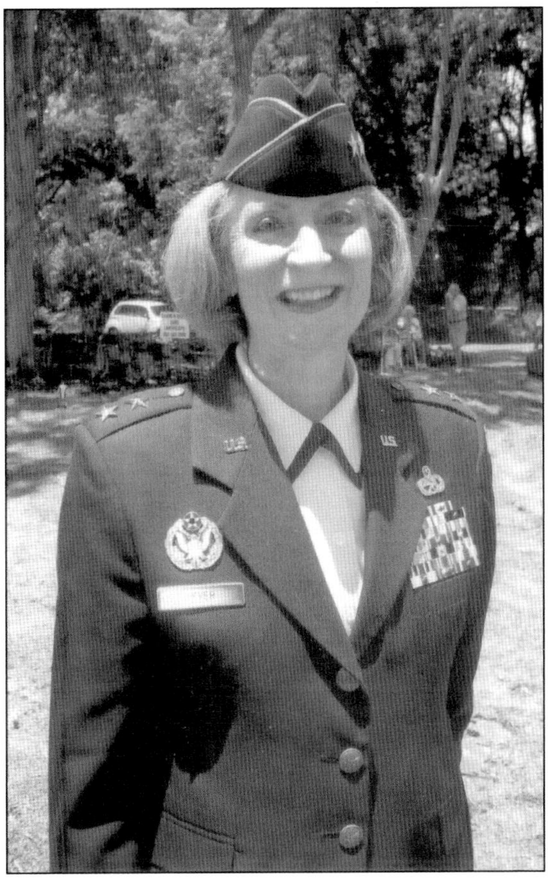

On November 18, 2010, at the US Capitol, Rep. Jim Marshall paid tribute to Maj. Gen. Polly Peyer, a 1967 graduate of Leesburg High School, on the occasion of her retirement, stating, "Maj. Gen. Peyer distinguished herself through exceptionally meritorious service to the Air Force and to the nation during more than thirty-four years of active military service in peace and war." (Courtesy of the Bob Grenier collection.)

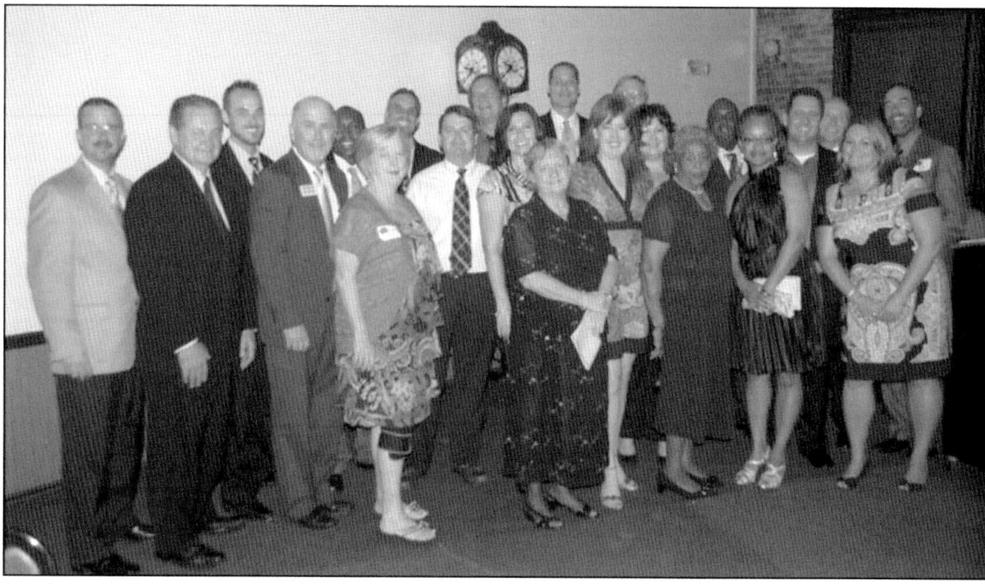

In 1996, the Downtown Merchants Association, the City of Leesburg, and the Leesburg Chamber of Commerce organized the Leesburg Downtown Partnership. In 2000, it changed its name to Leesburg Partnership to reflect its vision of improving other areas of the community as well. Its goal is to aid in the physical, economic, and social revitalization of the Leesburg community. The 2011 Leesburg Partnership board of directors is seen here. (Courtesy of Leesburg Partnership.)

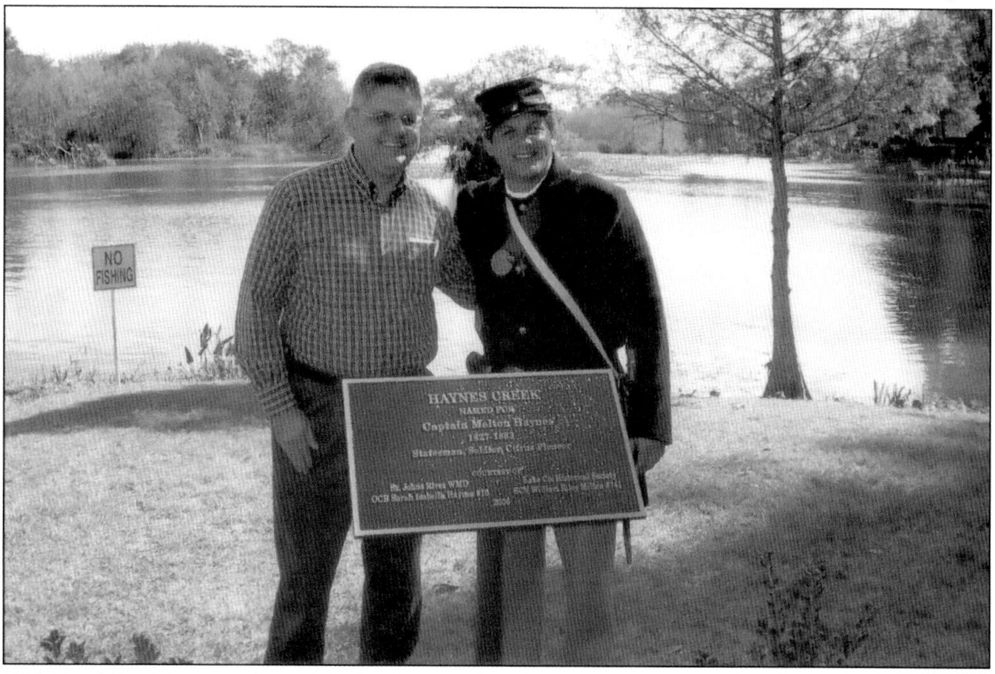

Rick Reed (left) is the author of the book *City of Leesburg: Sesquicentennial Celebration*. Since 1998, Reed has written a weekly local history column for the *Daily Commercial* called *Reminisce*. He is a recipient of the Florida Historical Society's Golden Quill Award. Seen here with Reed is the coauthor of this book, Bob Grenier, at the December 2006 dedication of the Haynes Creek historical marker at the Burrell Lock and Dam in Leesburg. (Courtesy of the Bob Grenier collection.)

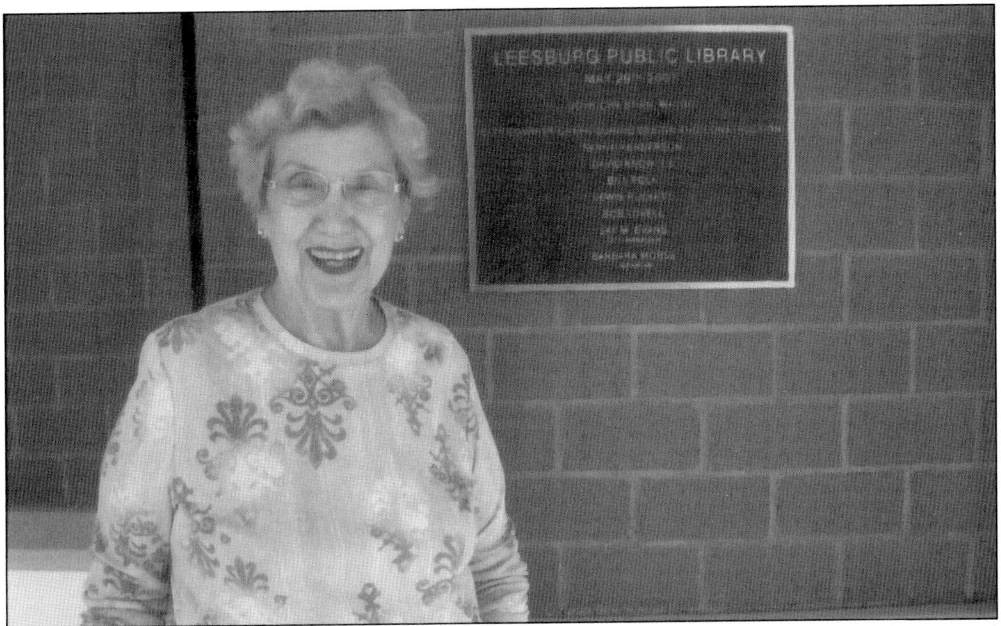

Sanna Henderson was first elected to the Leesburg City Commission in 1981. She has served as Leesburg's mayor five times, and has the distinction of being the city's longest-serving female commissioner. Of her many achievements, she ranks the Leesburg Public Library as her favorite project. She is also a past president of the Lake County Historical Society and the Leesburg Heritage Society. Her father was state representative Tim Sellars. (Courtesy of the Bob Grenier collection.)

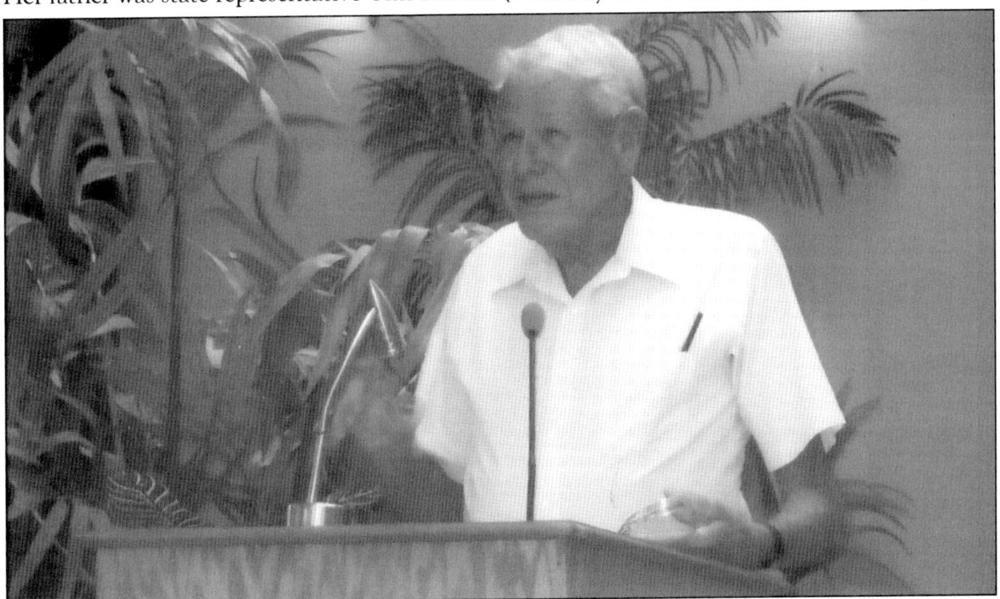

Dr. Joseph Branham is a 1951 graduate of Leesburg High School. In 1965, with degrees in zoology and marine biology, Dr. Branham worked in the laboratory of world-renowned scientist Conrad Hal Waddington at the University of Edinburgh in Scotland. He returned to Leesburg High School in 1973 and taught there until 1989. Dr. Branham, the foremost authority on Okahumpka, originally came to Bugg Spring in 1940, where he and his wife, Margaret, still reside today. (Courtesy of the Bob Grenier collection.)

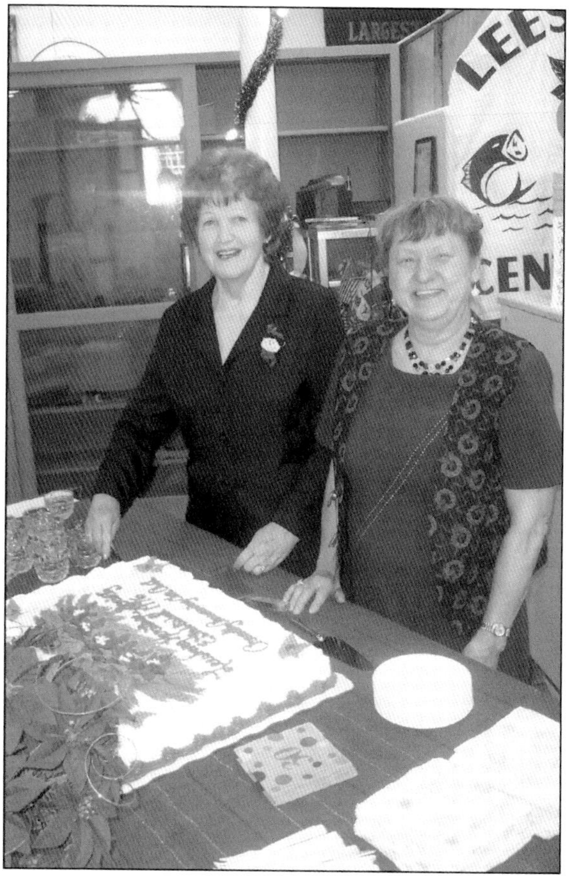

In 1973, historian Elisabeth Geiger began a movement to form a historical society in Leesburg. In 1976, the Leesburg Heritage Society, a name suggested by Nita A. Carter of Georgia, was established. Former mayor Burton Brown was elected as its first president. The society's objectives are "to preserve the past for the benefit of the future by promoting, encouraging, aiding and assisting in the collection, preservation, protection and exhibition of photographs, paintings, documents, relics and other memorabilia relating to the history of the Leesburg area." At left, in 2006, past president Laura Stoffel (left) and current president Glorianne Seymour Fahs, the coauthor of this book, celebrate the 30th anniversary of the Leesburg Heritage Society. Below, at the January 8, 2013, Leesburg Heritage Society meeting held at the Leesburg Public Library, members paused to have their photograph taken. (Below, courtesy of the Bob Grenier collection.)

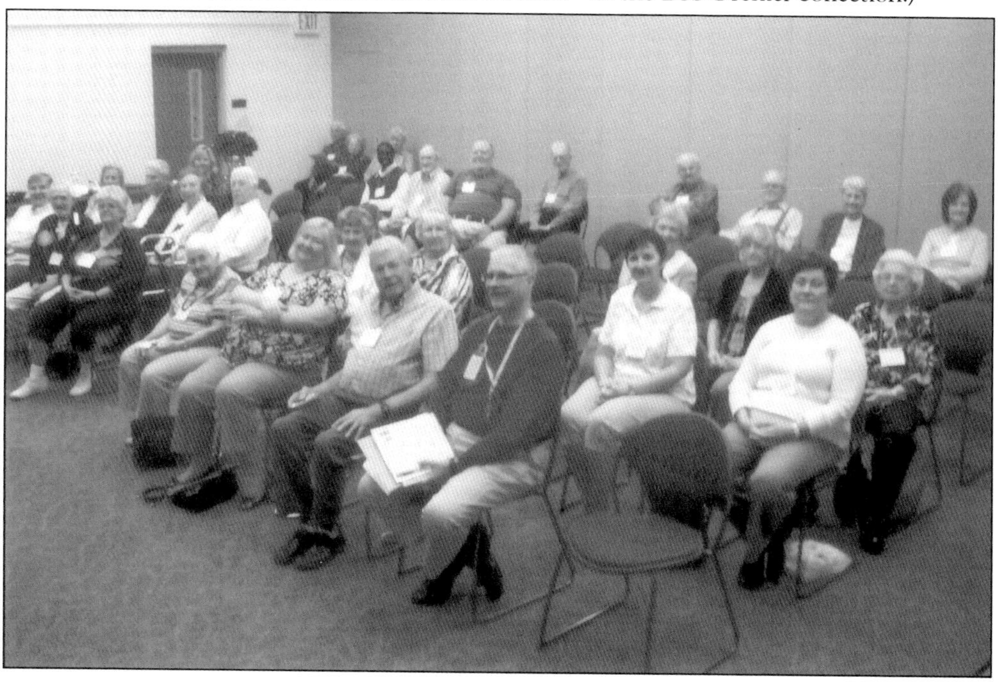

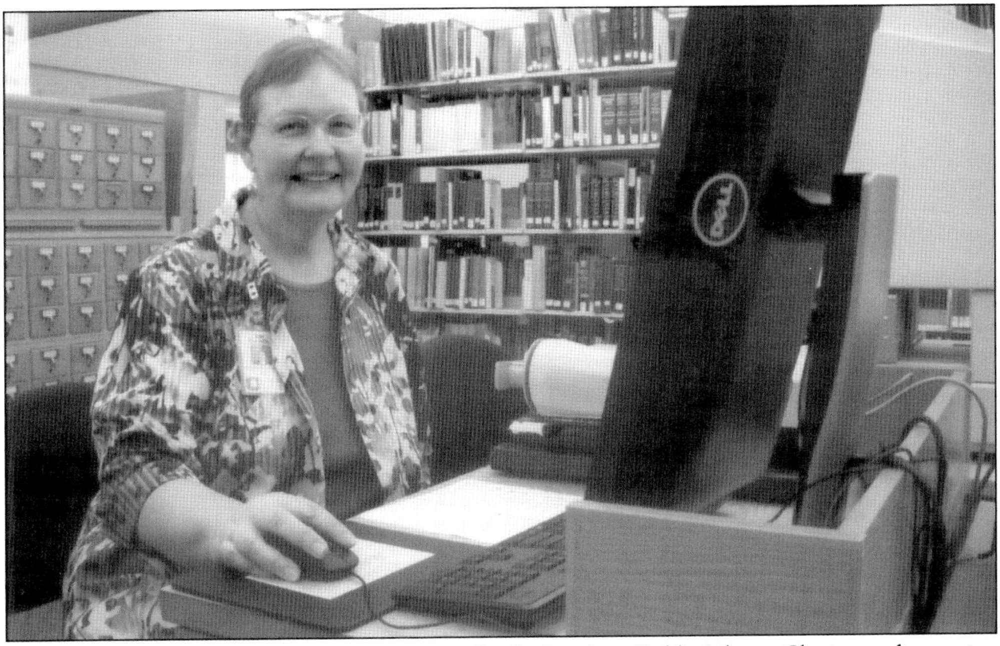

Carol Anderson is the adult services supervisor for the Leesburg Public Library. She is seen here using the library's new ScanPro 2000 digital microfilm viewer. The Leesburg Public Library houses a world-class genealogy collection that includes over 5,000 print sources, over 1,000 data CDs, genealogical magazines and journals, obituaries, and numerous microfilm and microfiche. The Leesburg Public Library is located at 100 East Main Street. (Courtesy of the Bob Grenier collection.)

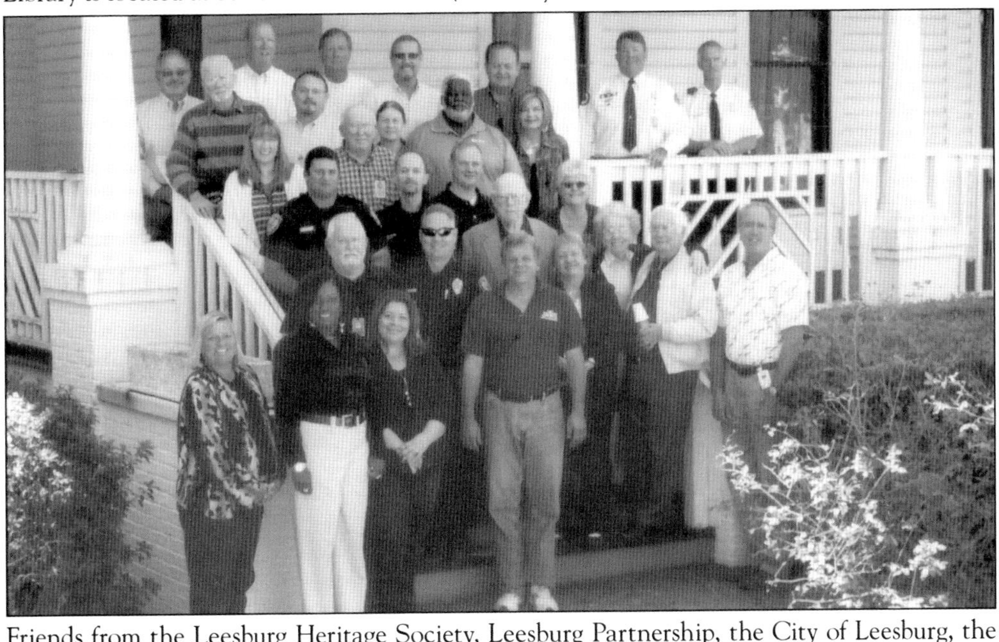

Friends from the Leesburg Heritage Society, Leesburg Partnership, the City of Leesburg, the Leesburg and Lake County Commissions, and those who assisted with this book join authors Bob Grenier (first row, center) and Glorianne Seymour Fahs (to Bob's left) to thank you for visiting Leesburg's historic past. We hope you enjoyed your trip down memory lane. (Courtesy of Bonnie Wicher Photography.)